AMERICAN PRESIDENTS

AMERICAN PRESIDENTS

David ⊠
LEVINE

Edited *by* DAVID LEOPOLD
And with an Introduction
by BILL MOYERS *and*
MICHAEL WINSHIP

Fantagraphics Books, Inc.
7563 Lake City Way
Seattle, WA 98115

Visit the publisher's website at: Fantagraphics.com. Please.

Distributed in the U.S. by W.W. Norton and Company, Inc. (1-212-354-5500)
Distributed in Canada by the Canadian Manda Group (1-416-516-0911)
Distributed in the UK by Turnaround Distribution (1-208-829-3009)
Distributed to comics stores by Diamond Comics Distributors (1-800-452-6642)

ISBN: 978-1-60699-130-5. Printed in China.

LIST of CHAPTERS

DAVID LEVINE'S VIVID SKETCHBOOK OF AMERICAN HISTORY

AN INTRODUCTION BY

BILL MOYERS AND MICHAEL WINSHIP

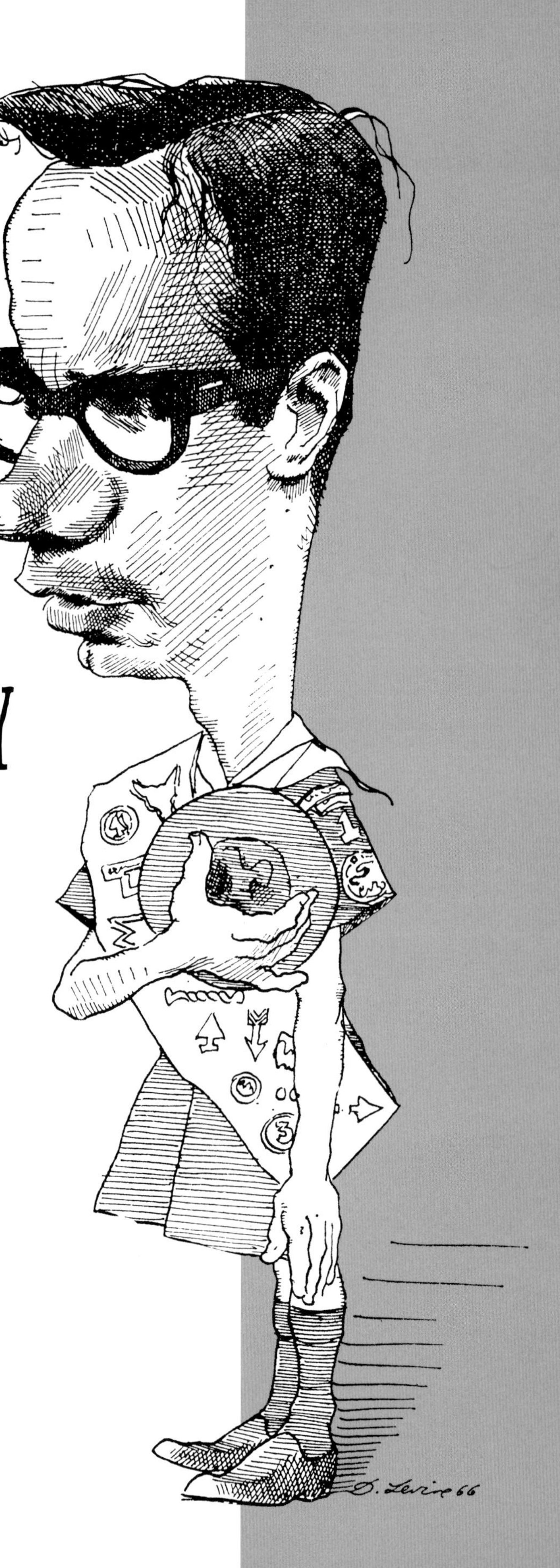

The Scottish poet Robert Burns died in 1796 still wishing for the "power the giftie gie us/To see oursels as ithers see us." If only he had waited around for David Levine, he would not have wished in vain.

For more than four decades, David Levine has pierced the public image of America's presidents and politicians with a fistful of sharpened pen nibs and gallons of India ink carefully tinctured with carbolic. "Politicians should be jumped on as often as possible," he once told *Time* Magazine. Levine pounced where many feared to tread.

He draws with the savage elegance of Daumier, the social conscience of Dickens' great illustrator Phiz and a flair for visual metaphor and exaggeration akin to the 19th century political cartoonist Thomas Nast, the man who brought down Boss Tweed, that 19th century Tony Soprano of New York's Tammany Hall; symbol of all things venal and corrupt in big city politics.

You may recall the story: so vexed was Tweed by Nast's cartoons, he offered the artist a bribe of half a million dollars and a vacation abroad to cease and desist. Turned down, Tweed is said to have exclaimed, "I don't give a straw for the newspaper articles. Most of my voters can't read. But they can't help seeing them damned pictures!"

Of course, one big difference between the contemporary viewers of Nast and Levine is that Levine's followers *can* read—in fact, they're probably the most literate folks in America. Most of the work contained in these pages first appeared in the *New York Review of Books*, that journal of commentary so intelligent and cultured that even its singles ads read as stylishly as a Petrarchan sonnet. So while Levine brings a Nast-like ferocity to his work, there is, too, a literacy and awareness of history and popular culture that bring to his wicked caricatures an added wink and zing of knowing recognition.

Our favorite is one of his most famous: A wily but rueful Lyndon Johnson, pointing to the scar from his gall bladder surgery, shaped like a map of Vietnam drawn down his midsection. Nothing so captured the forlorn and unforgiving reality of LBJ, his fate, and the dilemma for America that had been forged by his decisions.

There's Hillary Clinton as Samson pulling down the pillars of the temple, but this time the temple is our health care system and the fleeing Philistines are doctors and nurses. Richard Nixon as Don Corleone, Truman in the vortex of a mushroom cloud, Eleanor Roosevelt as the ugly duckling turned swan by the sheer grace of her warmth and eloquence, Jimmy Carter as both Alfred E. Newman and the Emperor Nero. Attorney General John Mitchell has on one of those crazy, Ruritanian uniforms Nixon briefly tried to make the White House guards wear.

Detail. So knowledgeable is Levine that his President Benjamin Harrison sports an outsized hat, a now-obscure reference to his grandfather, President William Henry Harrison, to whom he was said to be grossly inferior (an anti-Harrison campaign song of the time began, "His grandfather's hat is too big for his head/but Ben tries it on just the same.")

Forty plus years of these drawings are a vivid sketchbook of American history, drawn by a man who does not suffer fools gladly. As you flip through these pages, you're reminded over and over of events large and small and men and women of great or fleeting fame. Whatever happened to David Stockman, you ask yourself? Or Larry Speakes, or John Anderson?

OPPOSITE: **BILL MOYERS**, 1966

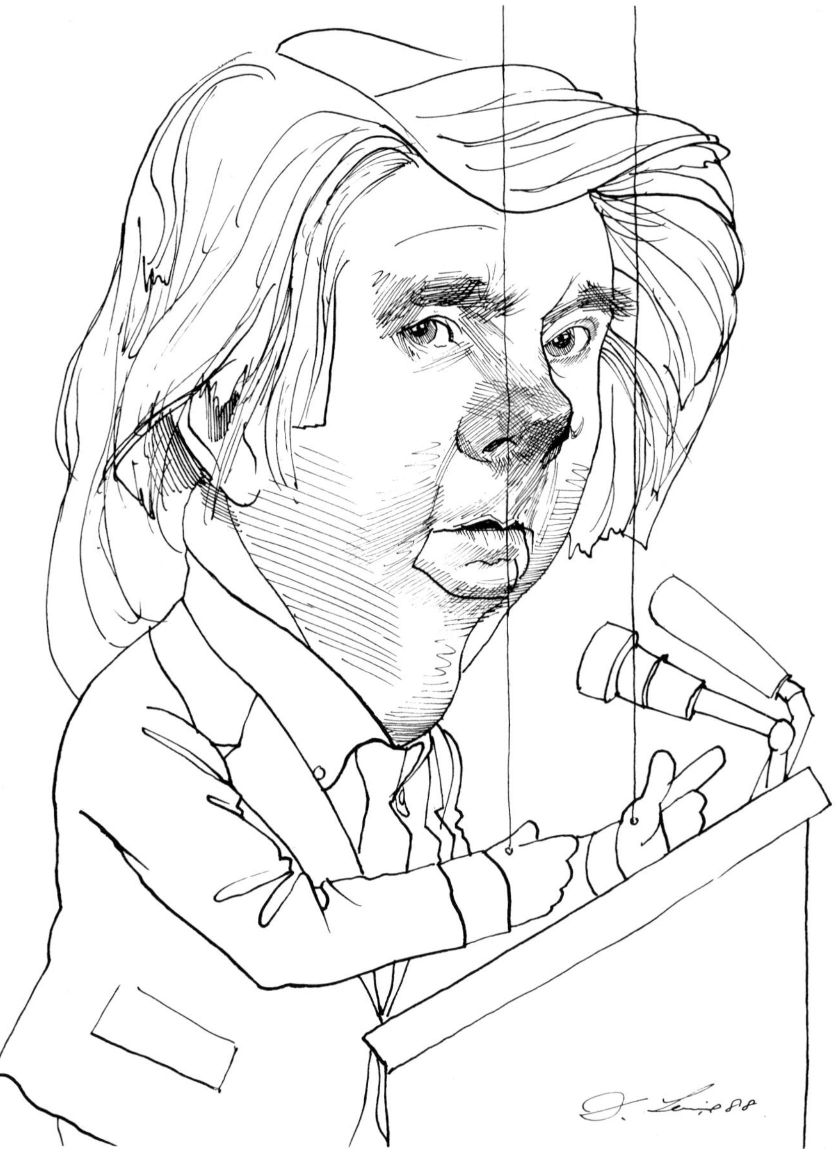

You notice that Levine has a propensity for outsized noses on his outsized heads—prodigious proboscises that lead you upward to that most important and telling facial feature—the eyes. The way Levine draws, you see in his characters' eyes every aspect of human ambition, frailty and failure. His aim is true.

One of the artists David Levine most admires is the great American painter Thomas Eakins. So unerring and unforgiving was Eakins' own eye that his friend the illustrator Edwin Justin

ABOVE: **LARRY SPEAKES**

Abbey once said he would never let Eakins paint his portrait because he "would bring out all those characteristics of mine I've been trying to hide from the public for years."

So, too, with David Levine. Certainly many of his subjects must have shuddered at the incisive satire—and accuracy—inflicted by his heat-seeking wit and sardonic imagination.

Of another contemporary American political cartoonist it has been said that had he not become an artist he would have found his calling as a professional assassin. Not so with Levine. He has far too much class. With his eye for detail and meticulous crosshatching, as a criminal, we see him more master forger than hit man, creating immaculate copies of currency. Of course, on the one, Washington's lips are a little too tightly pressed, to cover his wooden teeth; on the five, Lincoln has far too much of a twinkle in his eye; and Grant's beard is much too untidy on the twenty.

By the way, when you're done with this book, check out David Levine's watercolors, especially the ones of Coney Island and the Connecticut shore. Wonderful and brilliant in an entirely different way. What a talent.

But remember this, too, about a man who could be so merciless and devastating in his portrayal of our poo-bahs: A great intelligence guided his hand, and also a great heart. Even as he held their flaws and foibles high on the skewer, he never seems driven by malevolence. "I love my species," he once said. And why not? He could not have had better material.

Bill Moyers is managing editor of *Bill Moyers Journal* on PBS. Michael Winship is Senior Writer for the same broadcast and president of the Writers Guild East. Both are long-time admirers of David Levine.

AMERICAN PRESIDENTS

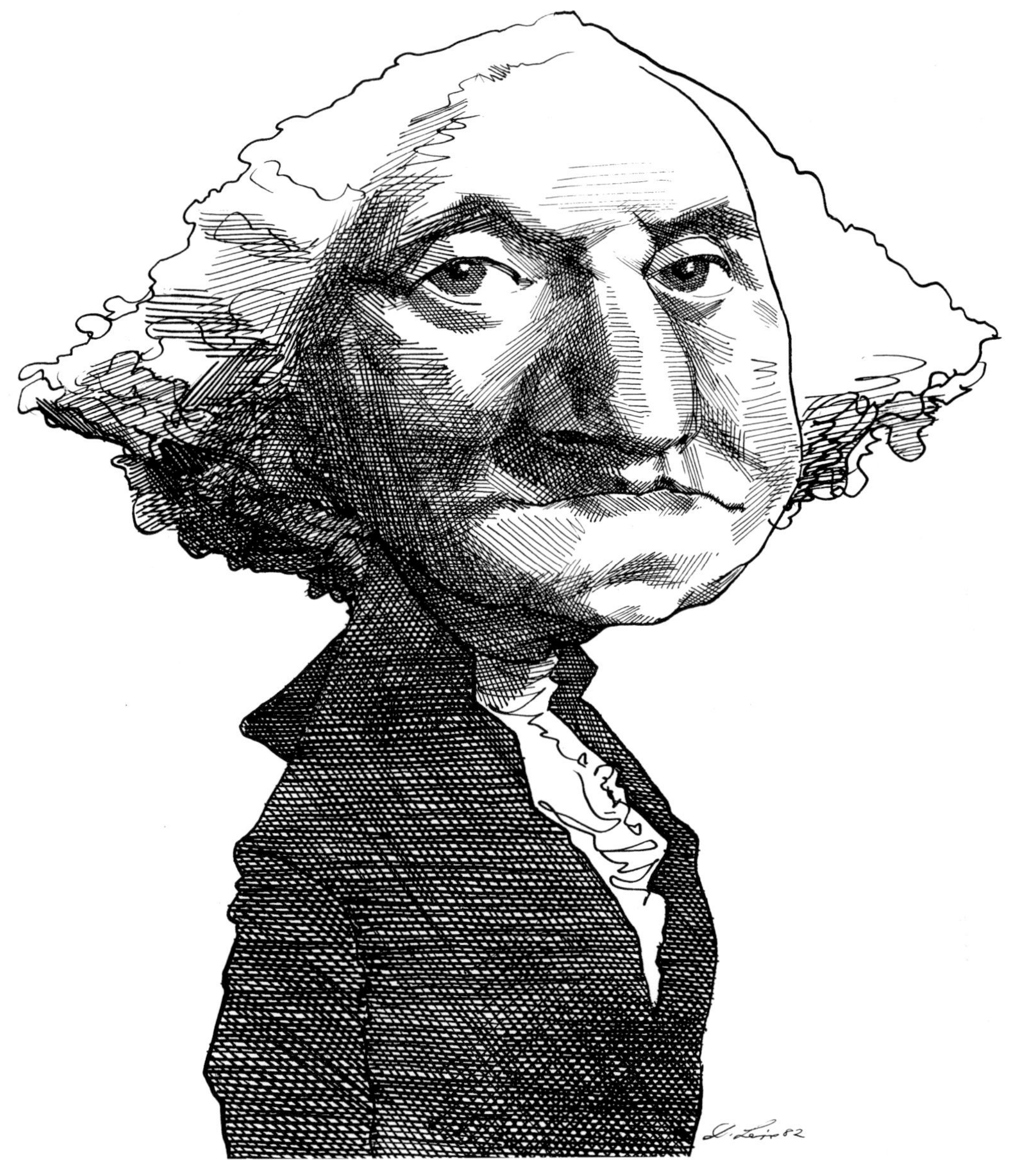

FOUNDING ★ FATHERS

➧ Call them the Founding Philosophers because fatherhood does not indicate greatness necessarily. I go back to the Greeks in thinking of them. I have commented on the clothing because clothing still makes the man. But these are references also to their openness and general thinking. I see our time as just a beginning of a really new democracy. We still have a lot more to do. The Constitution is never done, and it never can be done. It has to be worked for, fought for, understood, and read about. To think that half the people in this country are rejected in the sense that they have never had an image of themselves in the White House means there is work to be done.

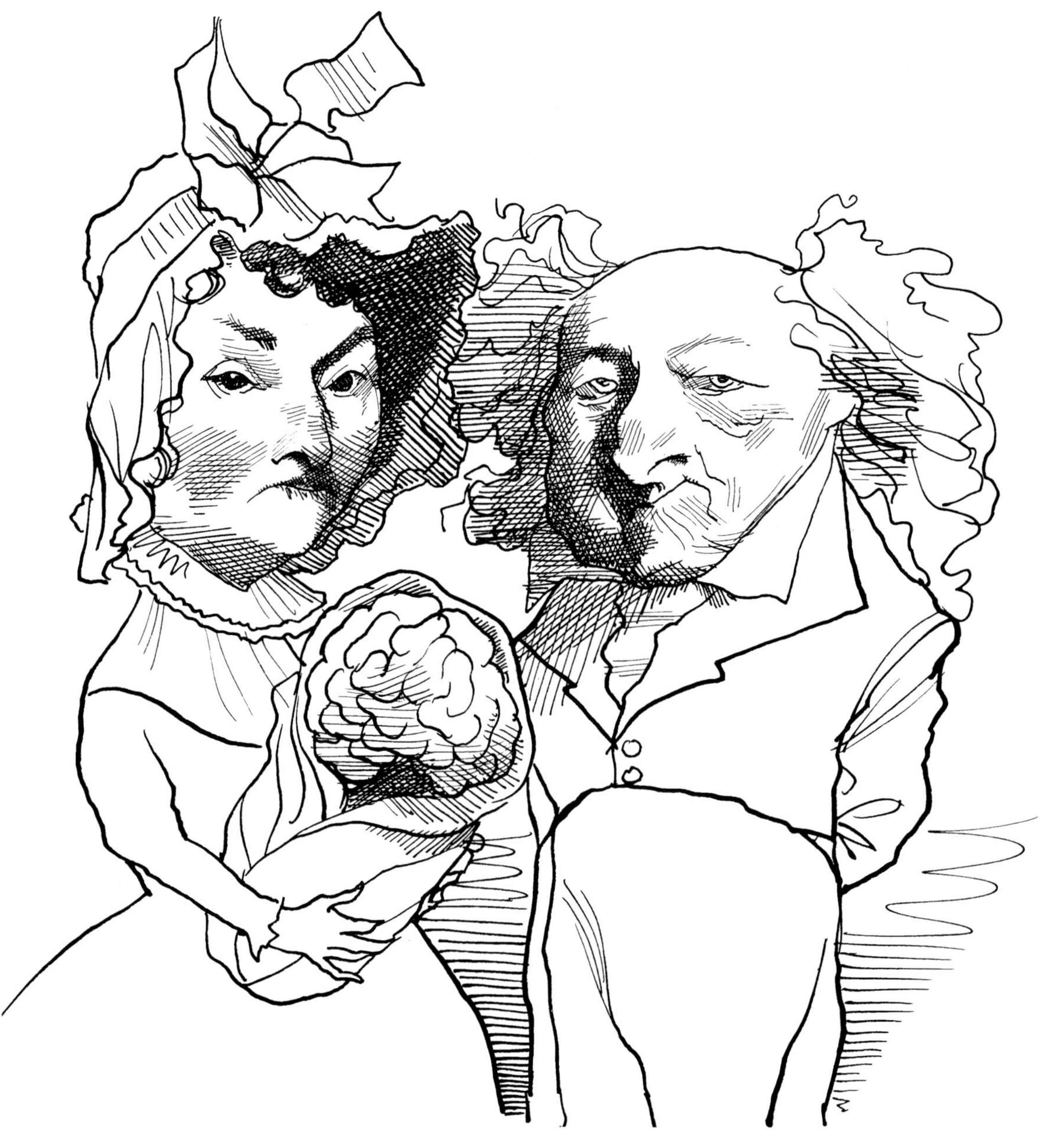

ABOVE: **JOHN & ABIGAIL ADAMS**

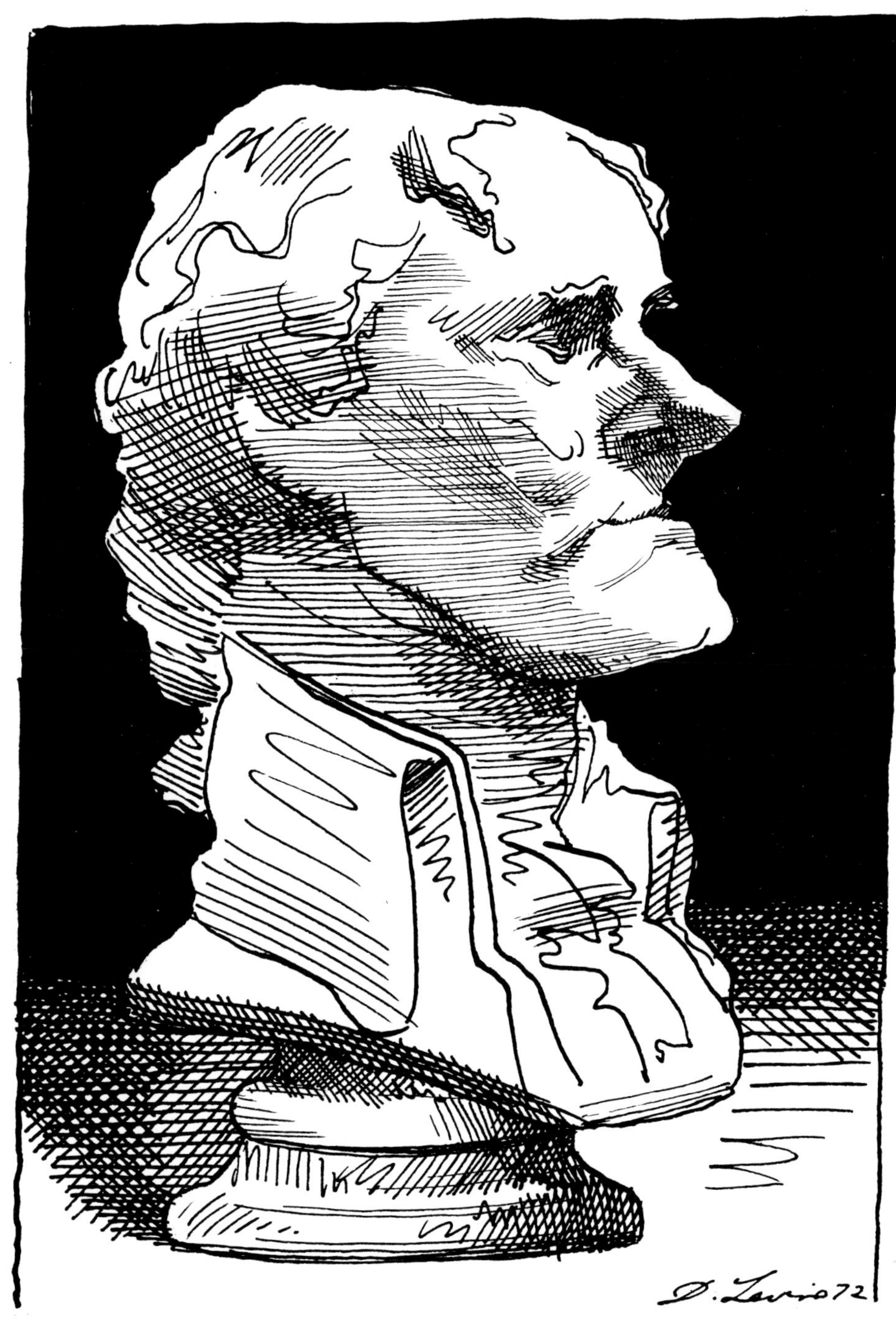

THOMAS JEFFERSON, after Hudon.

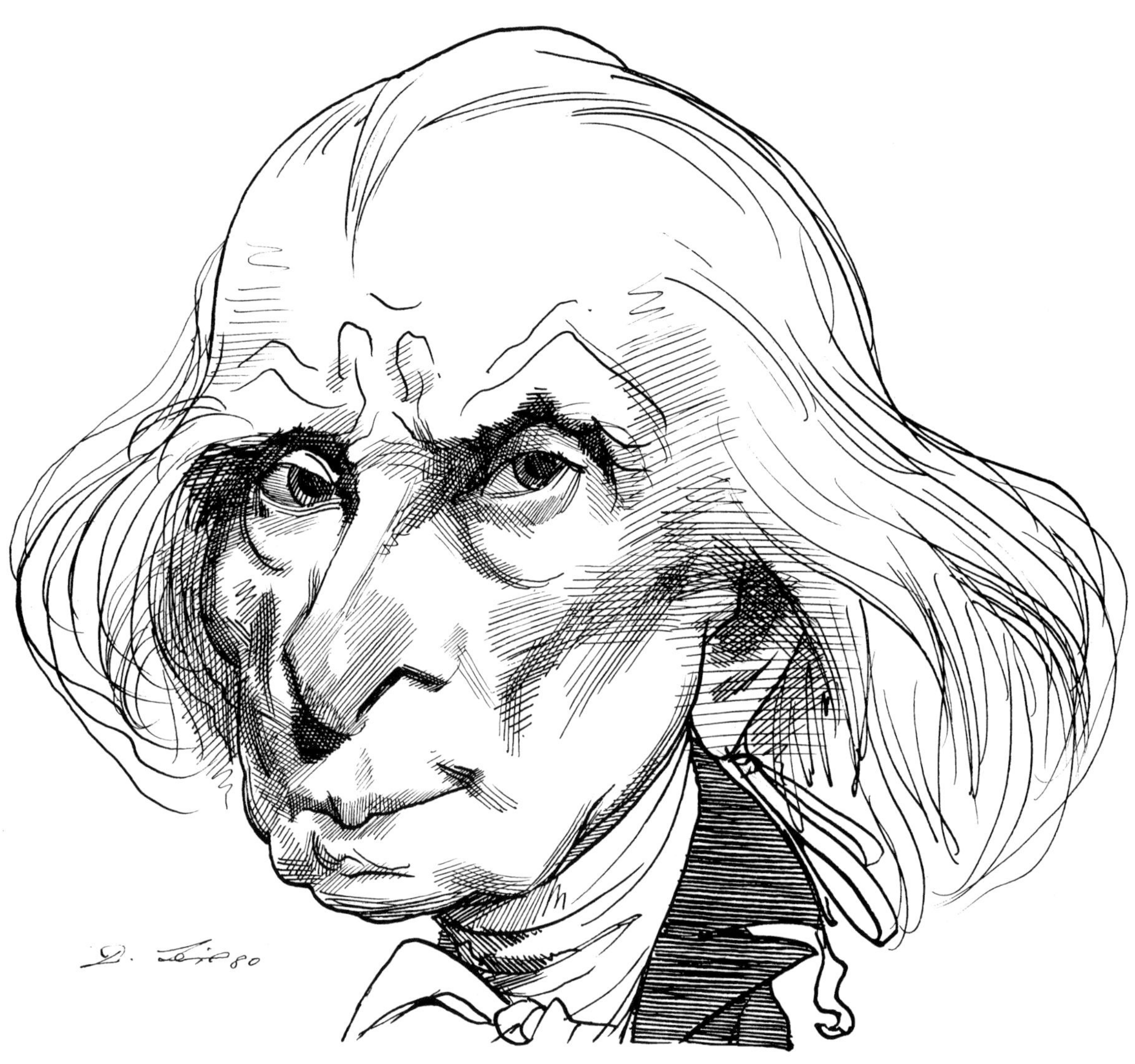

James Madison

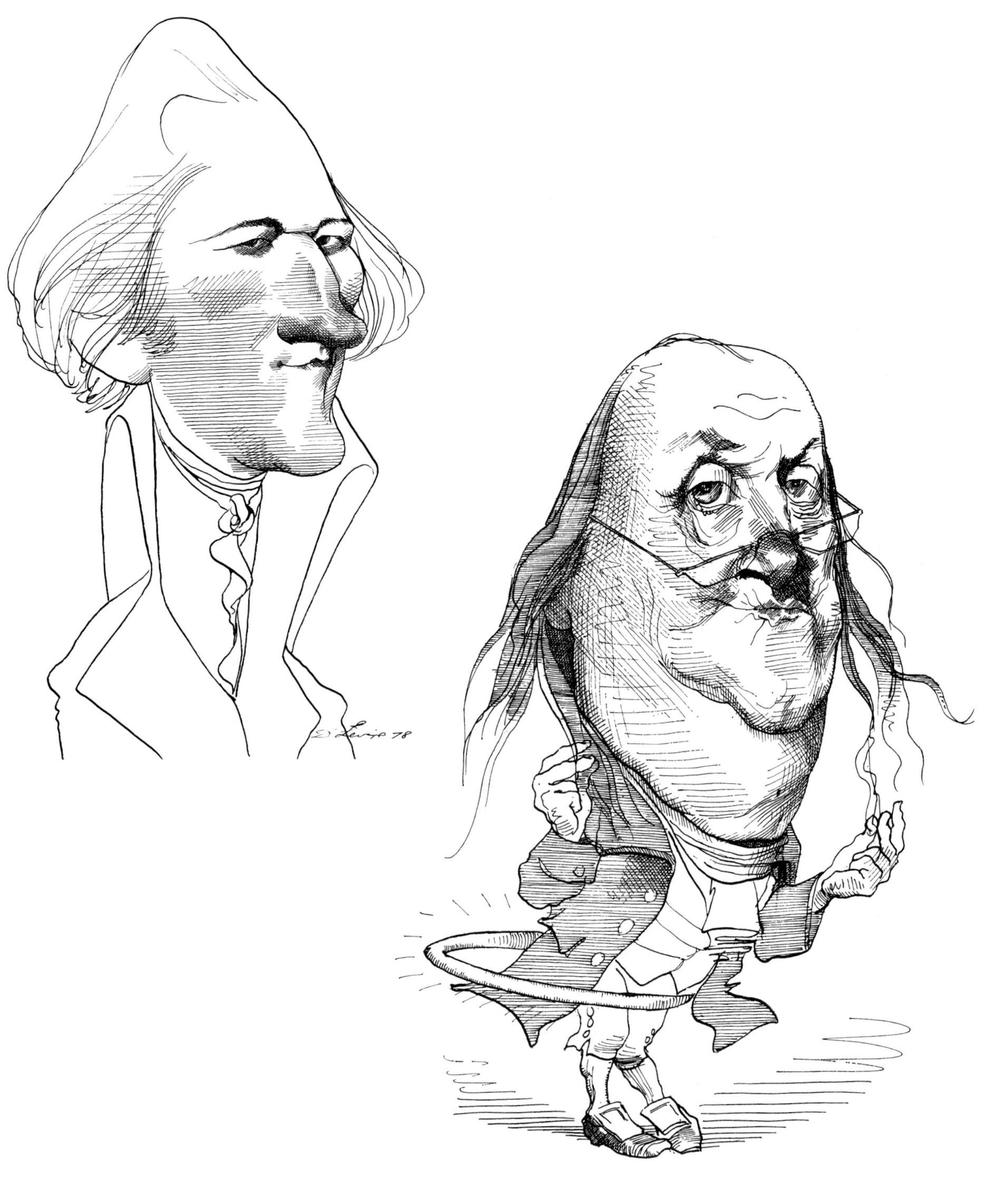

Alexander Hamilton (top), **Benjamin Franklin** (bottom)
While these men were not presidents, their role in the founding of the nation earned them a place on our money, which arguably is more important than the presidency.

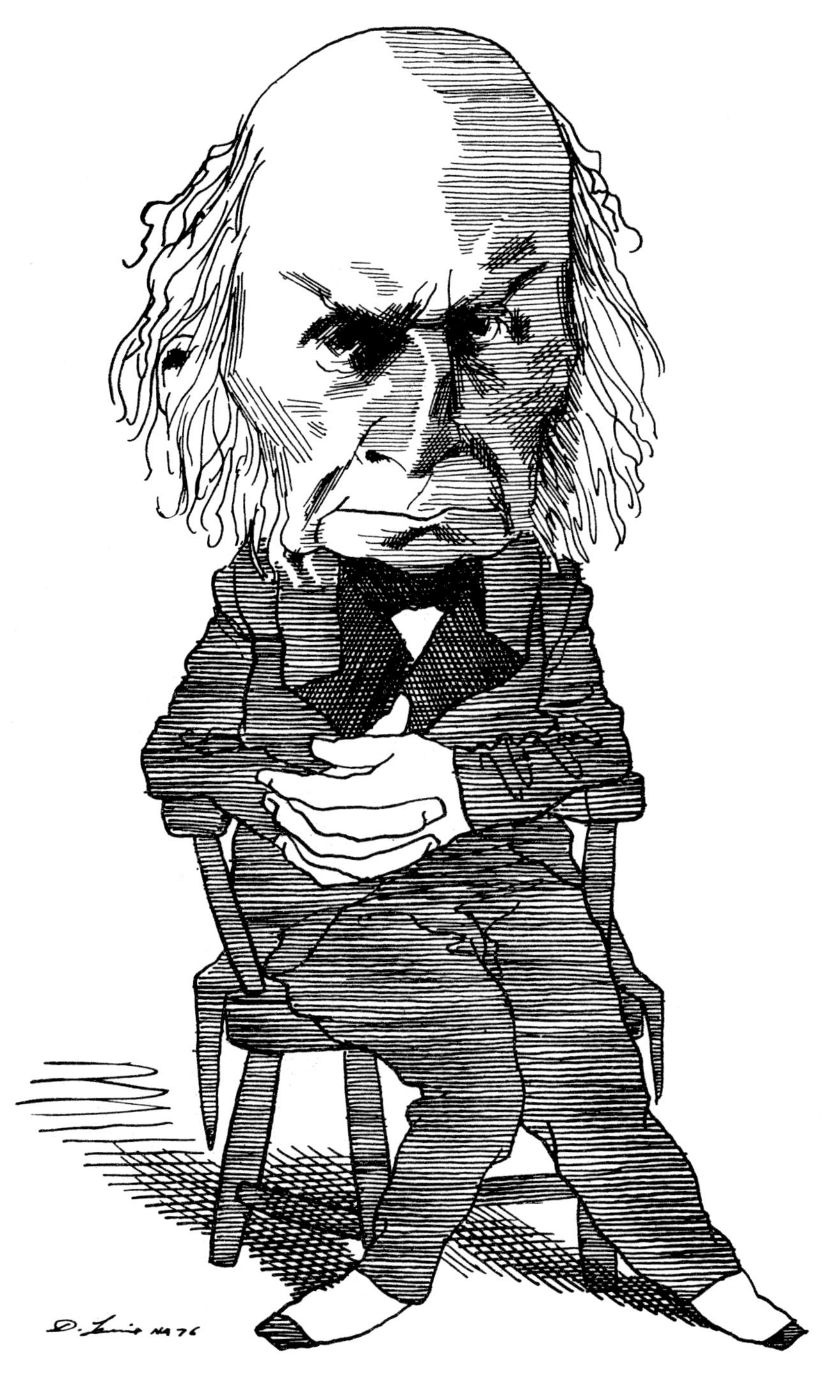

JOHN QUINCY ADAMS

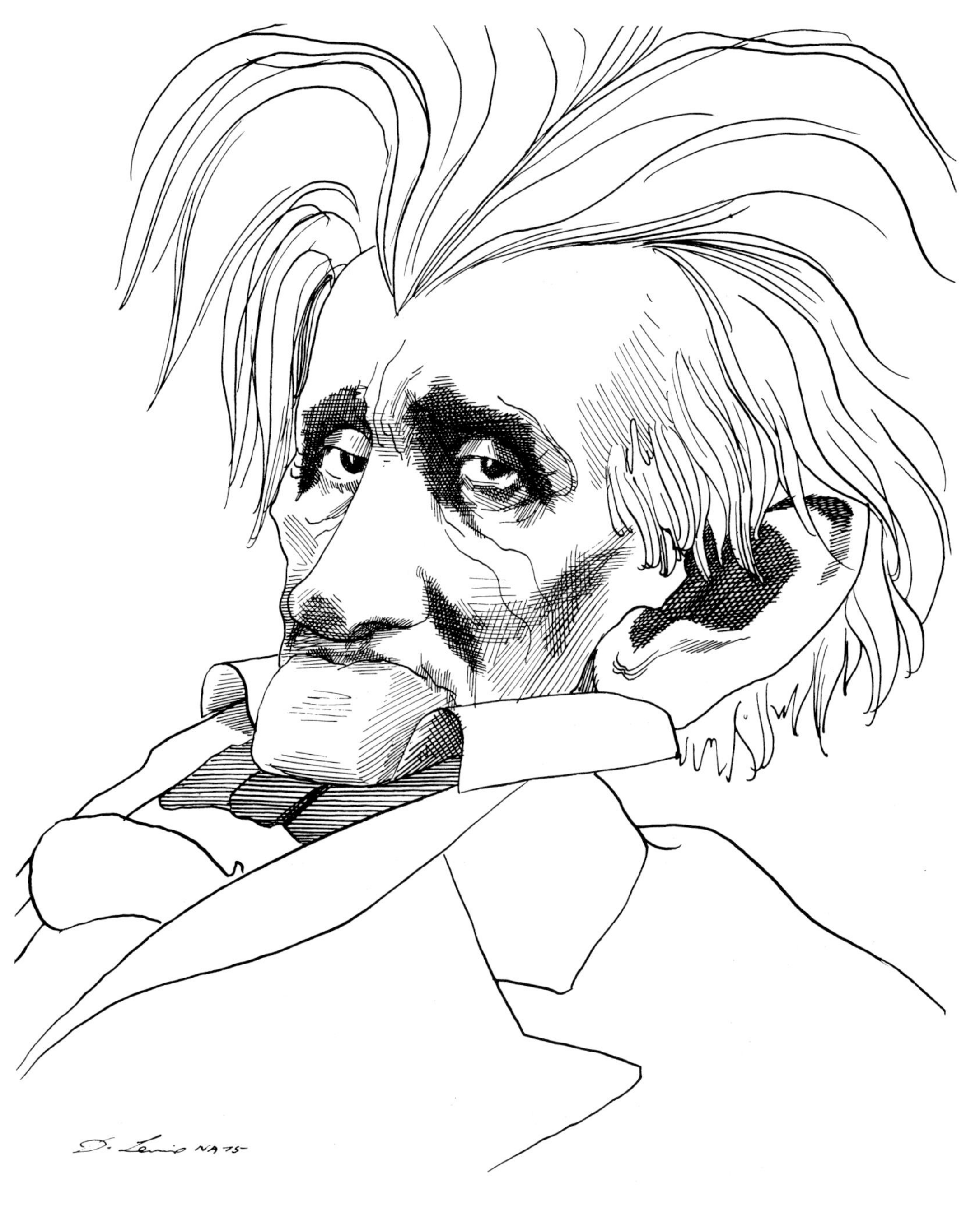

Andrew Jackson

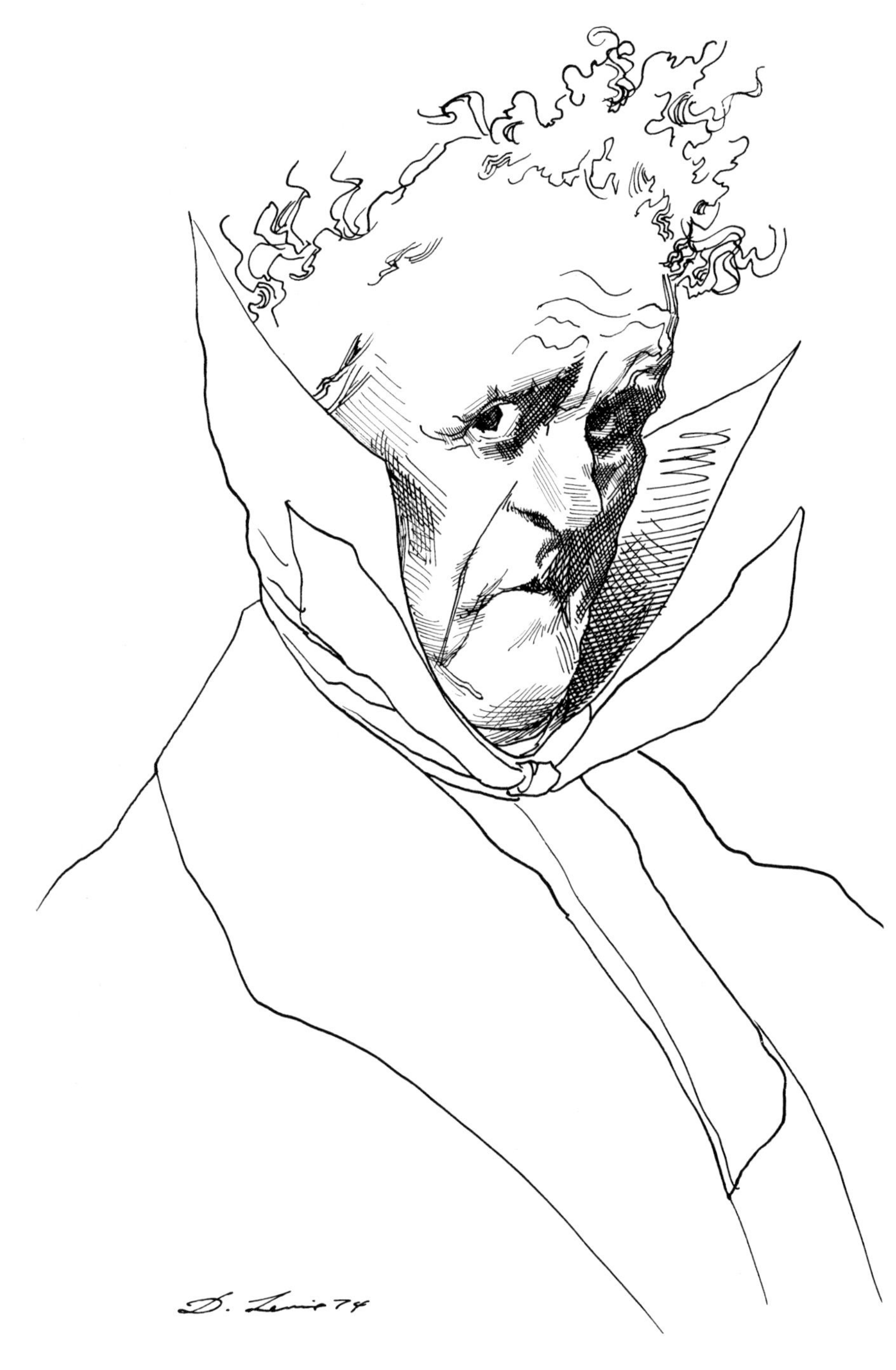

James Buchanan

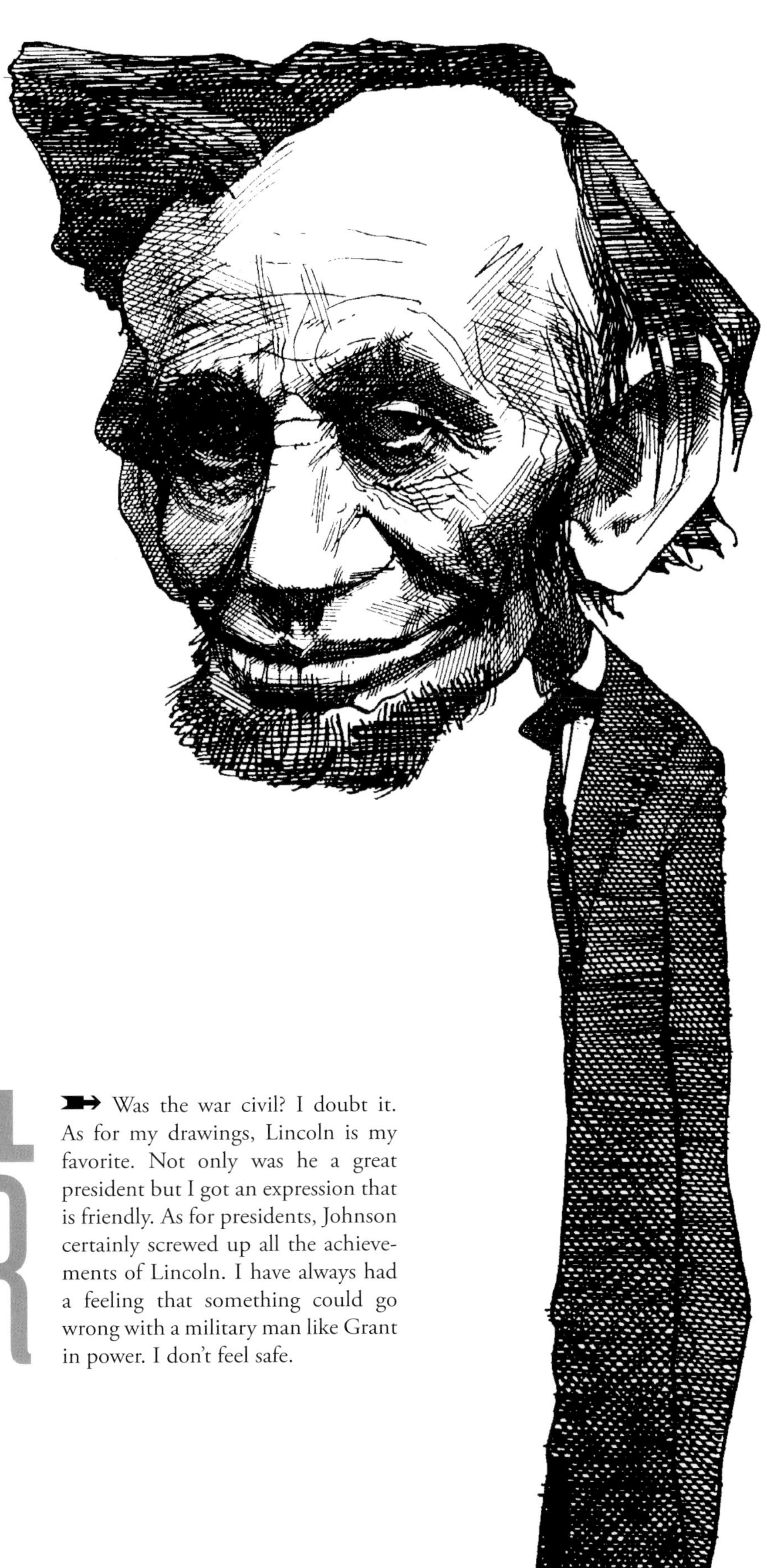

CIVIL WAR

➡ Was the war civil? I doubt it. As for my drawings, Lincoln is my favorite. Not only was he a great president but I got an expression that is friendly. As for presidents, Johnson certainly screwed up all the achievements of Lincoln. I have always had a feeling that something could go wrong with a military man like Grant in power. I don't feel safe.

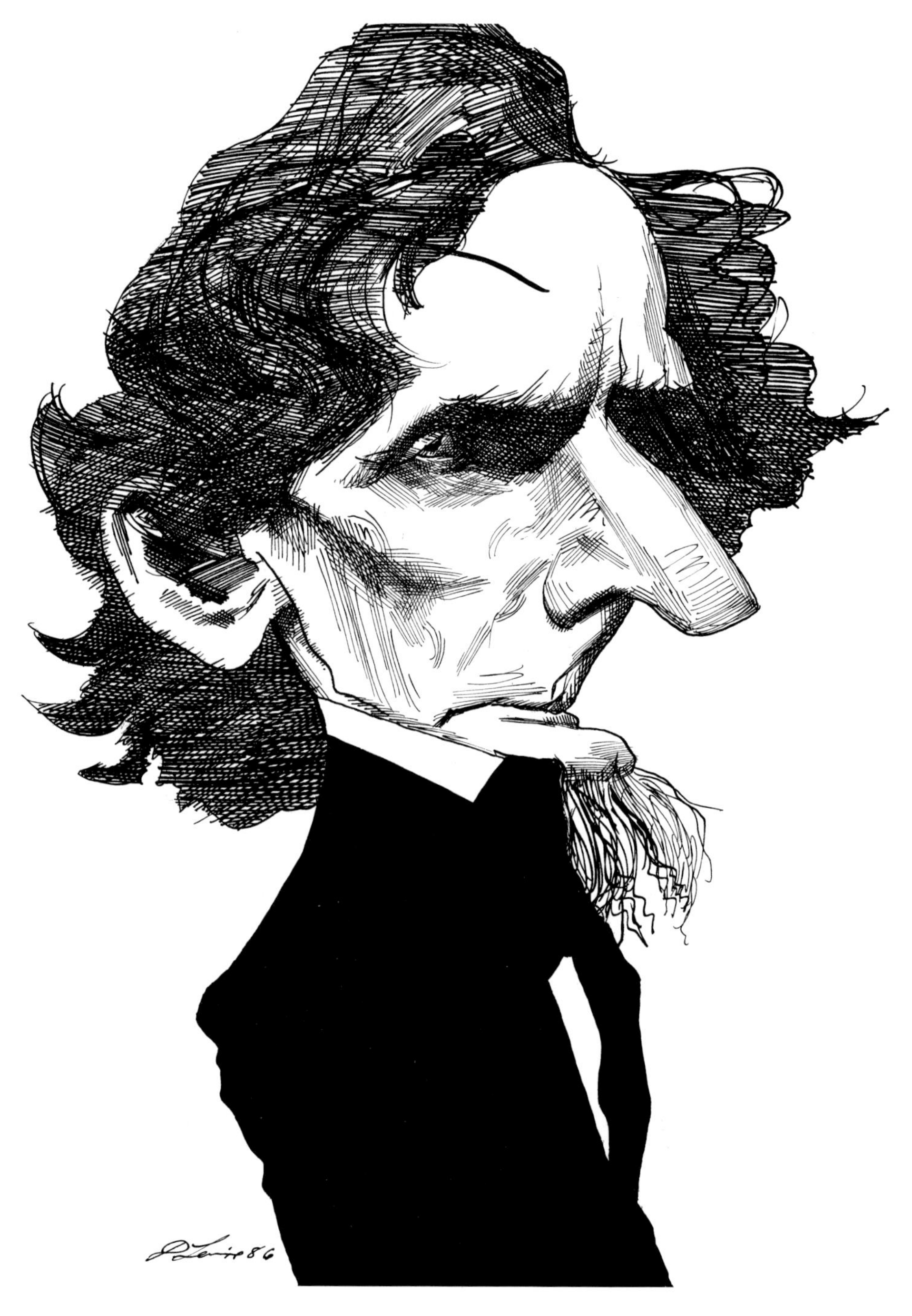

ABOVE: **JEFFERSON DAVIS**. The only man to declare himself the President and have an army to back him up.

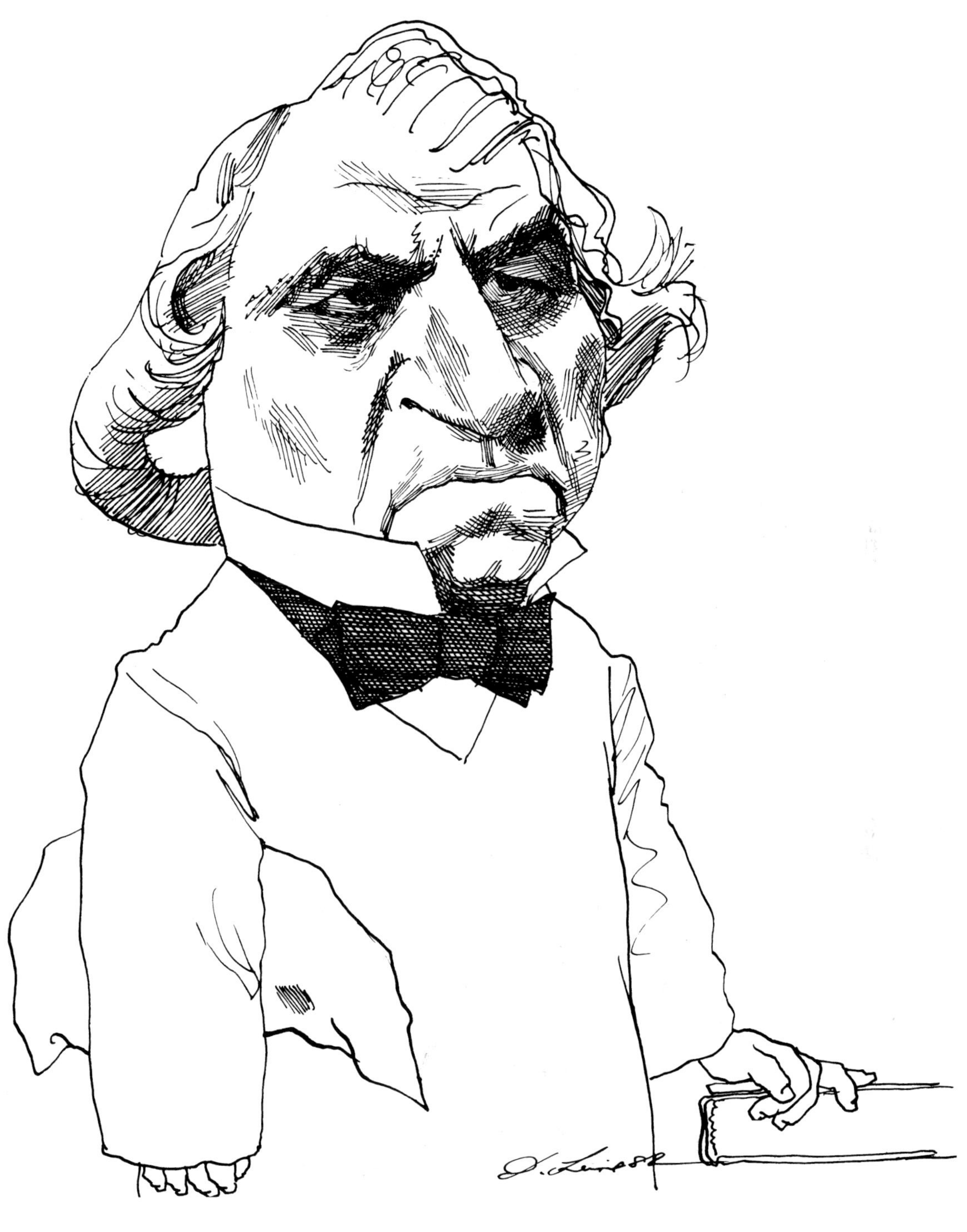

ANDREW JOHNSON

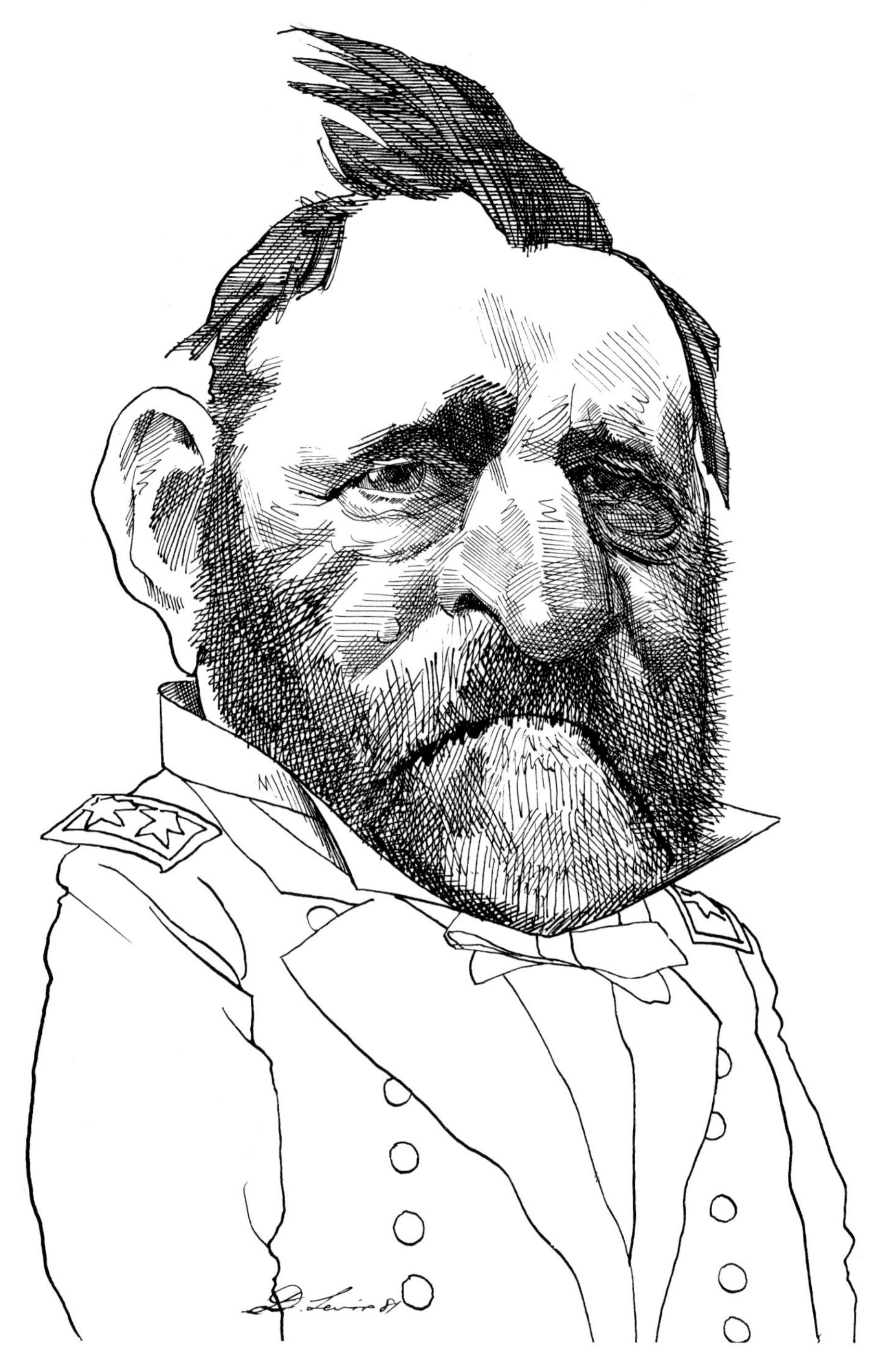

ULYSSES S. GRANT

EARLY 20TH CENTURY

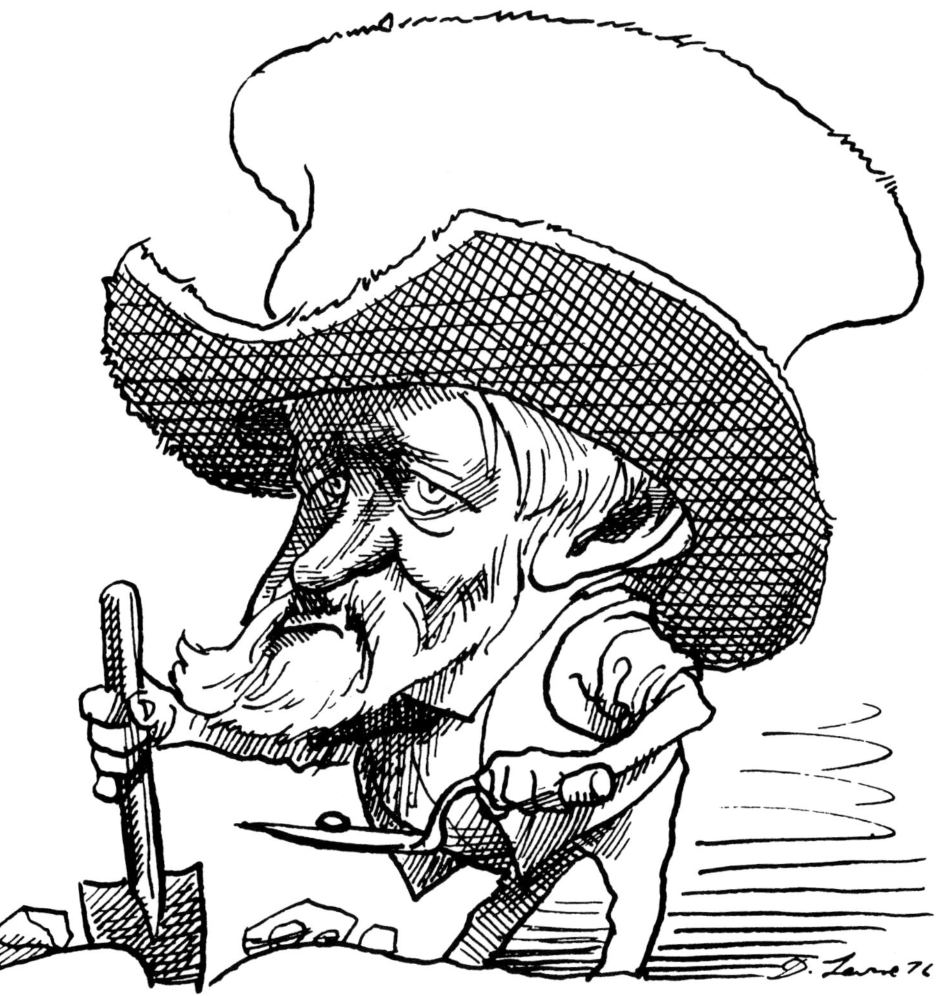

➡ The dawn of a new century saw a procession of unlikely men as president. I show Teddy Roosevelt shooting the wrong animal. When I think of Harding, I laugh at the jokes where people hold a baby up and say "You made this!" due to his affairs while in office. Woodrow Wilson shows that Bush is not the first to carry out warrantless searches. Wilson created the American Protective League which checked up on people who failed to buy Liberty Bonds and spoke out against the government's policies. Finally, Hoover, who ran on a platform of economic modernization, did not seem up to the task when faced with the Depression. Almost forty years later, Nixon showed he was another Hoover when faced with tough economic times.

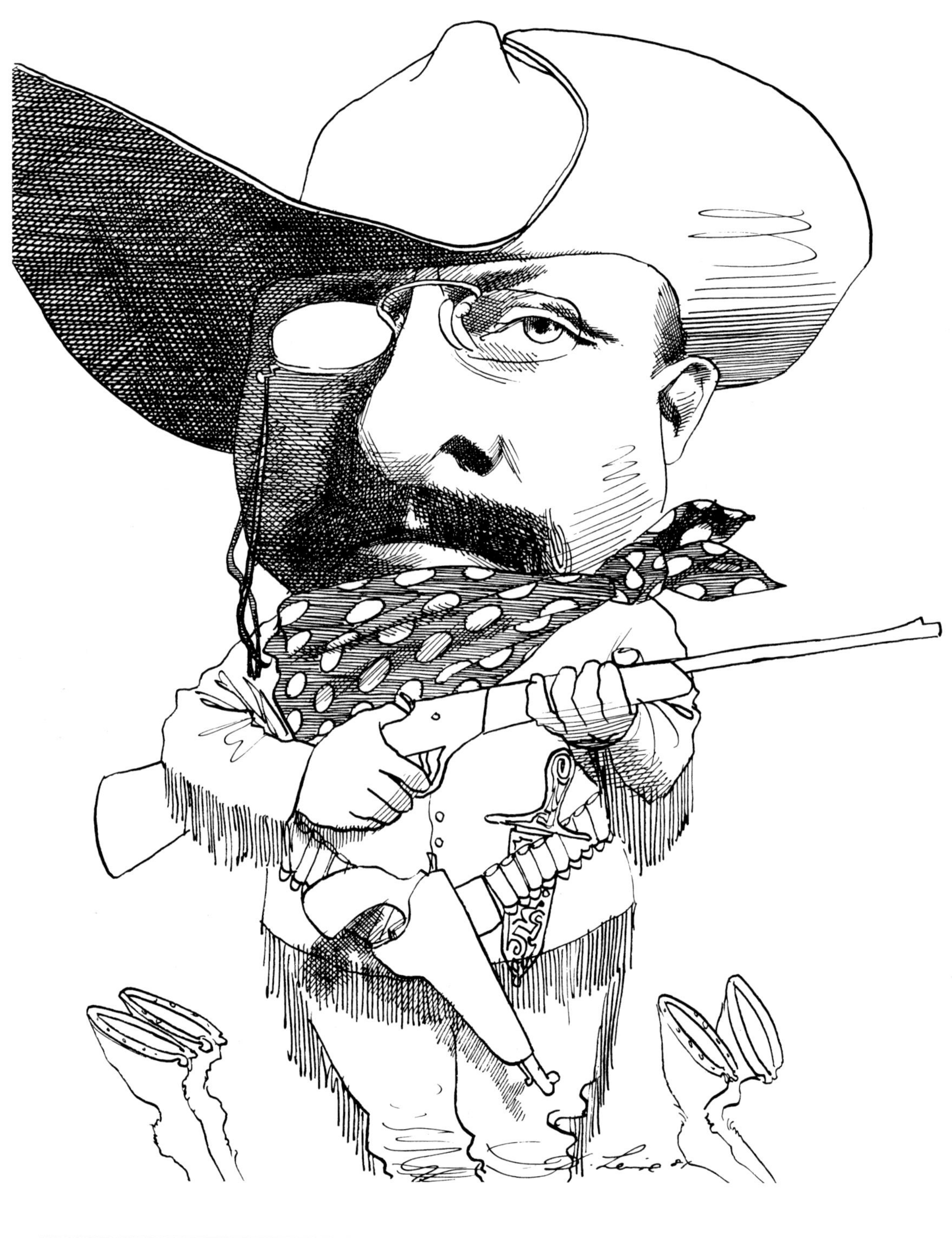

ABOVE: **THEODORE ROOSEVELT**
PREVIOUS PAGE: **BENJAMIN HARRISON**

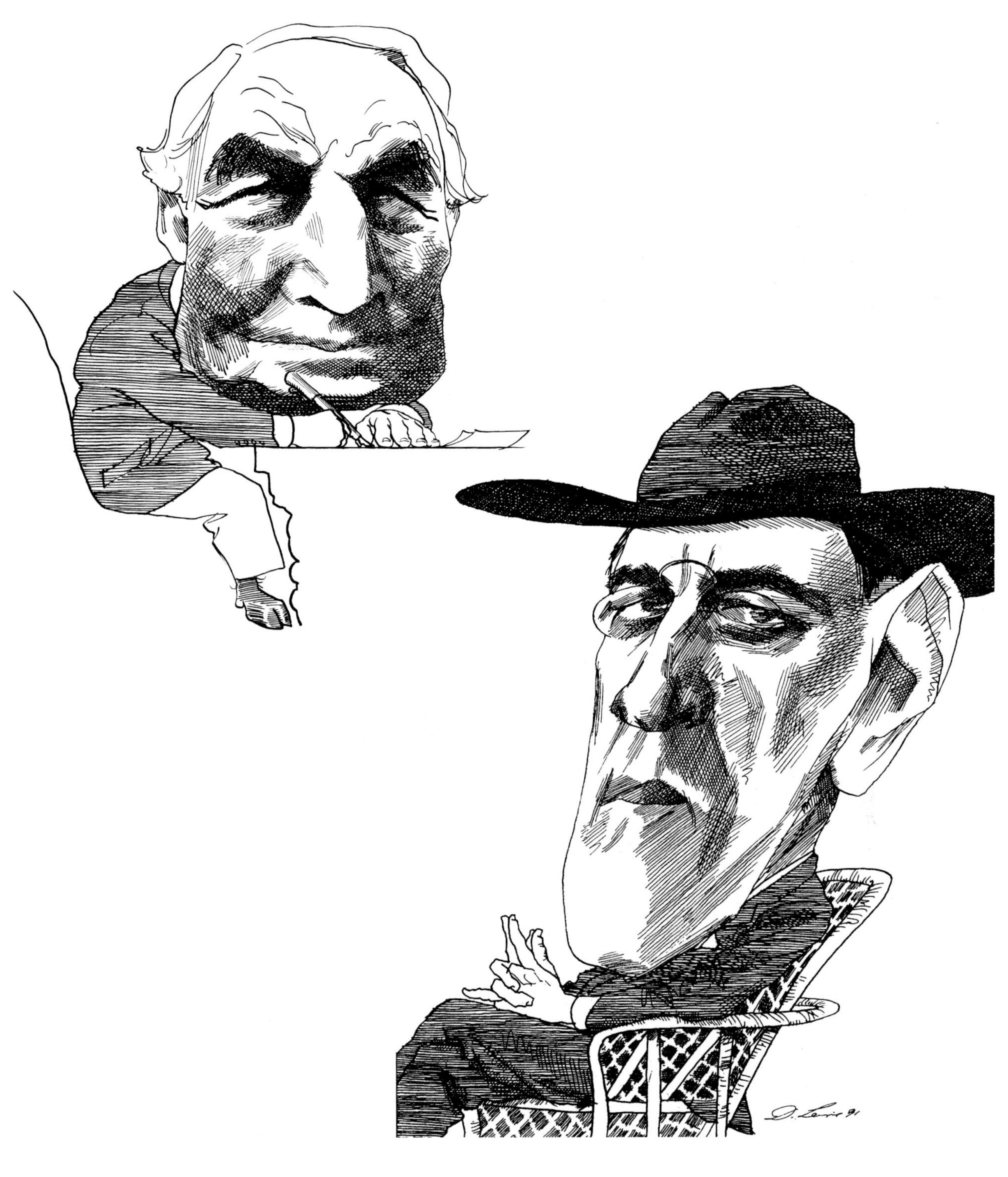

Warren G. Harding (top)
Woodrow Wilson (bottom)

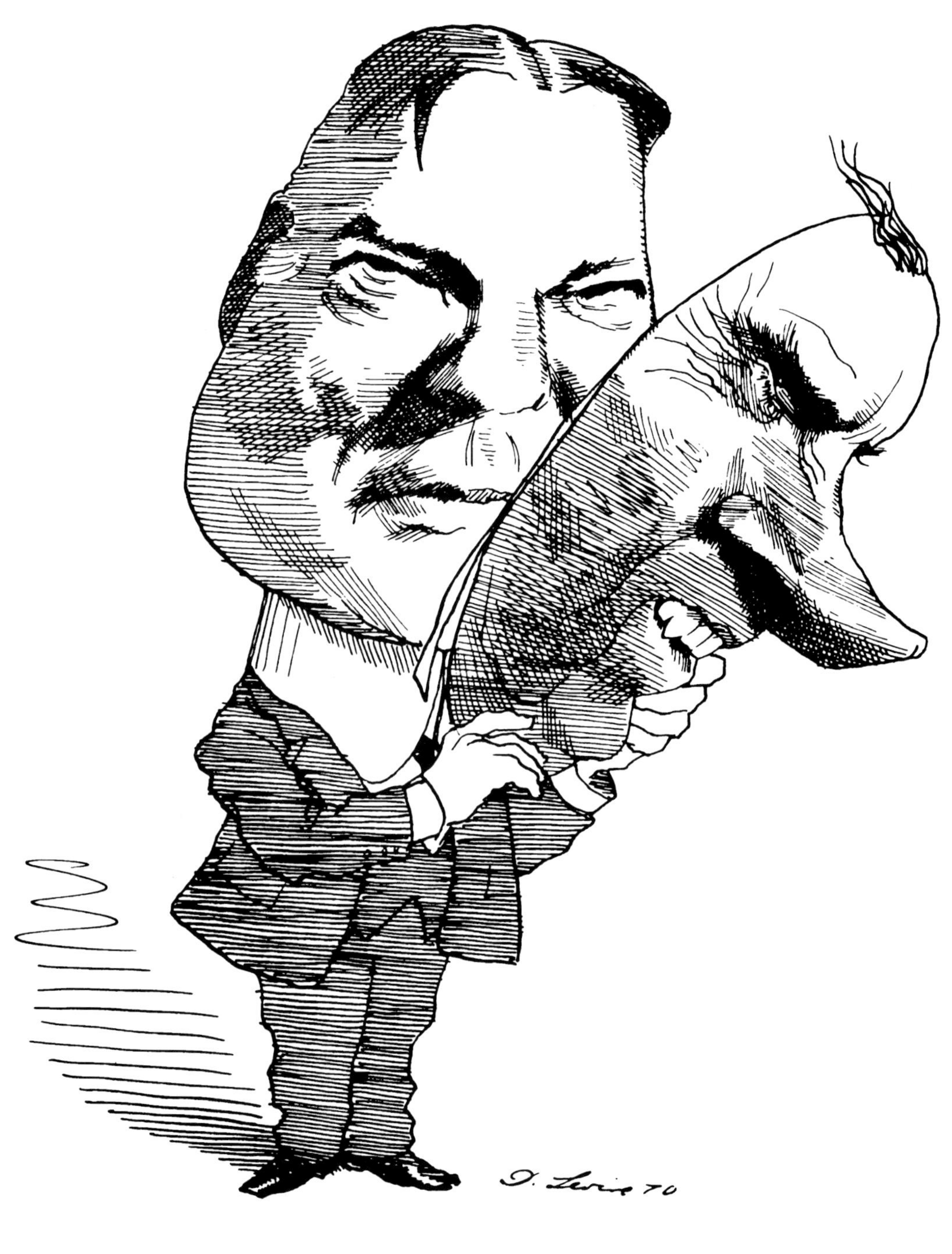

HERBERT HOOVER, "Depression 1970." The recession of 1969-70, and the Nixon administration's refusal to call it such, conjured memories of another president who assured citizens that "prosperity is just around the corner."

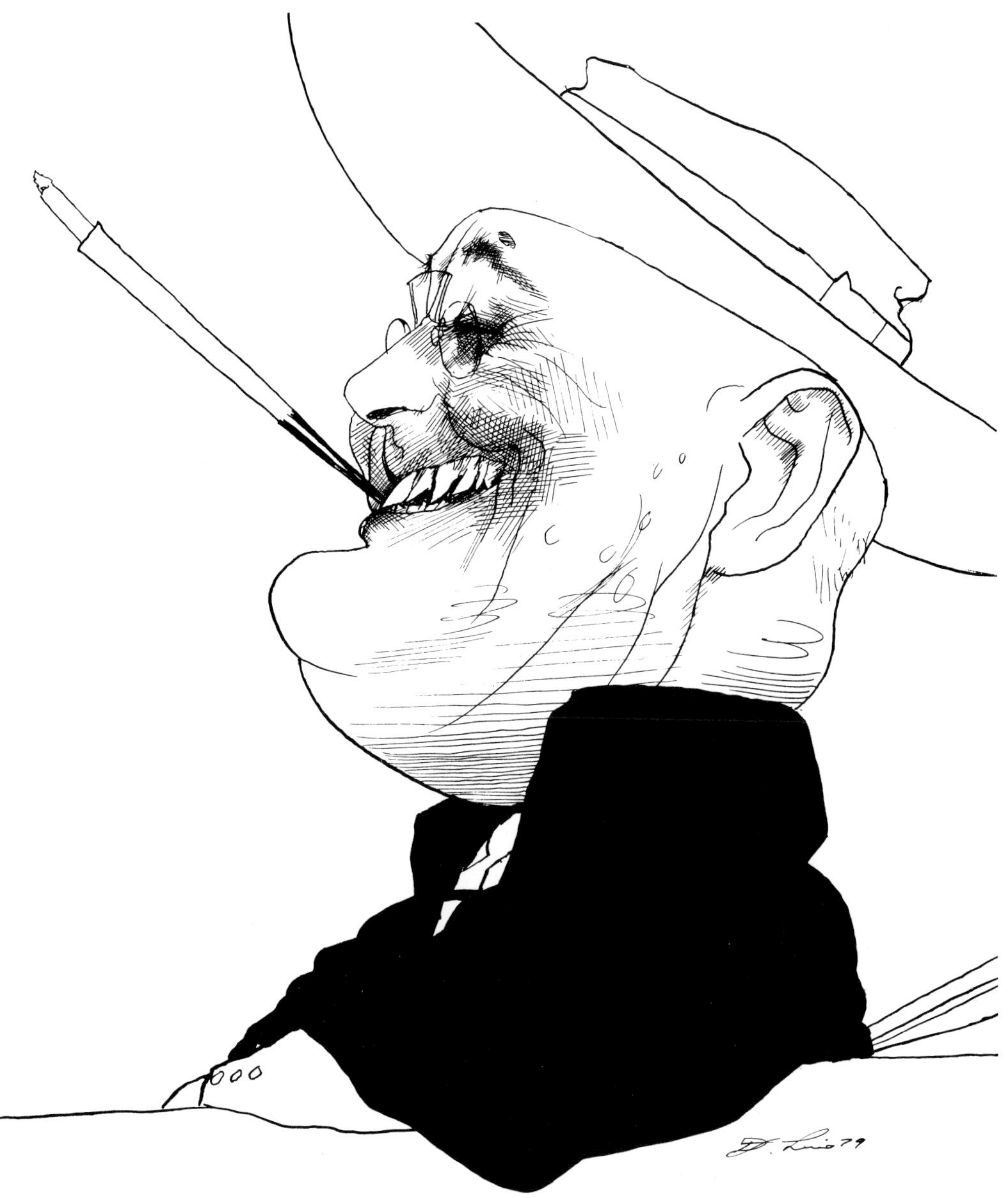

★ FRANKLIN D. ★

ROOSEVELT

Franklin Roosevelt is the only President I have shaken hands with. I was 10 or 12 at the time, and he came to Ebbets Field in Brooklyn and we all ran toward him. I think he is the 20th century's great President. He understood the social issues facing the county and with his mix of wit, social interests, and intelligence, worked to make things better for many people. I think the greatest move socially in this country was the GI Bill introduced by the Roosevelt administration. Eleanor aided and encouraged her husband. And their tremendous education, which was made fun of, I wished I had.

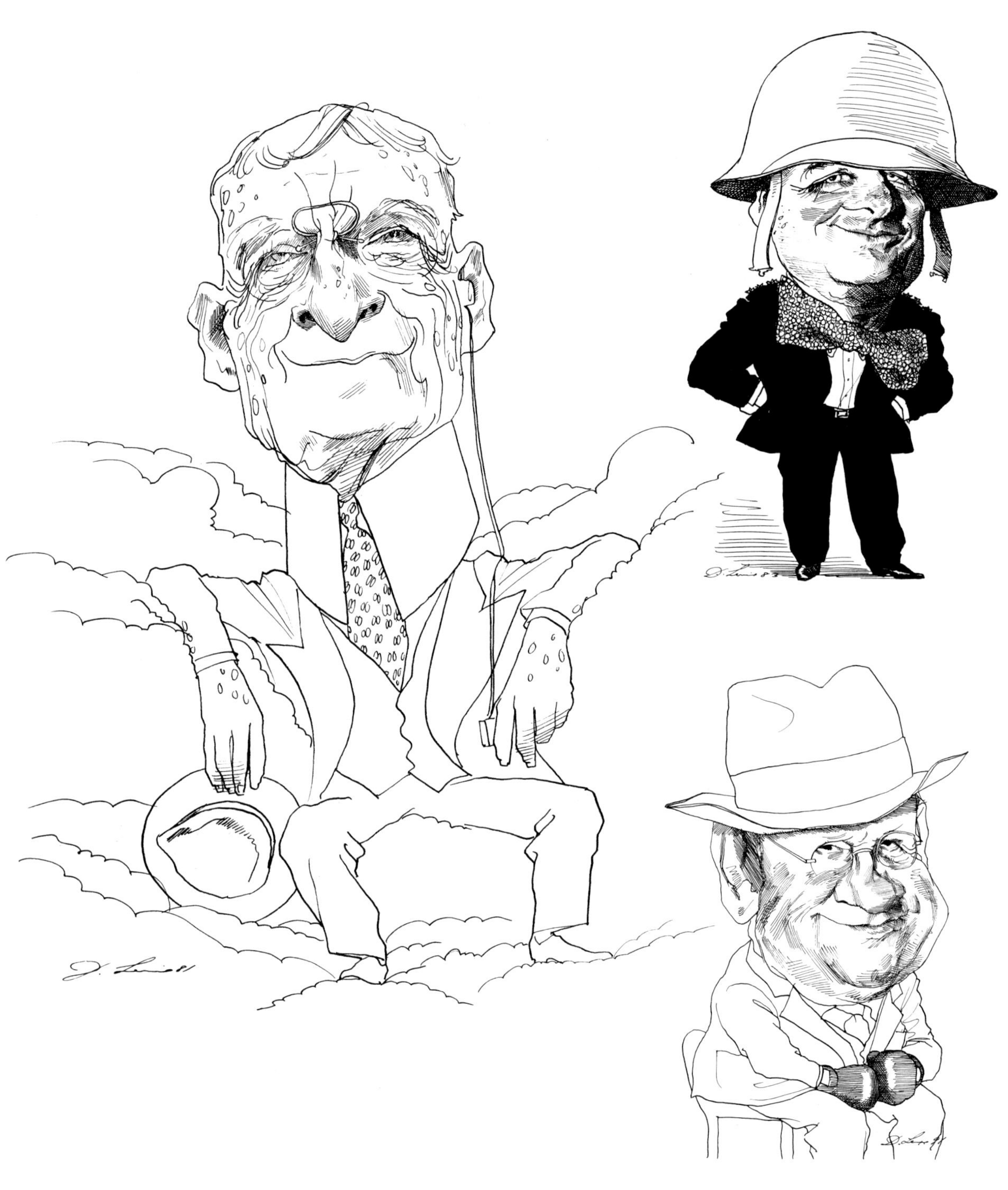

CLOCKWISE FROM LEFT: Financier **BERNARD BARUCH** provided important economic advice from a park bench located near the White House. **WILD BILL DONOVAN**, head of wartime intelligence, is considered the father of the CIA. **HAROLD ICKES**, a Republican in the quintessential Democratic administration; The "Aggressive Progressive" was Director of the Public Works Administration for the New Deal, and later Secretary of Interior.

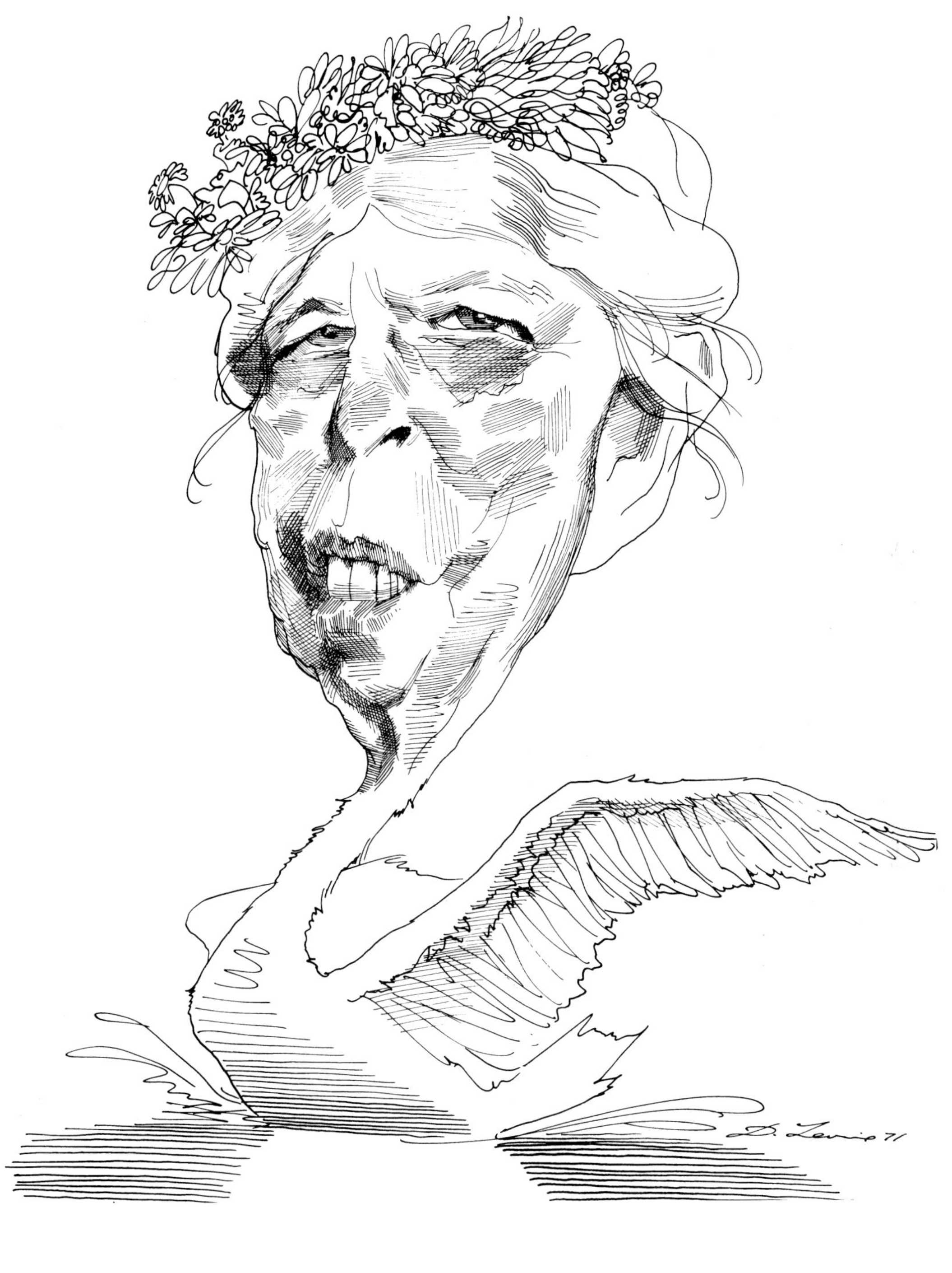

Eleanor Roosevelt

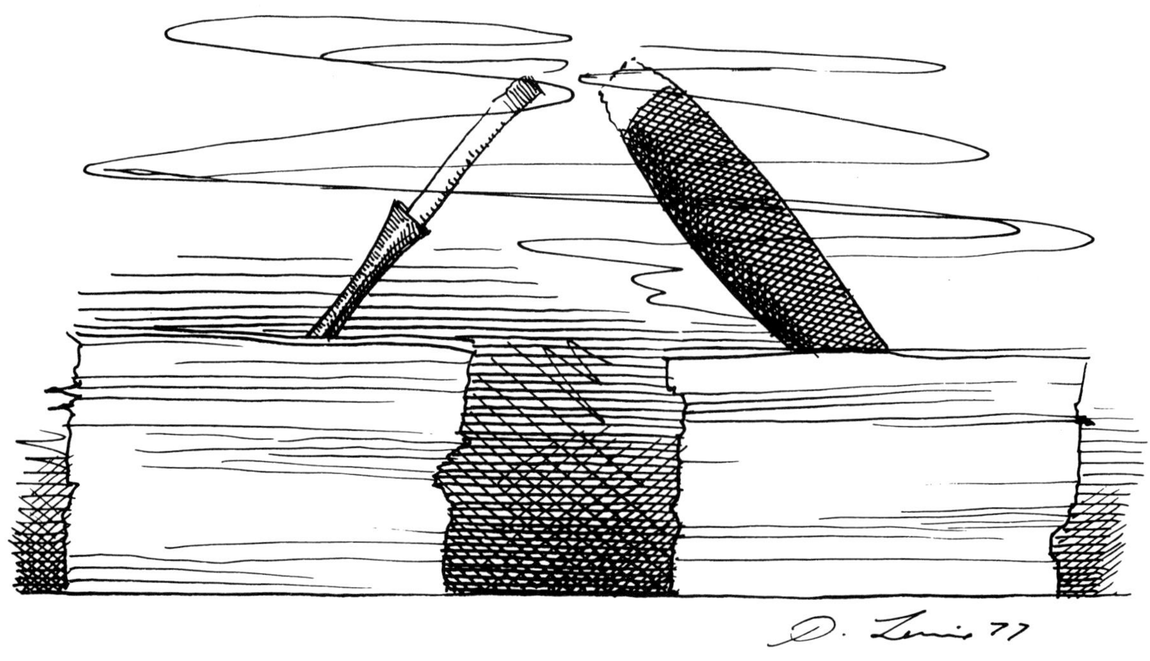

Franklin D. Roosevelt & Winston Churchill

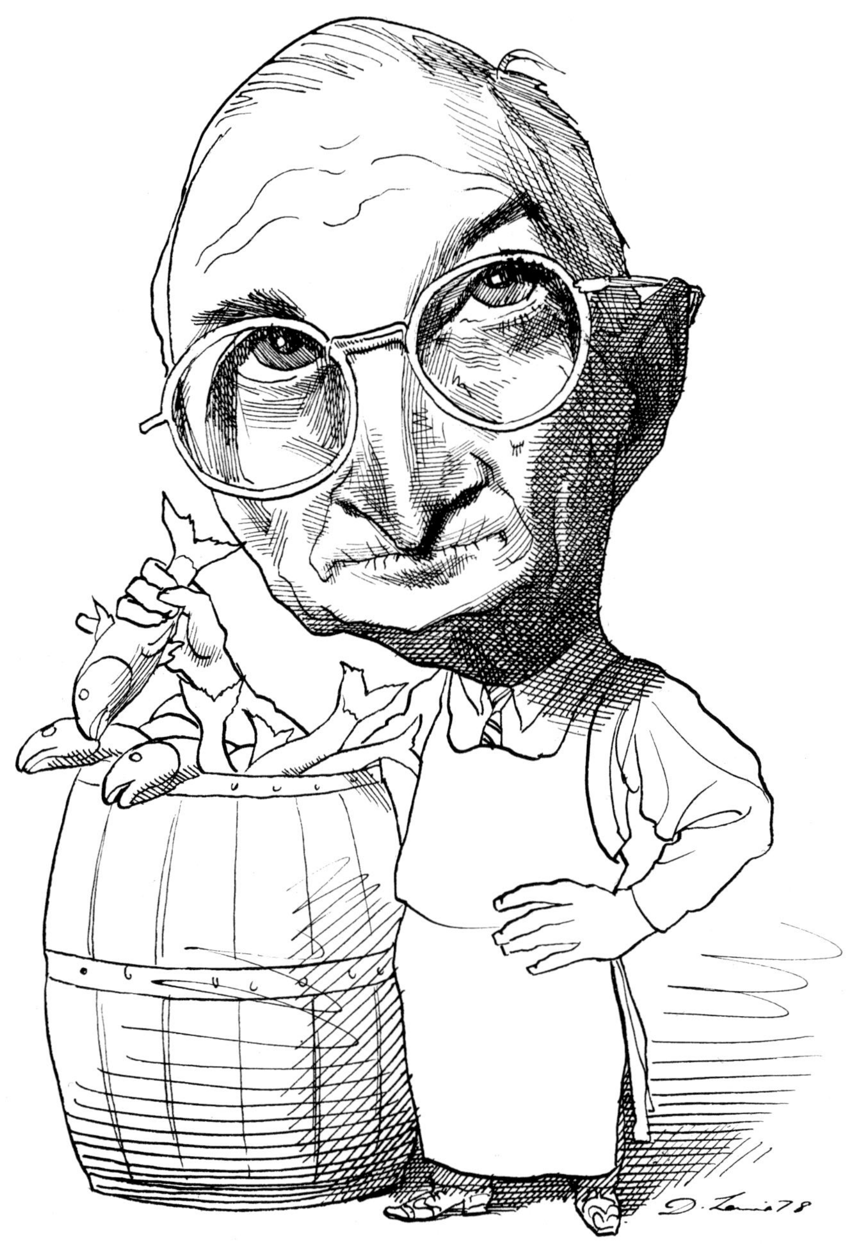

HARRY S. ★★★★★ TRUMAN

➡ The Great Liberal used the bomb and took my passport. I've shown him with a barrel full of red herrings. There were plenty of reactionary things accomplished by Truman such as limiting—almost eliminating—unions whereas Roosevelt had gone along with the development of the CIO. Right there is a true indication of who stands where on social issues. Around the world, the American imperialism that we have today is in part because of Truman's Secretary of State, Dean Acheson. Yet compared to General MacArthur and Senator McCarthy, he doesn't seem so bad. MacArthur would have had us in total war. McCarthy would have had us informing on each other.

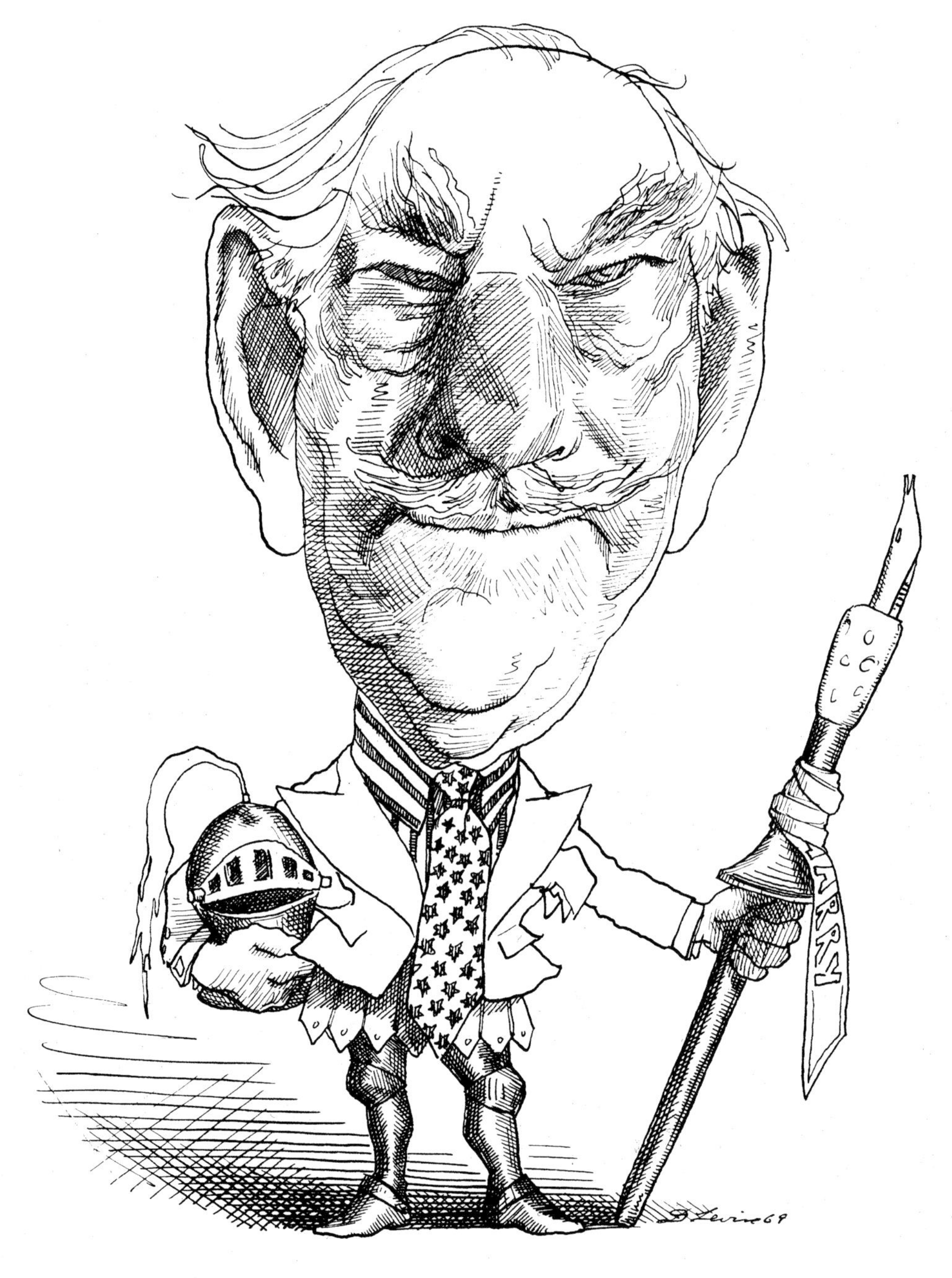

Dean Acheson. The Secretary of State was a committed cold warrior who defended State Department personnel against McCarthy's witch hunt. He wrote the Truman Doctrine, yet also designed the Marshall Plan.

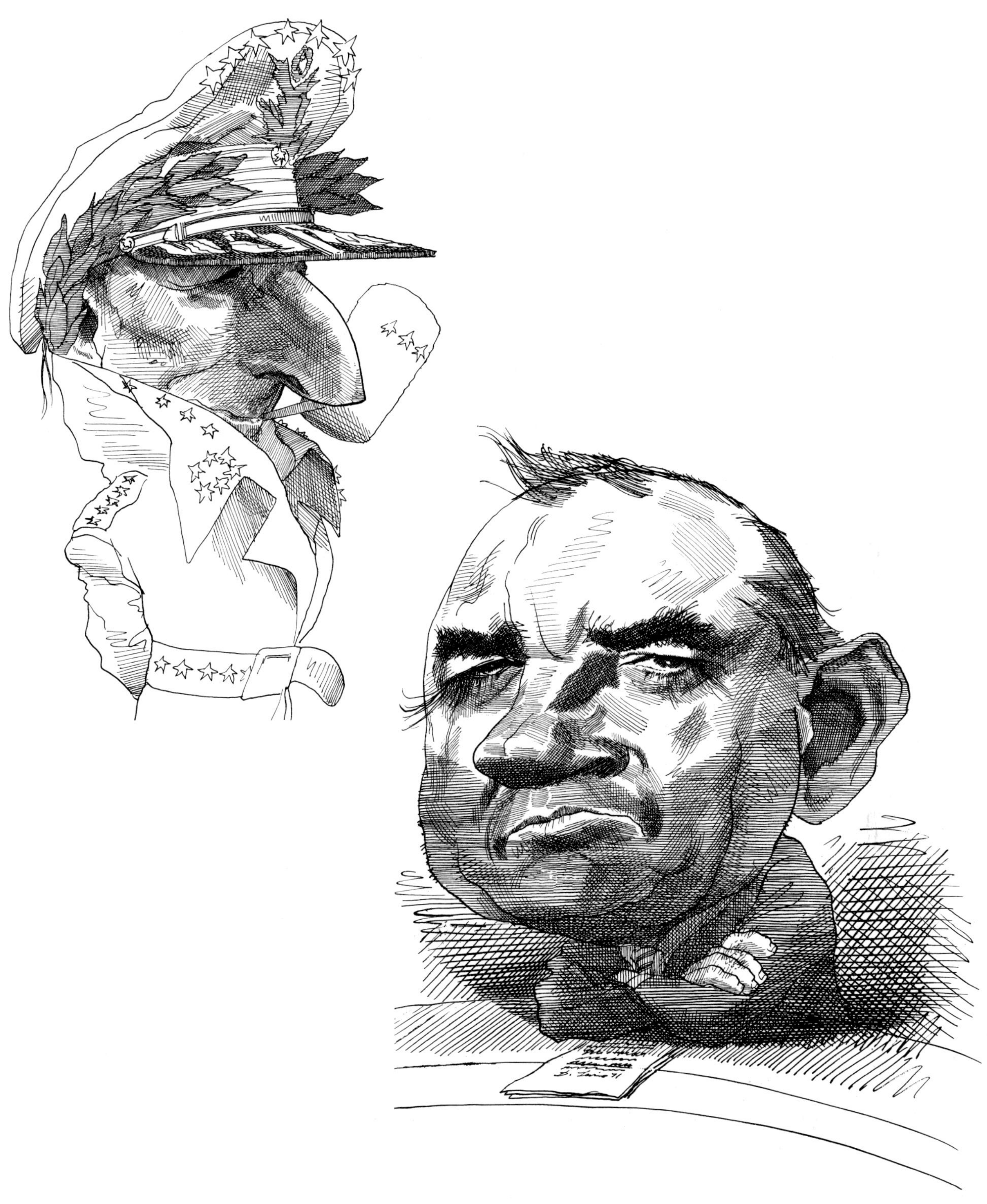

Two thorns in Truman's side: General **DOUGLAS MACARTHUR** (TOP), the leader of the US forces in the Pacific, he eventually was dismissed by Truman for publicly, and repeatedly, disobeying Truman's Korean War Policy. Senator **JOSEPH MCCARTHY** (BOTTOM) frequently characterized Truman as soft or in league with Communists during McCarthy's discredited search for Soviet spies in the government.

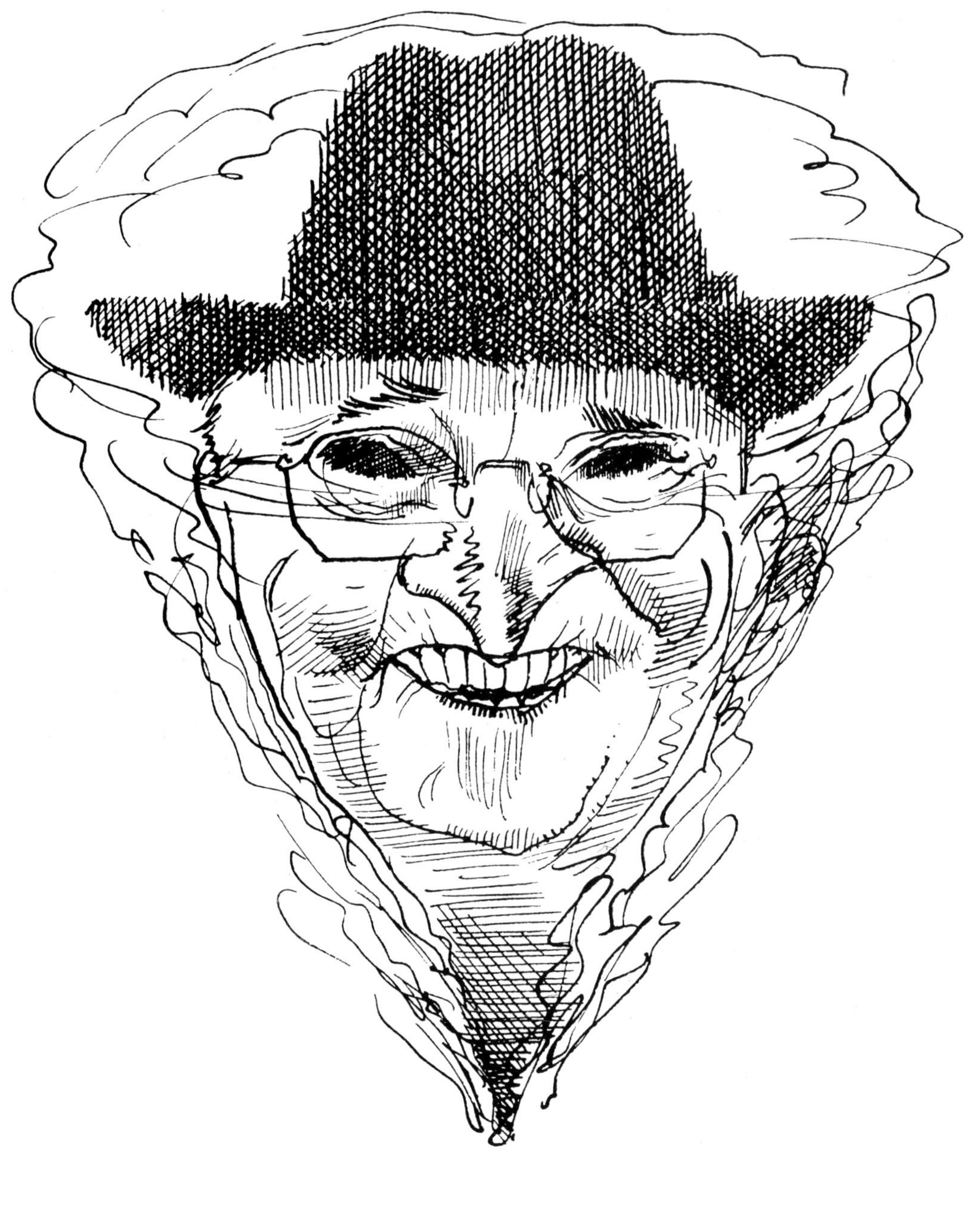

Harry S. Truman

DWIGHT

★

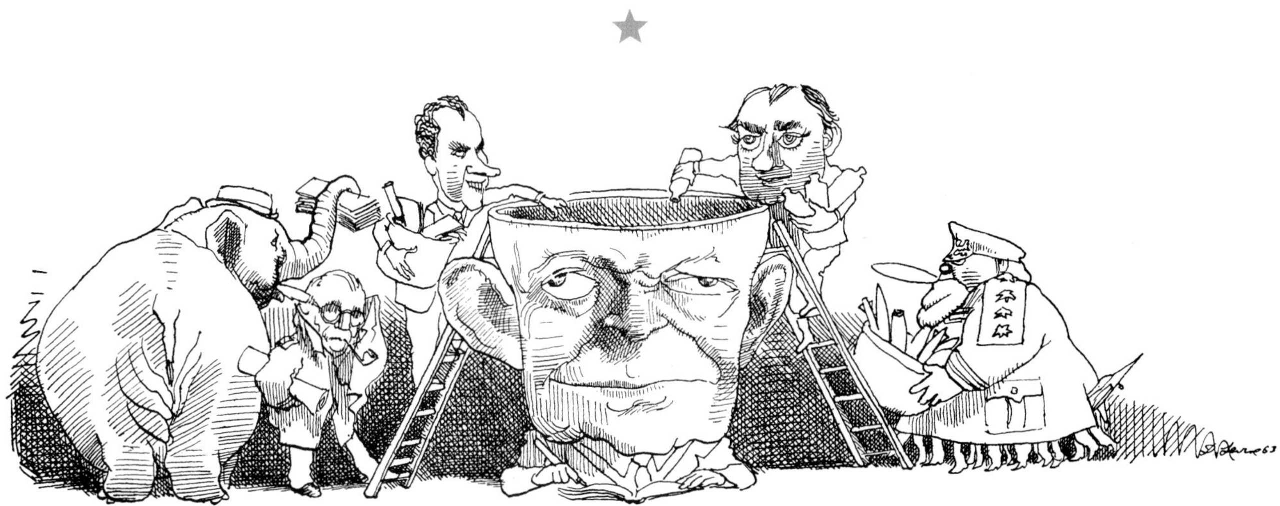

EISENHOWER

➽ Everyday they should print out Eisenhower's statement about the military industrial complex. Today he would be talking about lobbyists. It was during Eisenhower's administration that I got my passport back. Rockwell Kent had lost his as well, and he fought it all the way to the Supreme Court, and won.

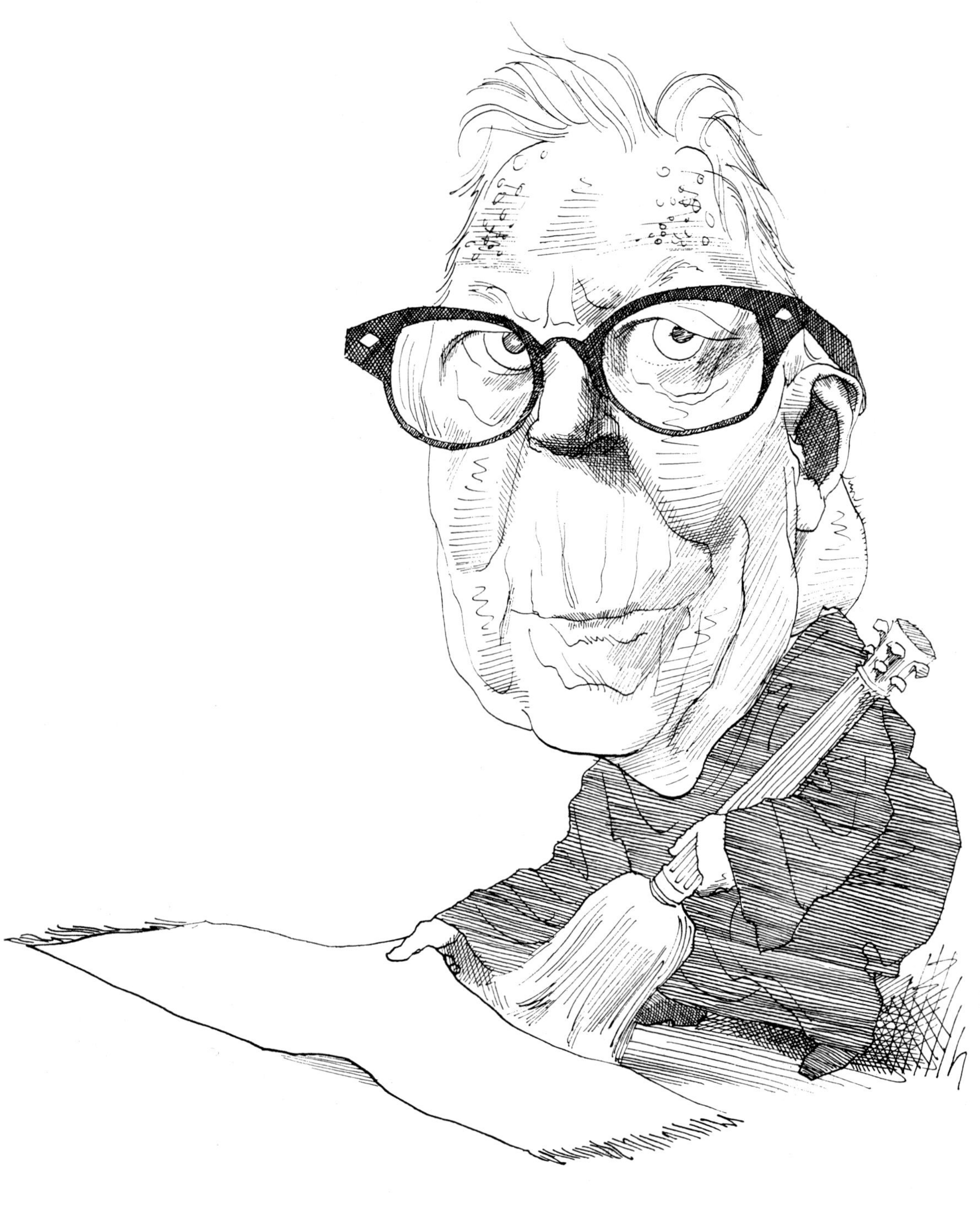

Justice Earl Warren. A one time Vice Presidential candidate in 1948, Warren was rewarded for his 1952 campaign support with a nomination as Chief Justice of the Supreme Court. The Warren Court was known for using its judicial powers to effect social change, although in this drawing I show what he did as the head of the Warren Commission that investigated the JFK assassination.

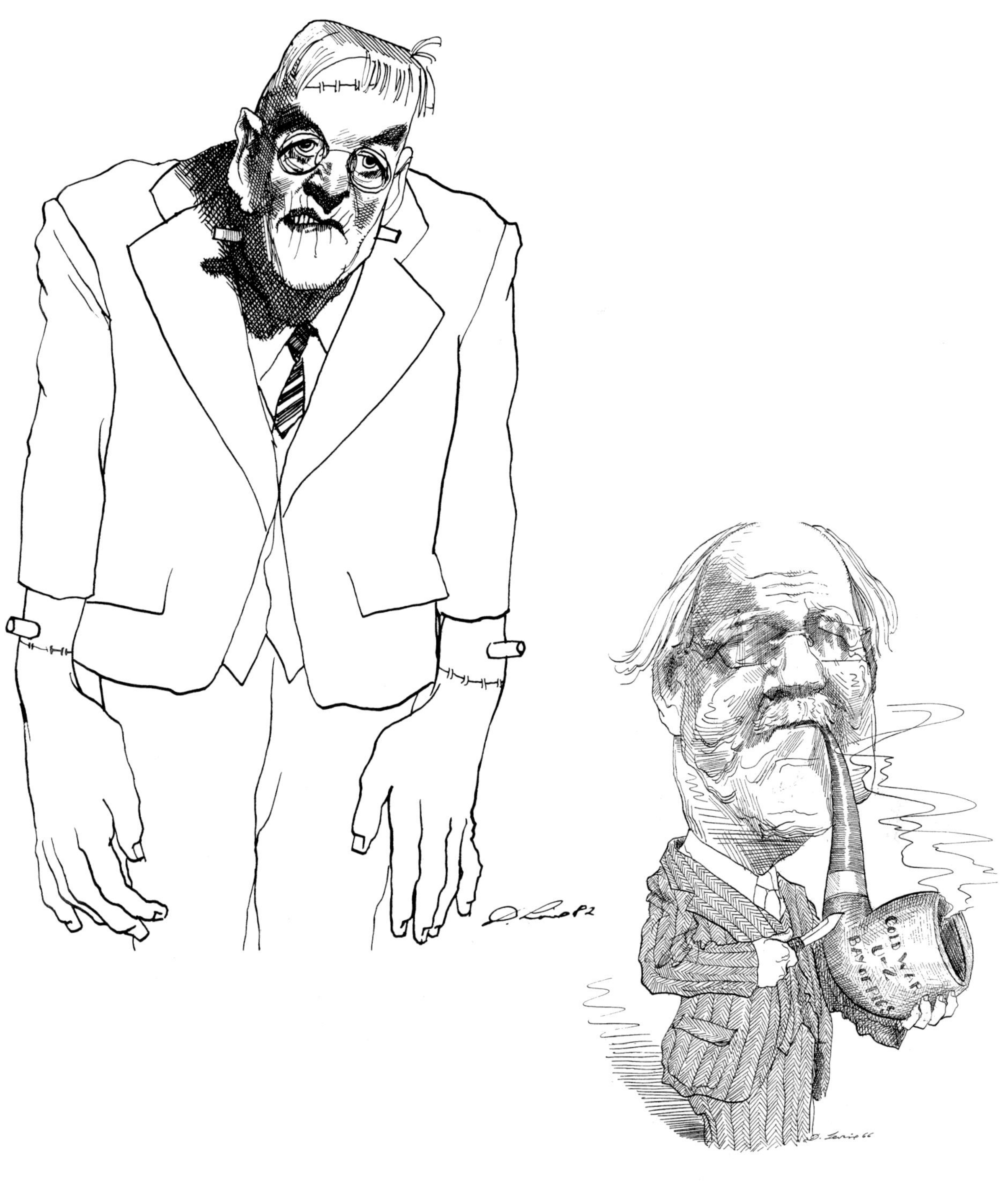

ALLEN W. DULLES (TOP) and **JOHN FOSTER DULLES** (BOTTOM). These two brothers shaped foreign policy throughout the 1950s. Allen was director of the CIA, while John was Secretary of State.

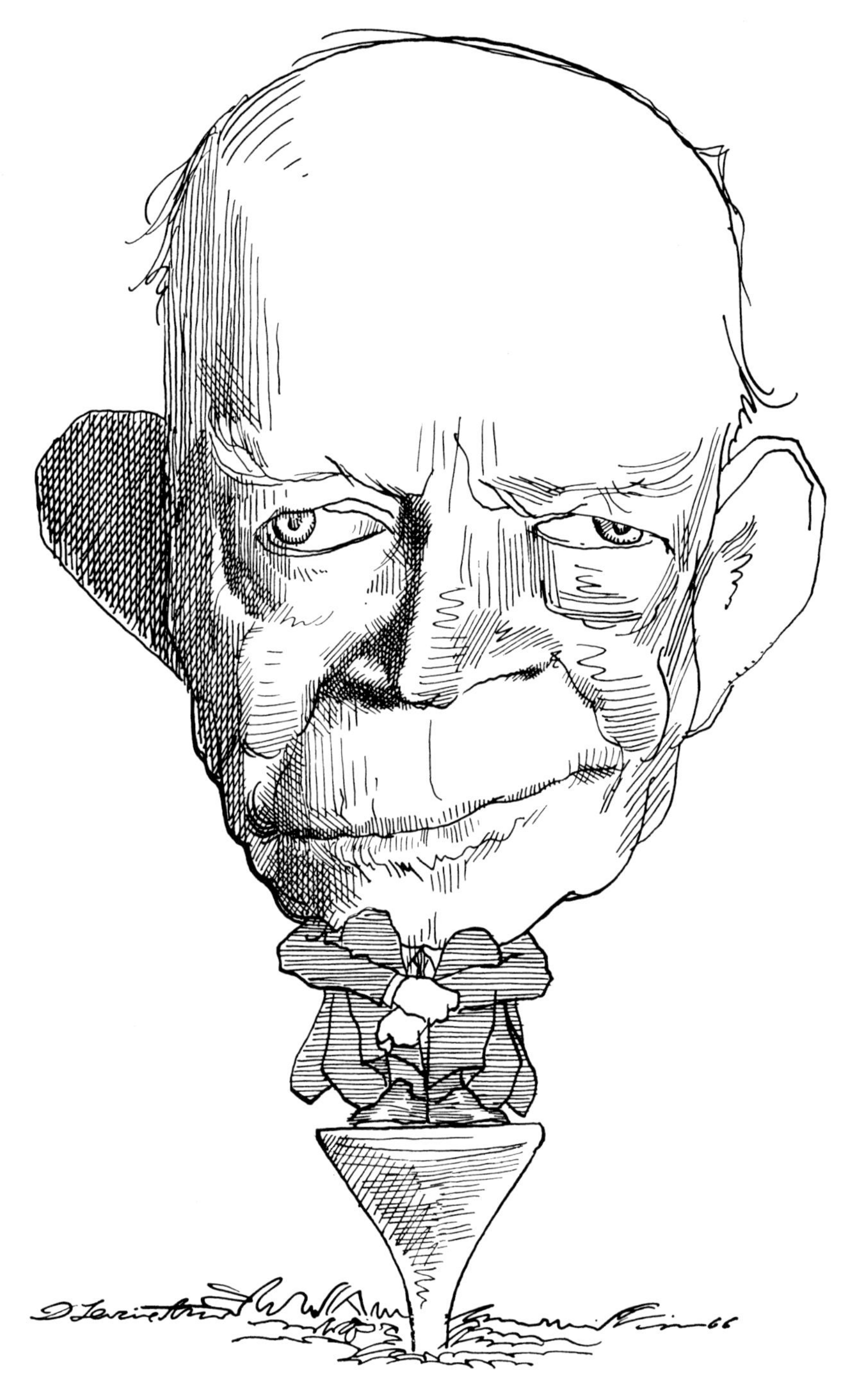

Dwight Eisenhower

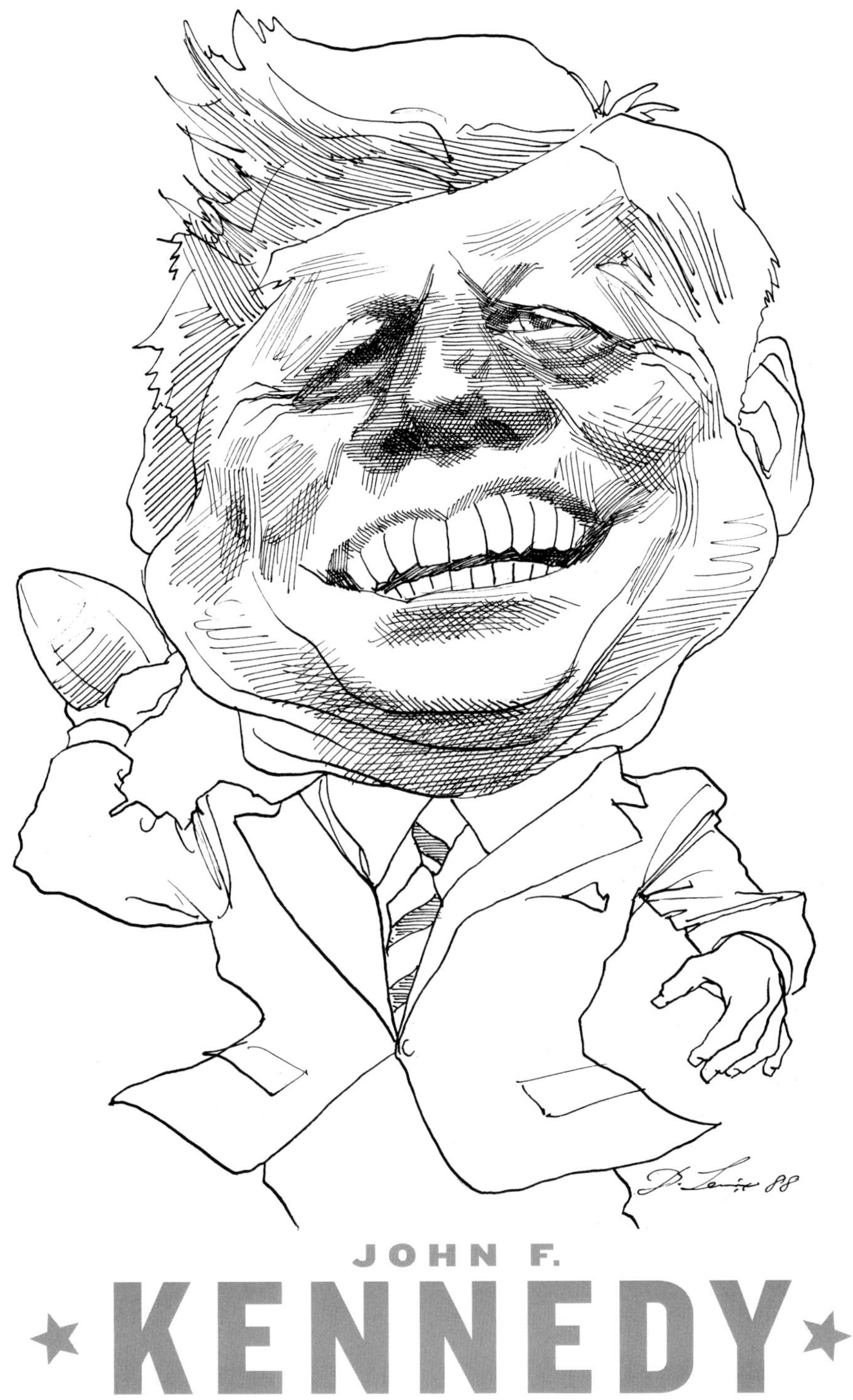

JOHN F.

★ KENNEDY ★

➥ The Kennedys didn't have a thread that starts here and leads to something as the Founding Fathers (who produced something very solid and which is now being whittled away). With the Kennedys there is usurpation. They occupied for a while and what did they produce? A hairdo?

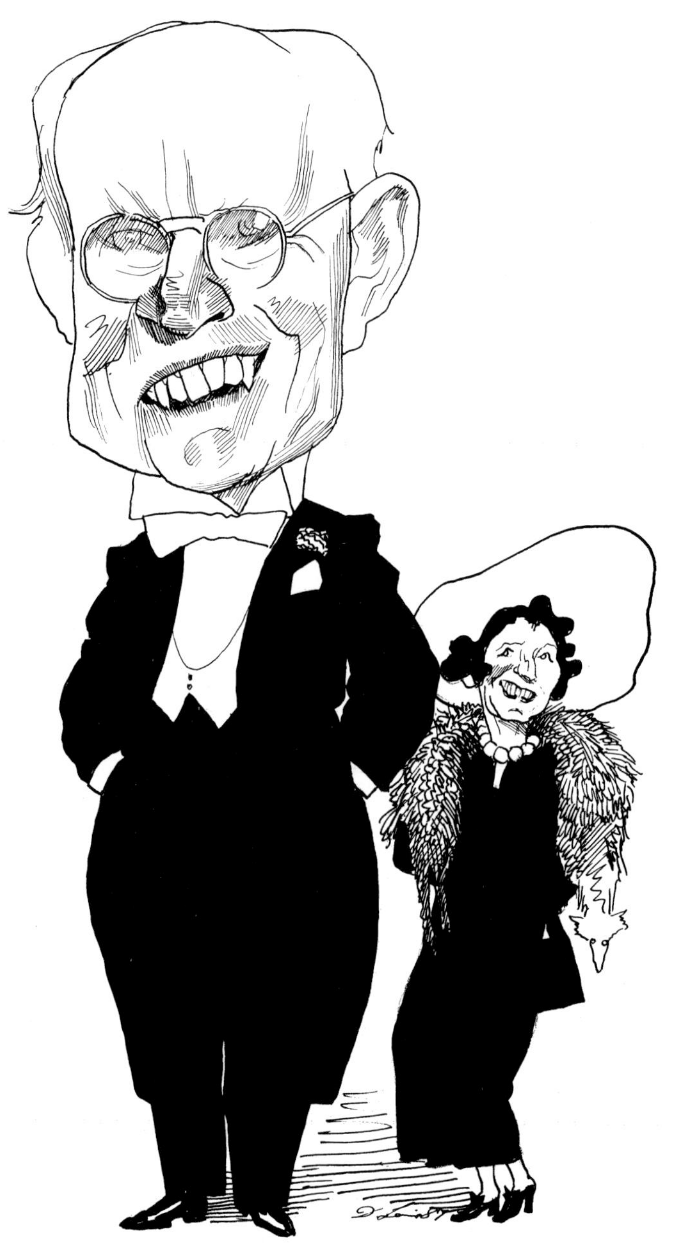

Joseph & Rose Kennedy

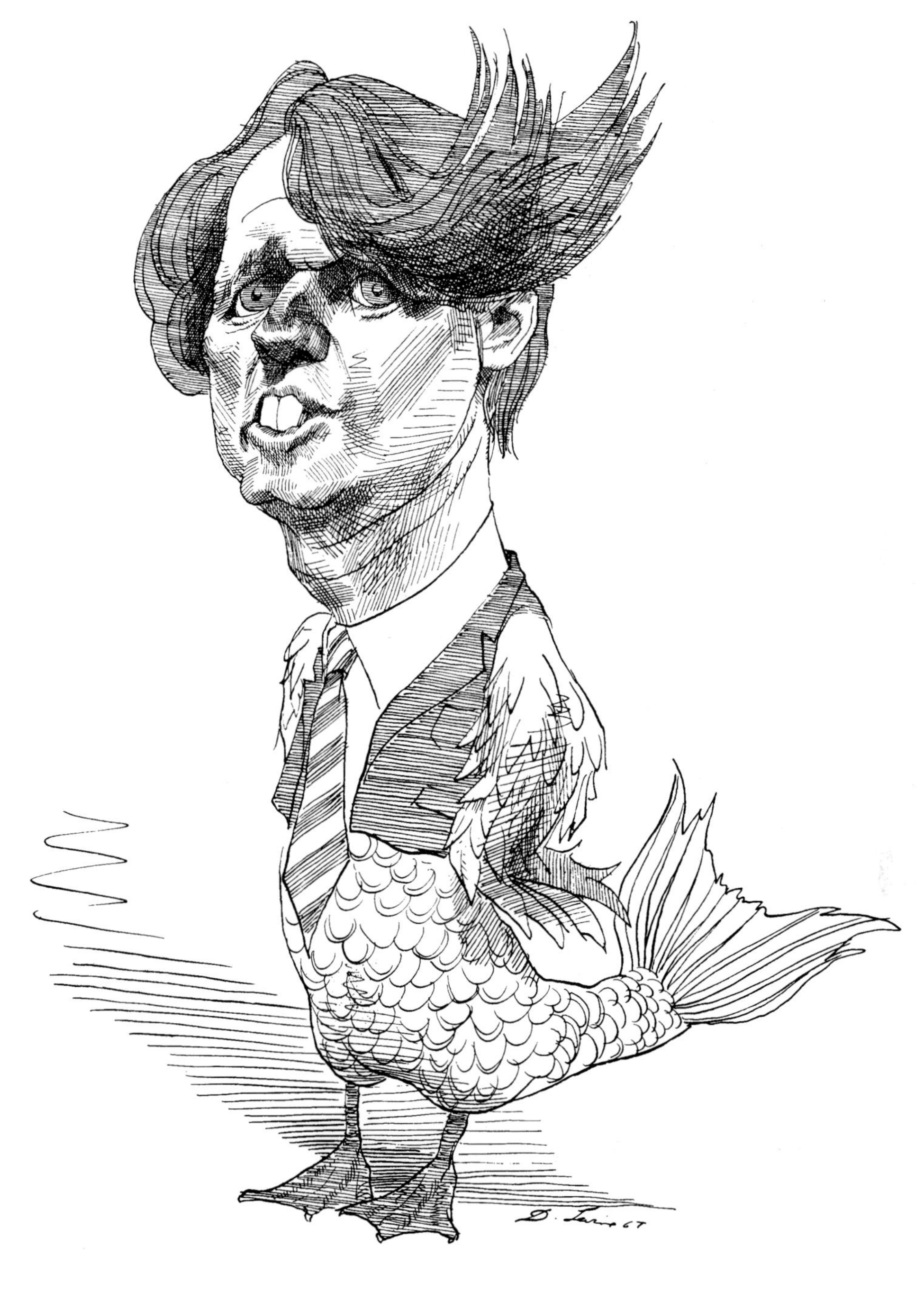

ROBERT KENNEDY

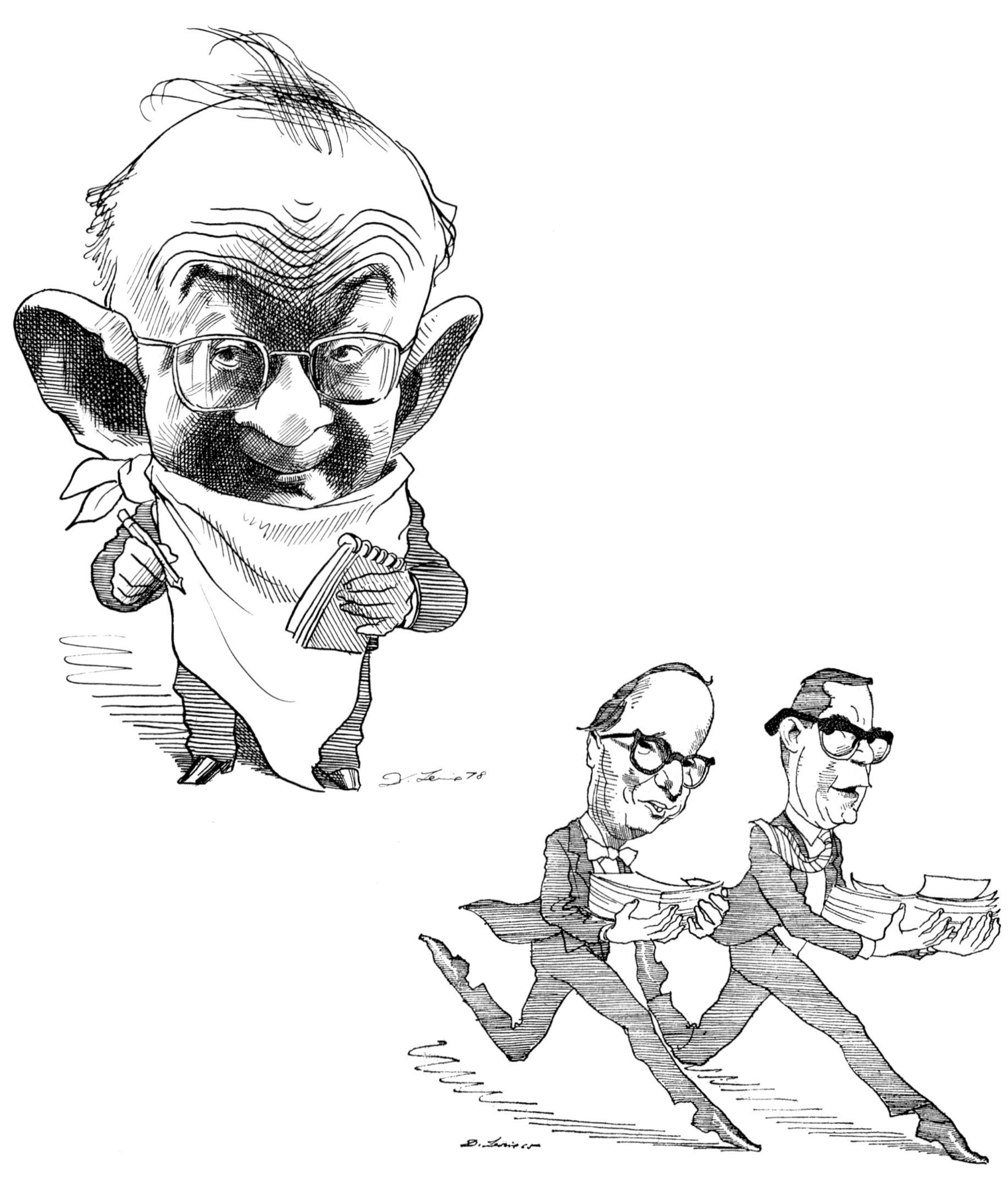

Theodore White (top) wrote a series of books titled "The Making of the President": the first and best documented Kennedy's election; **Arthur Schlesinger** (right) and **Theodore Sorensen** (left) were speechwriters for Kennedy. Schlesinger was the "court historian" of Camelot, while Kennedy referred to Sorensen as his "intellectual blood bank."

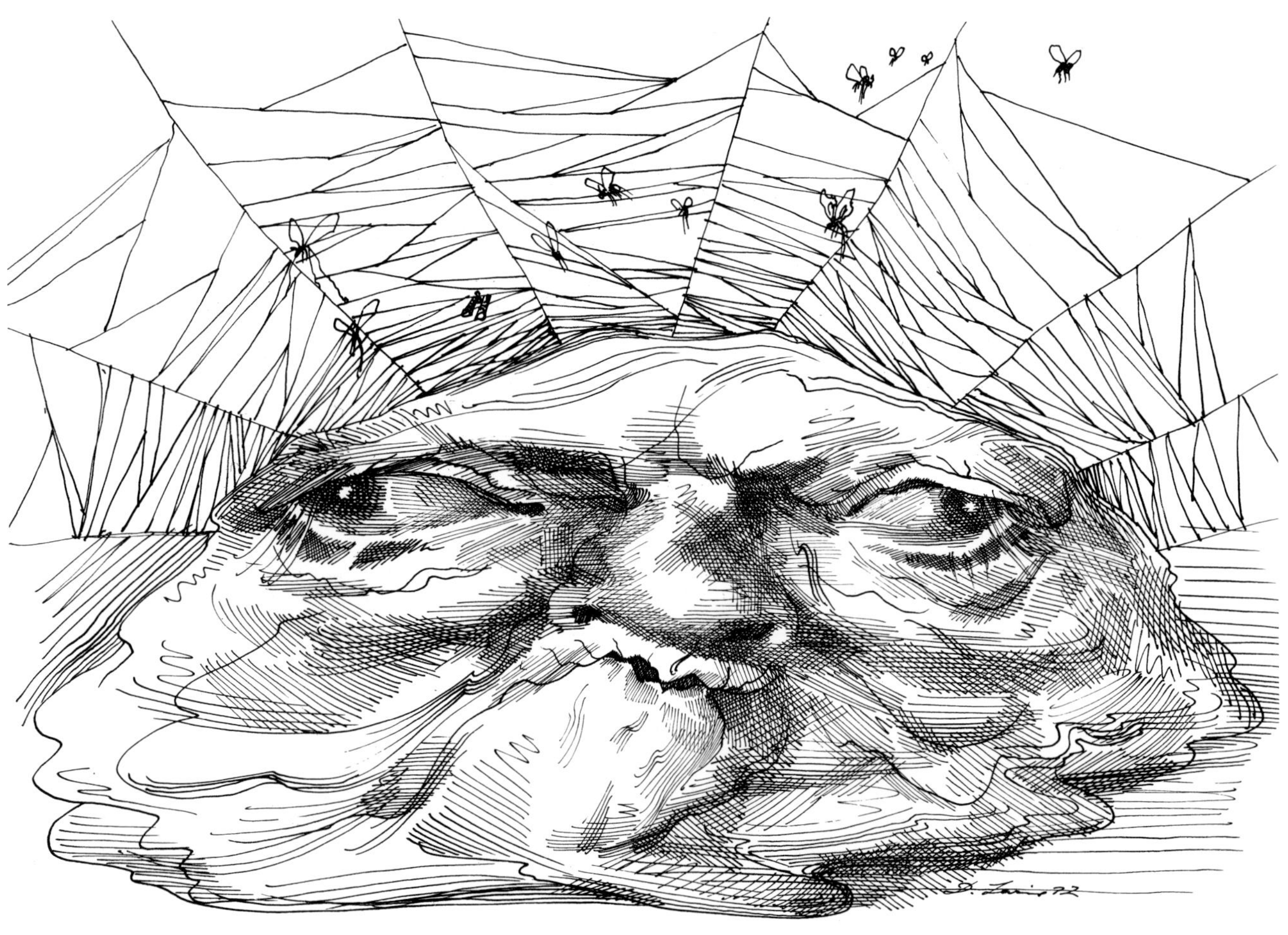

J. Edgar Hoover. Director of the FBI. A pile of corruption. Kennedy considered firing the FBI man, but concluded that the political cost was too high.

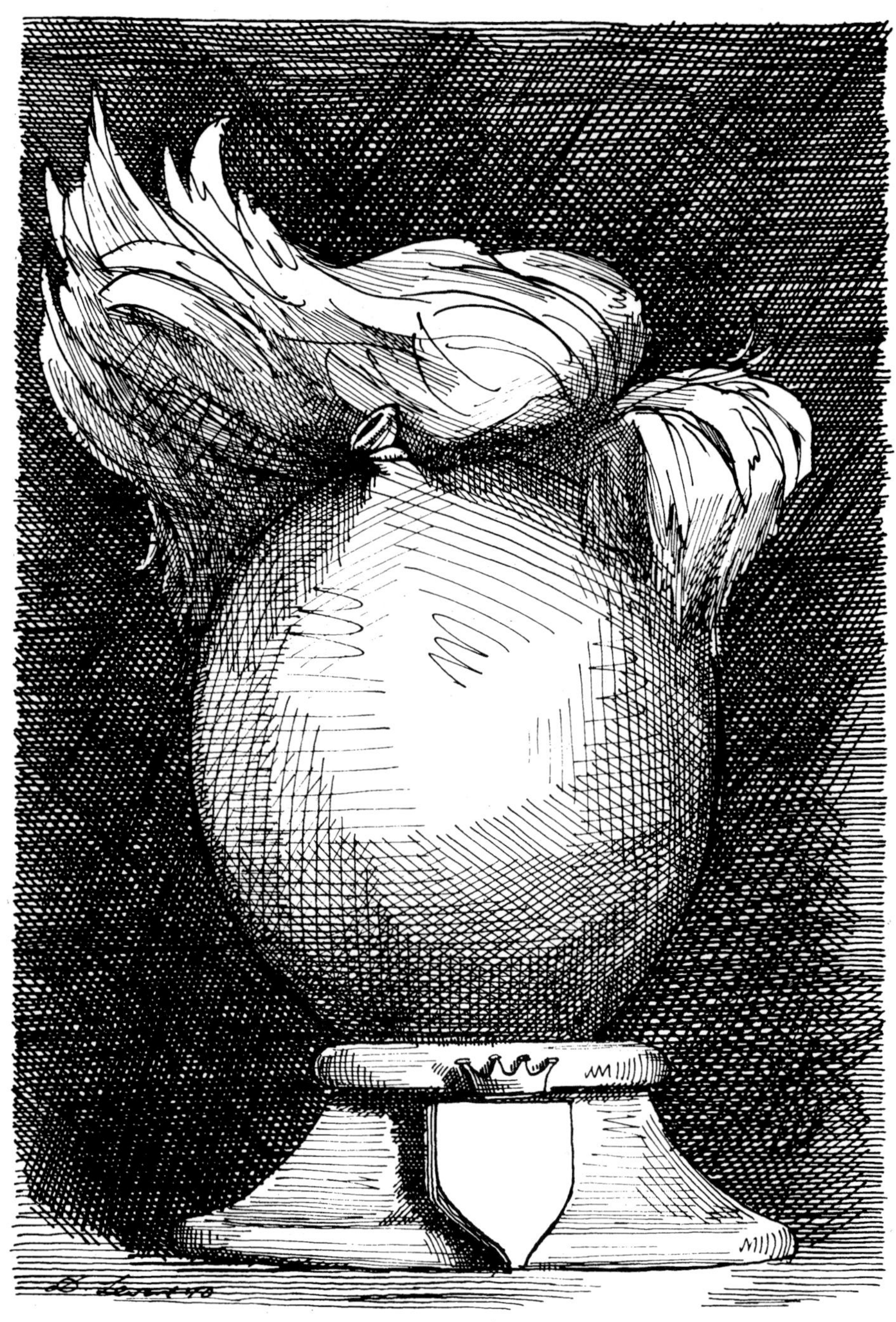

The Kennedy Legacy

LYNDON JOHNSON

Johnson took on a look of "I am doing this, I have to do this, they are forcing my hand." We murdered 50,000 of our own kids and we will never know how much talent we lost or what problems could have been solved by them. When I first started drawing caricatures, Johnson was in office and I drew him over sixty times for a wide variety of publications.

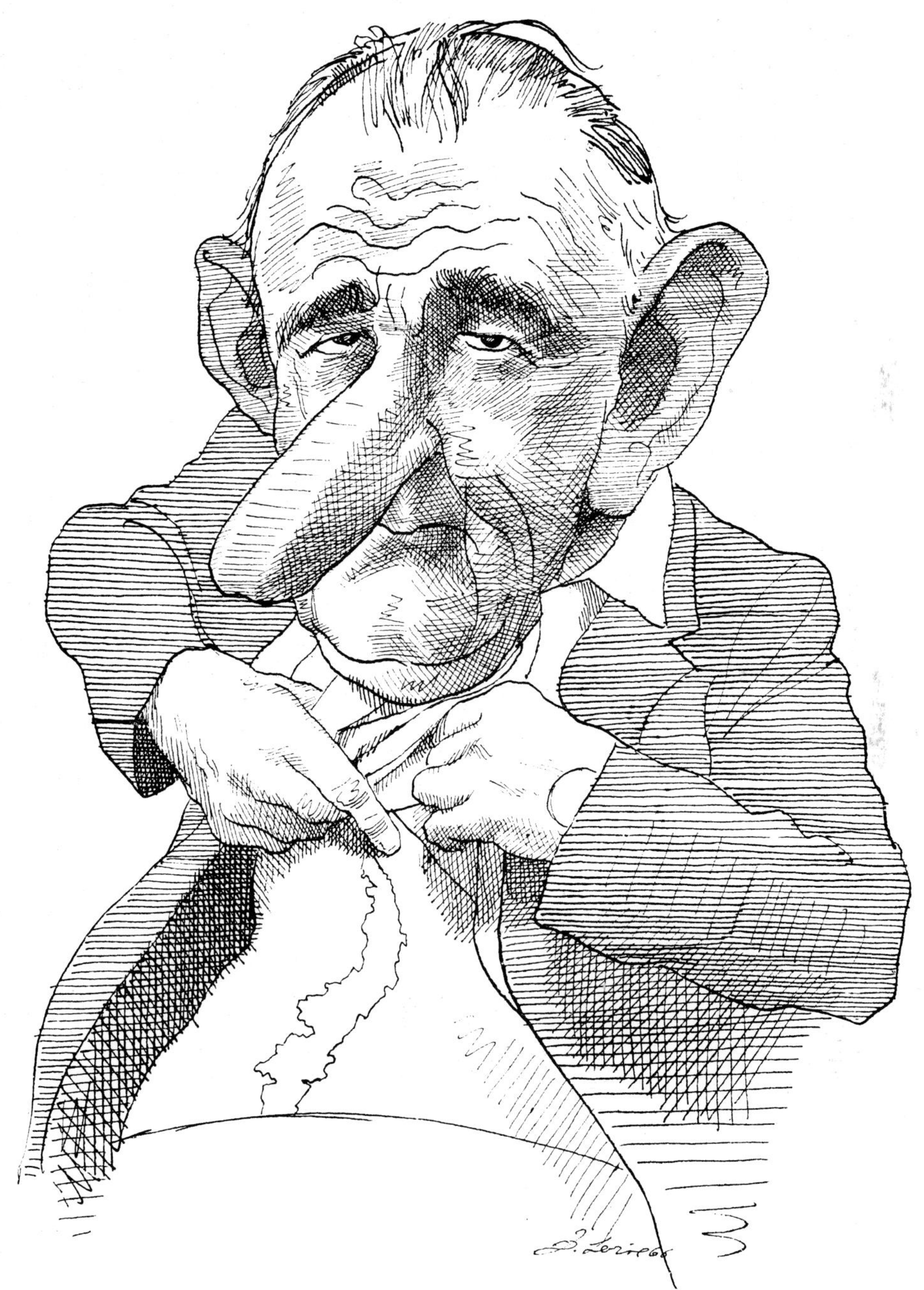

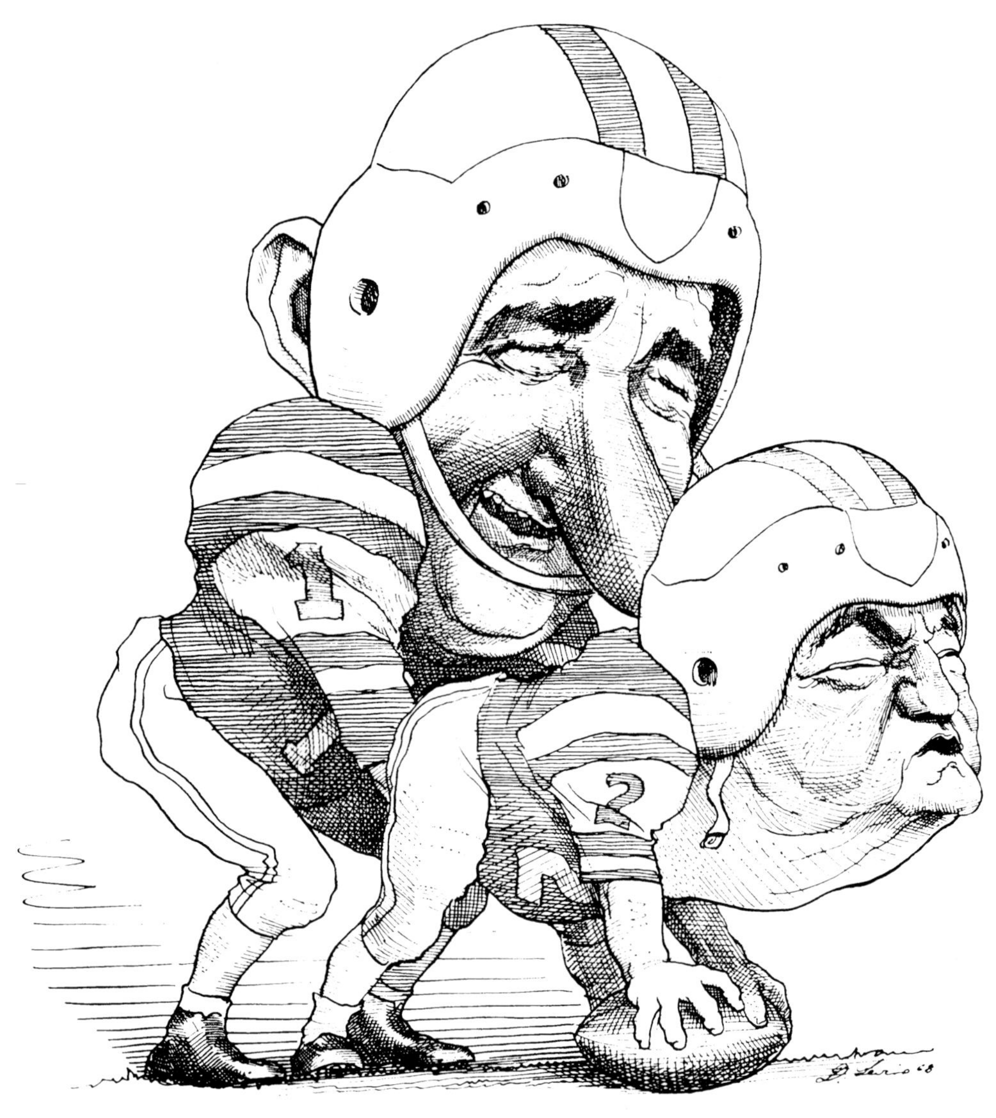

THE QUARTERBACK & THE CENTER

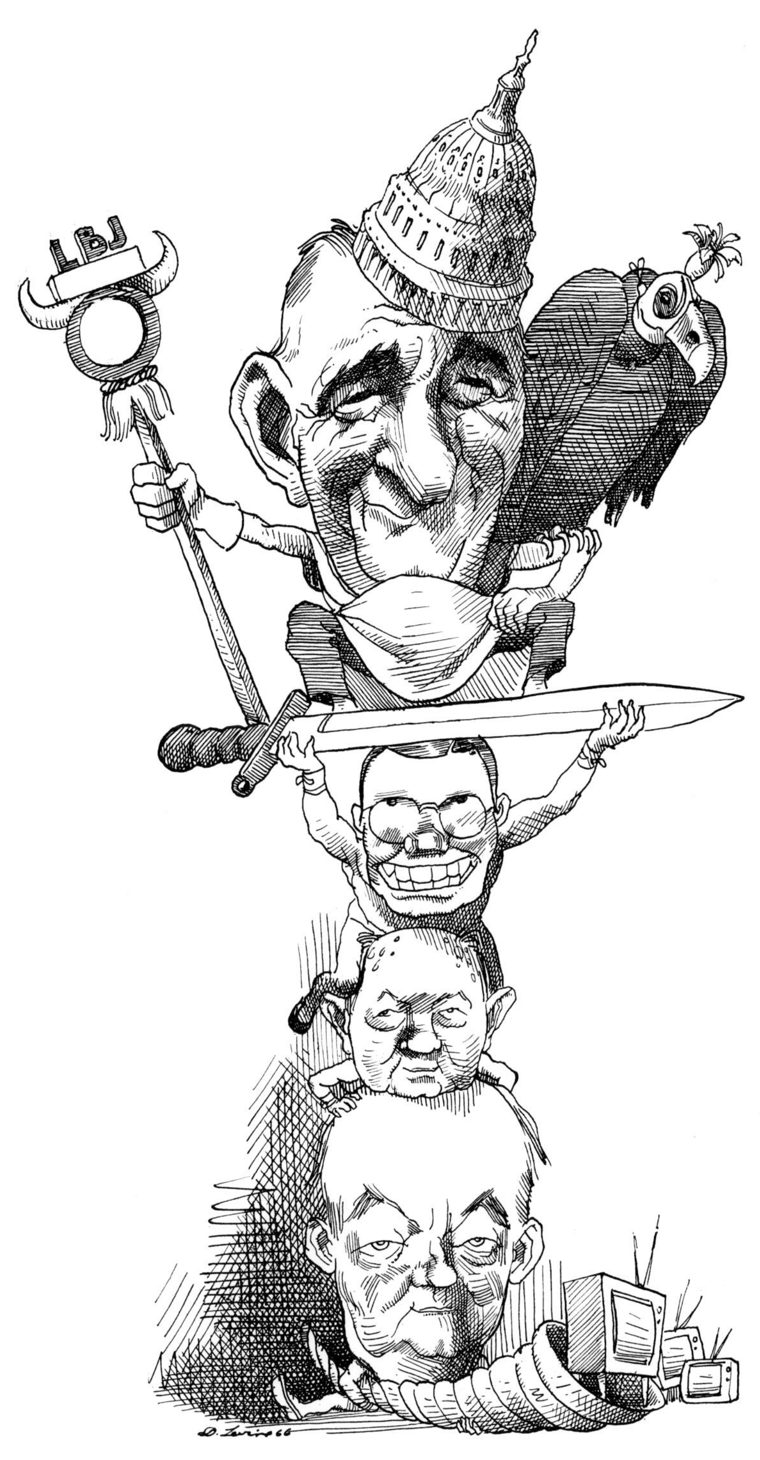

The Johnson Administration. (TOP TO BOTTOM) **JOHNSON**, Secretary of Defense **ROBERT MCNAMARA**, Secretary of State **DEAN RUSK**, and vice president **HUBERT HUMPHREY**.

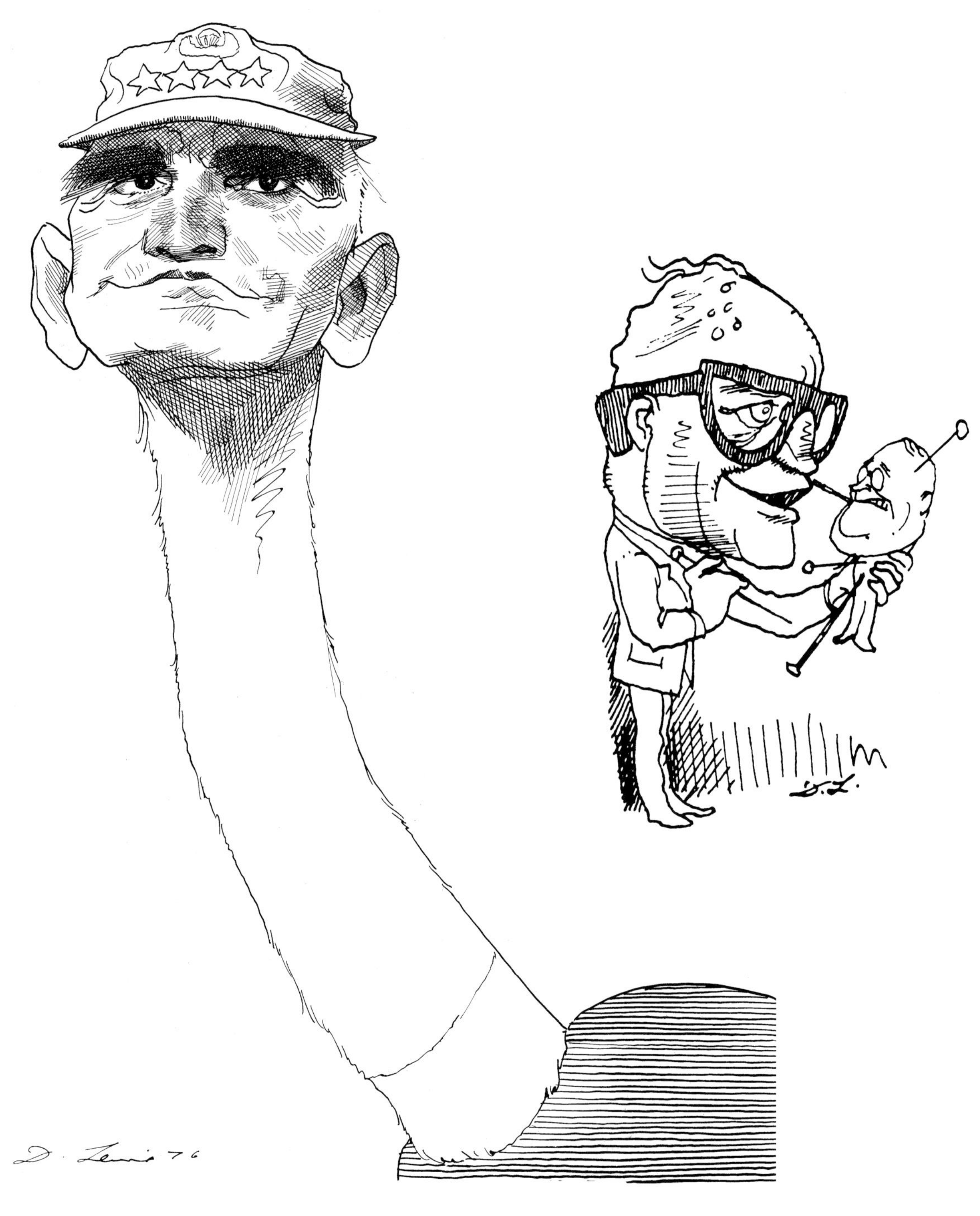

General **WILLIAM WESTMORELAND** (LEFT). Commander of Military operations in Vietnam at the peak of the war. Under Westmoreland's leadership, with his very public rosy assessments of the war, as Neil Sheehan wrote, the United States "won every battle until it lost the war." Father of the modern day conservative movement, **BARRY GOLDWATER** (RIGHT) lost by a wide margin to Johnson in the 1964 presidential election.

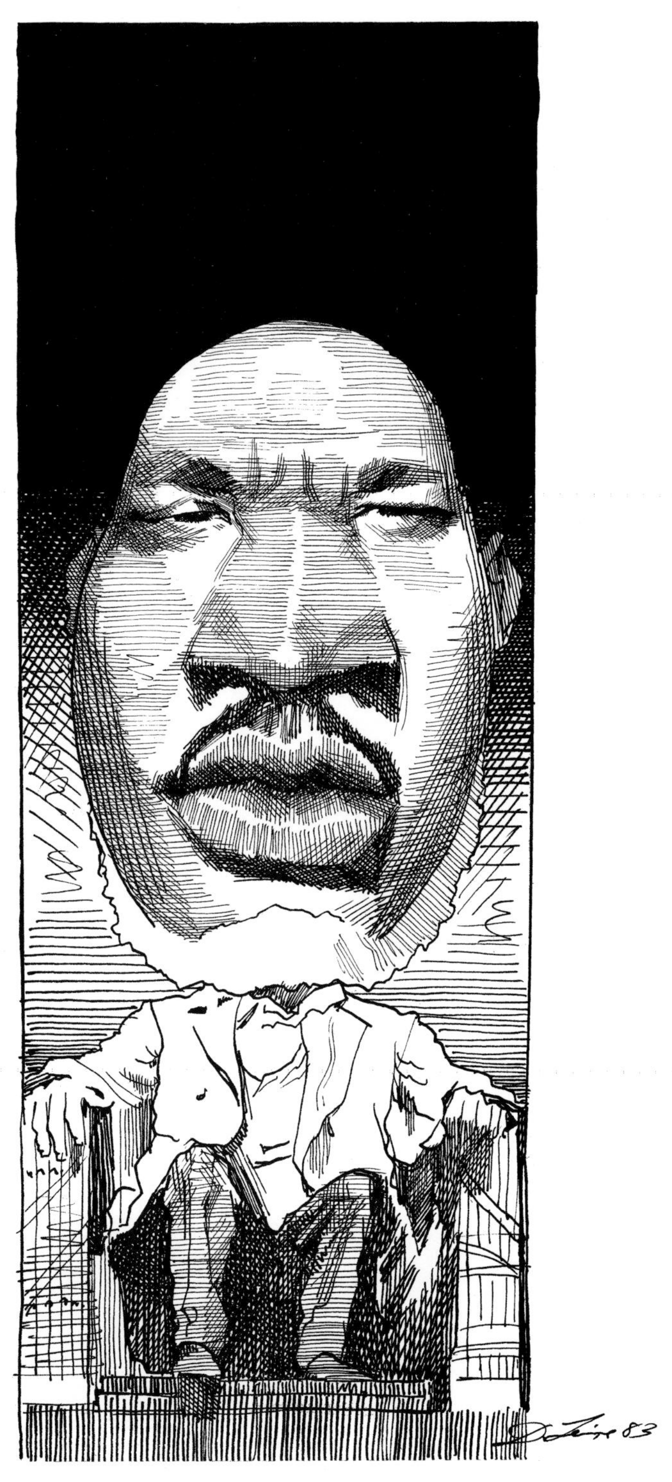

Martin Luther King Jr. and Johnson engaged in negotiations that led to the passage of the Civil Rights Act of 1964 and the Voting Rights Act of 1965, but this spirit of cooperation was irrevocably damaged in 1967 when King spoke publicly against the Vietnam War.

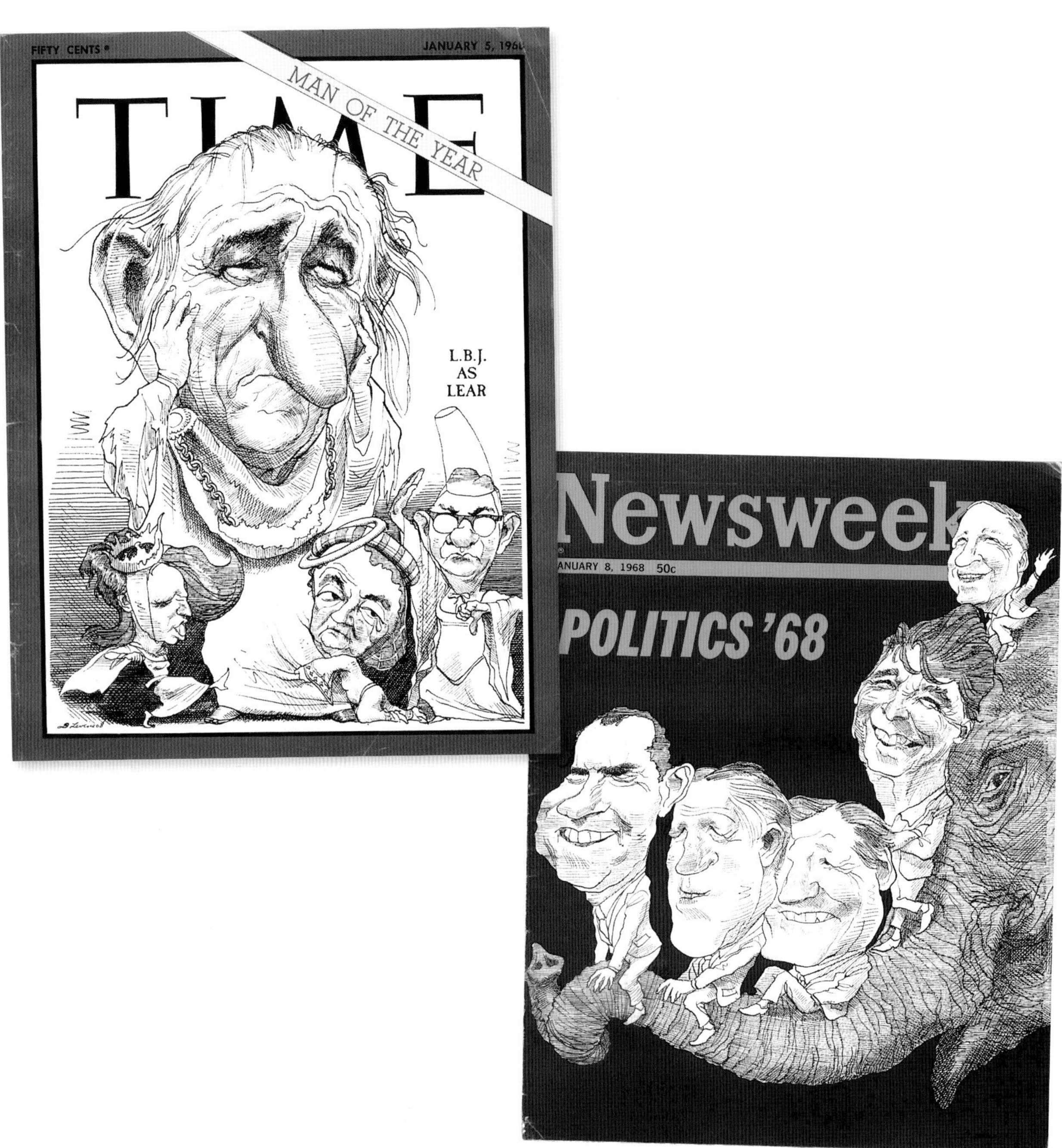

On January 8, 1968, editors of *Time* and *Newsweek* were chagrined to discover that both magazines had David Levine drawings on their covers. *Time*'s Man of the Year (LEFT) featured a Lear-like **JOHNSON** beset by **ROBERT KENNEDY**, **HUBERT HUMPHREY**, and **WILBUR MILLS**, while *Newsweek* (RIGHT) had the Republican Presidential candidates: **RICHARD NIXON**, **GEORGE ROMNEY**, **NELSON ROCKEFELLER**, **RONALD REAGAN**, and **CHARLES PERCY**.

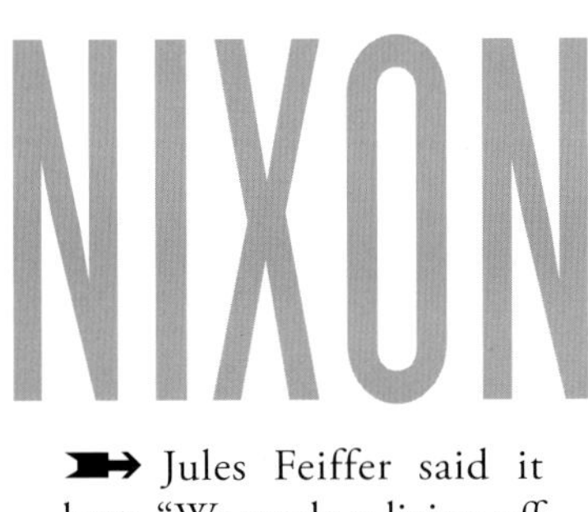

Jules Feiffer said it best: "We made a living off this guy." Even physically he was interesting to draw. The shifty look, the eyebrows, the nose. Once one of the last issues of *Life* magazine showed him as a criminal, I knew I could do anything.

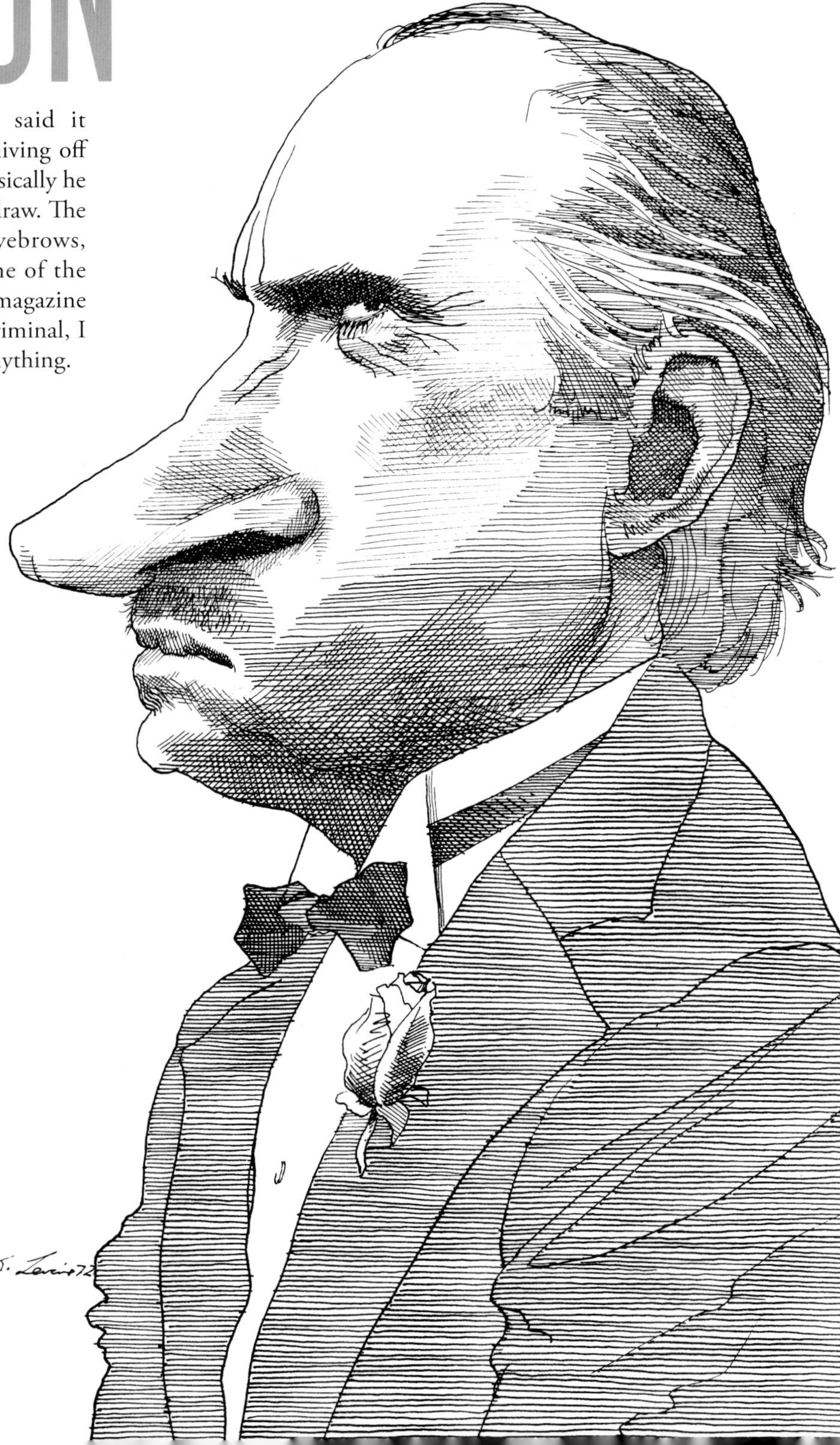

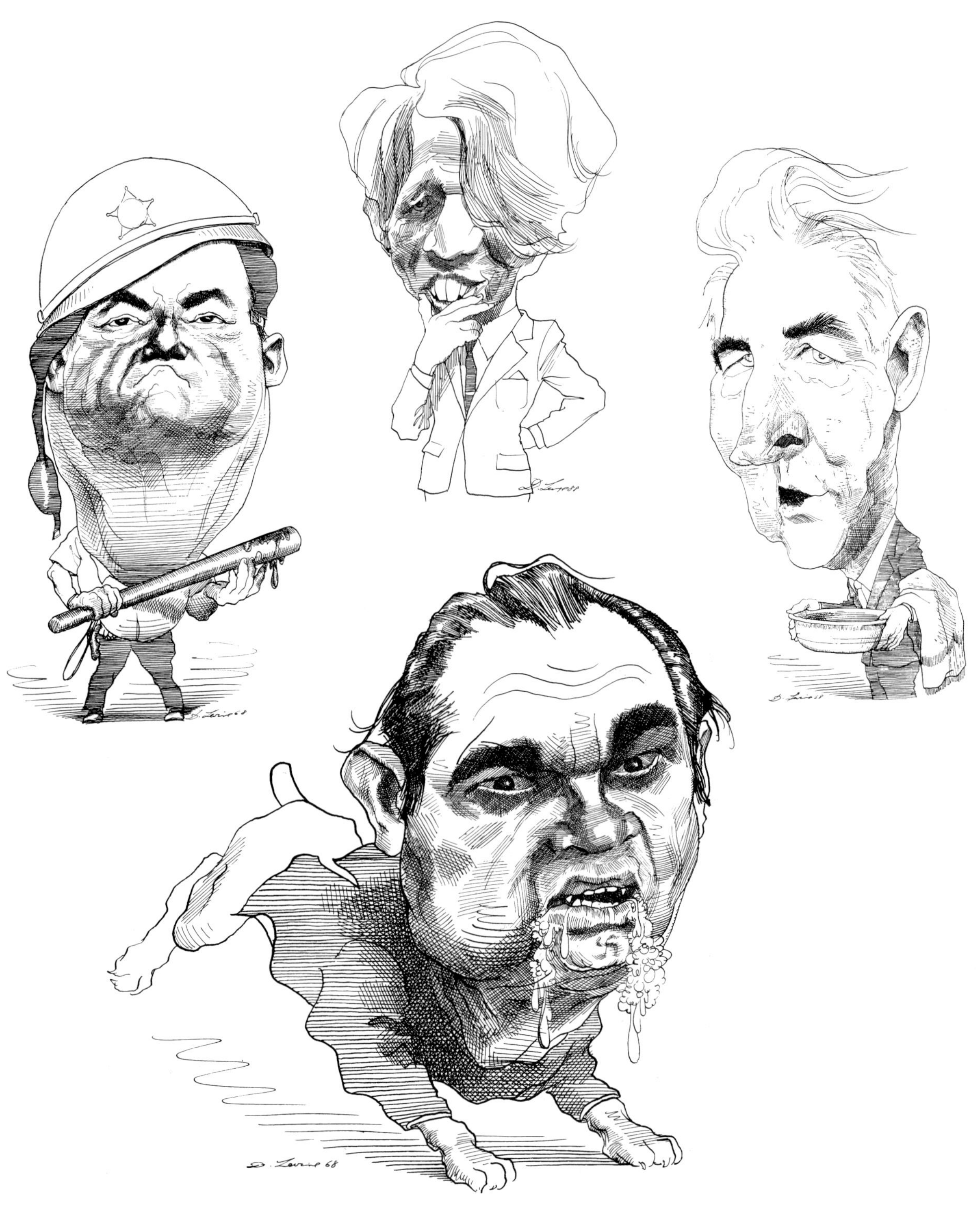

Nixon's rivals for the Presidency in 1968 included (CLOCKWISE FROM LEFT) the eventual Democratic nominee, **HUBERT HUMPHREY**; **ROBERT KENNEDY**, who was assassinated during his primary bid; anti-war candidate **EUGENE MCCARTHY**; and the racist American Independent Party nominee, **GEORGE WALLACE**.

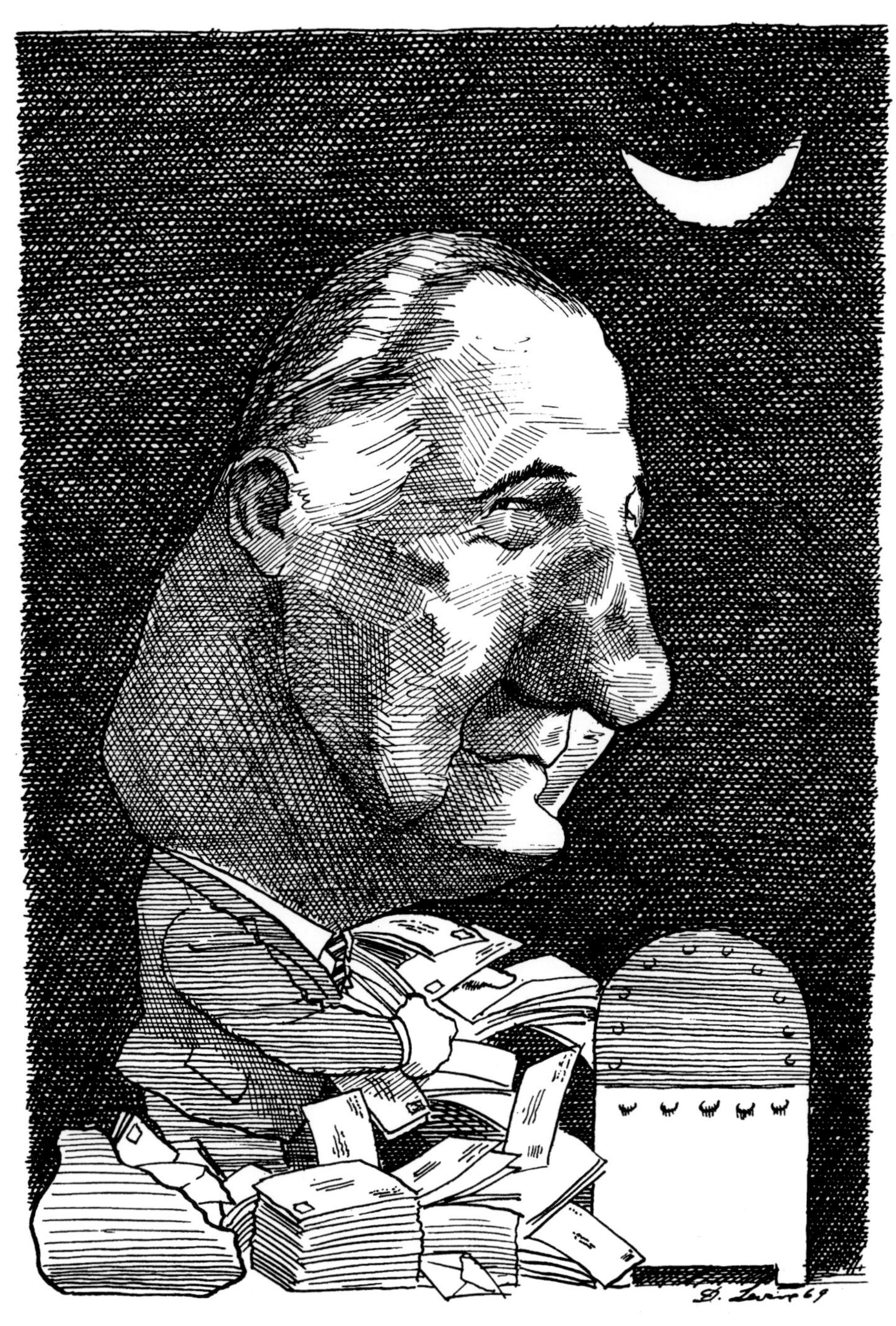

SPIRO AGNEW. A Greek man threatened to break both my knees over this drawing. It is the only threat of physical violence I have ever received.

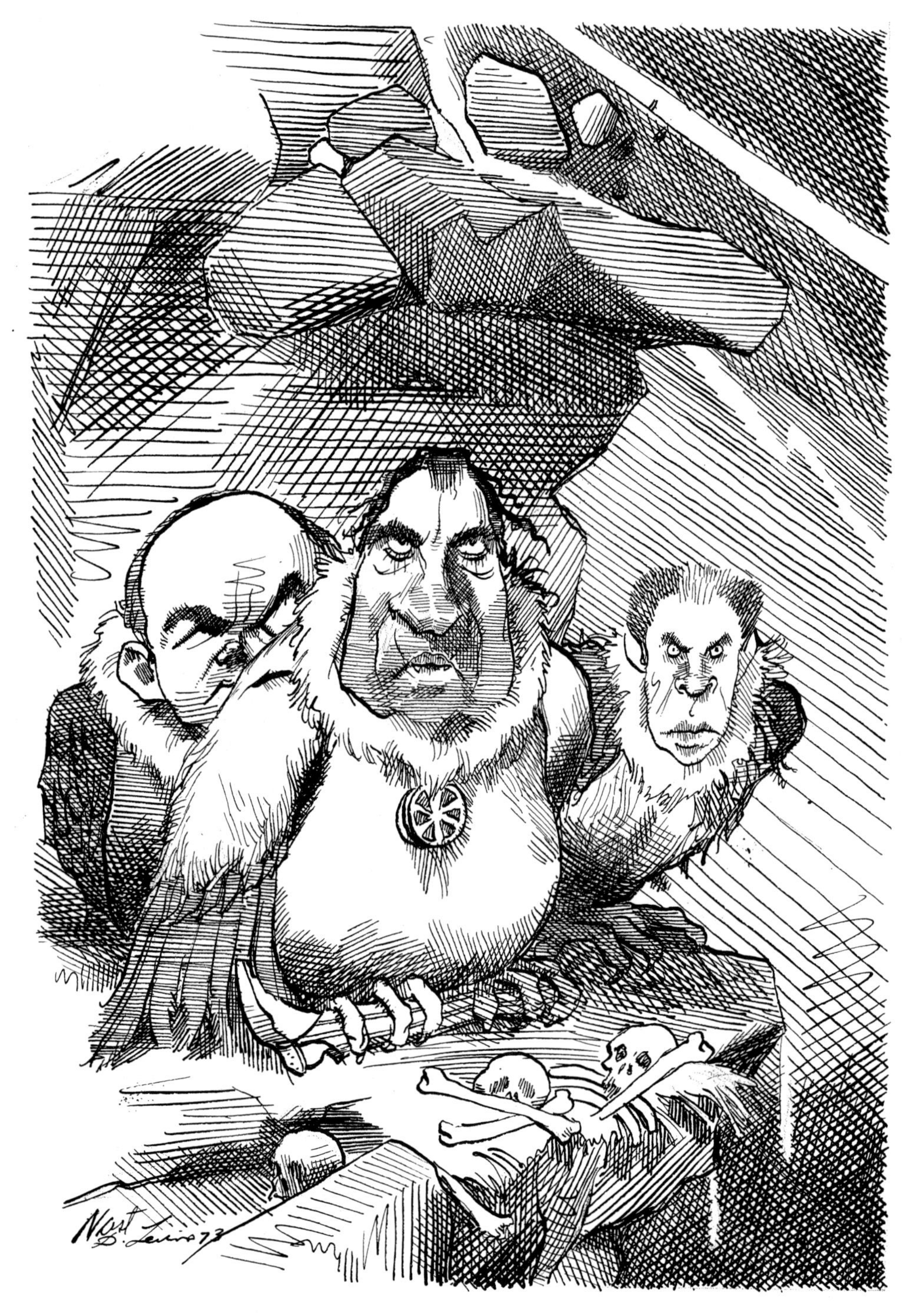

"Let Us Prey or Waiting out the Storm." A homage to political cartoonist Thomas Nast (1840-1902), this work shows **Ehrlichman**, **Nixon**, and **Haldeman** waiting out the storm of accusations from Watergate.

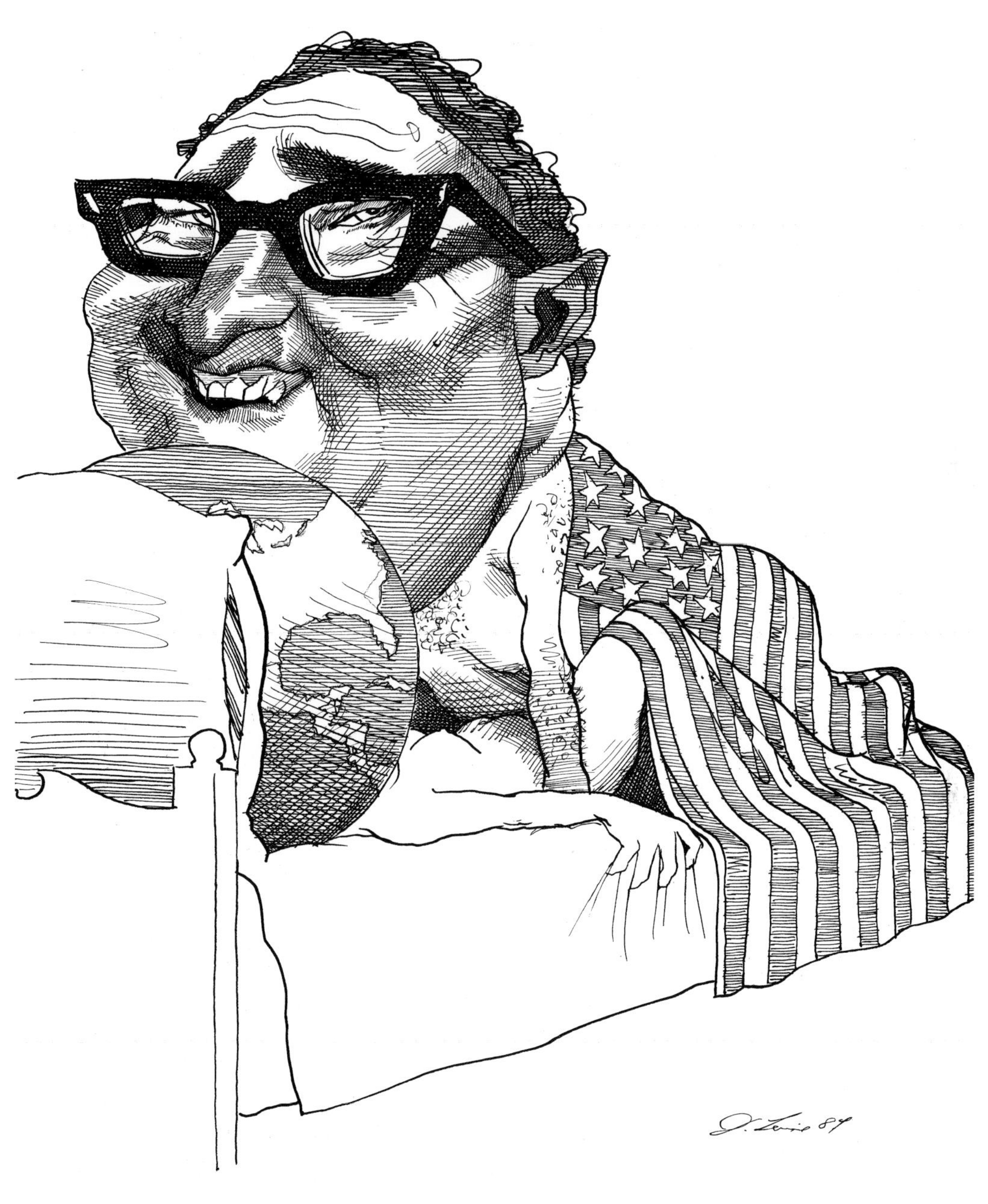

National Security Advisor and Secretary of State "**Henry Kissinger** F**king the World."

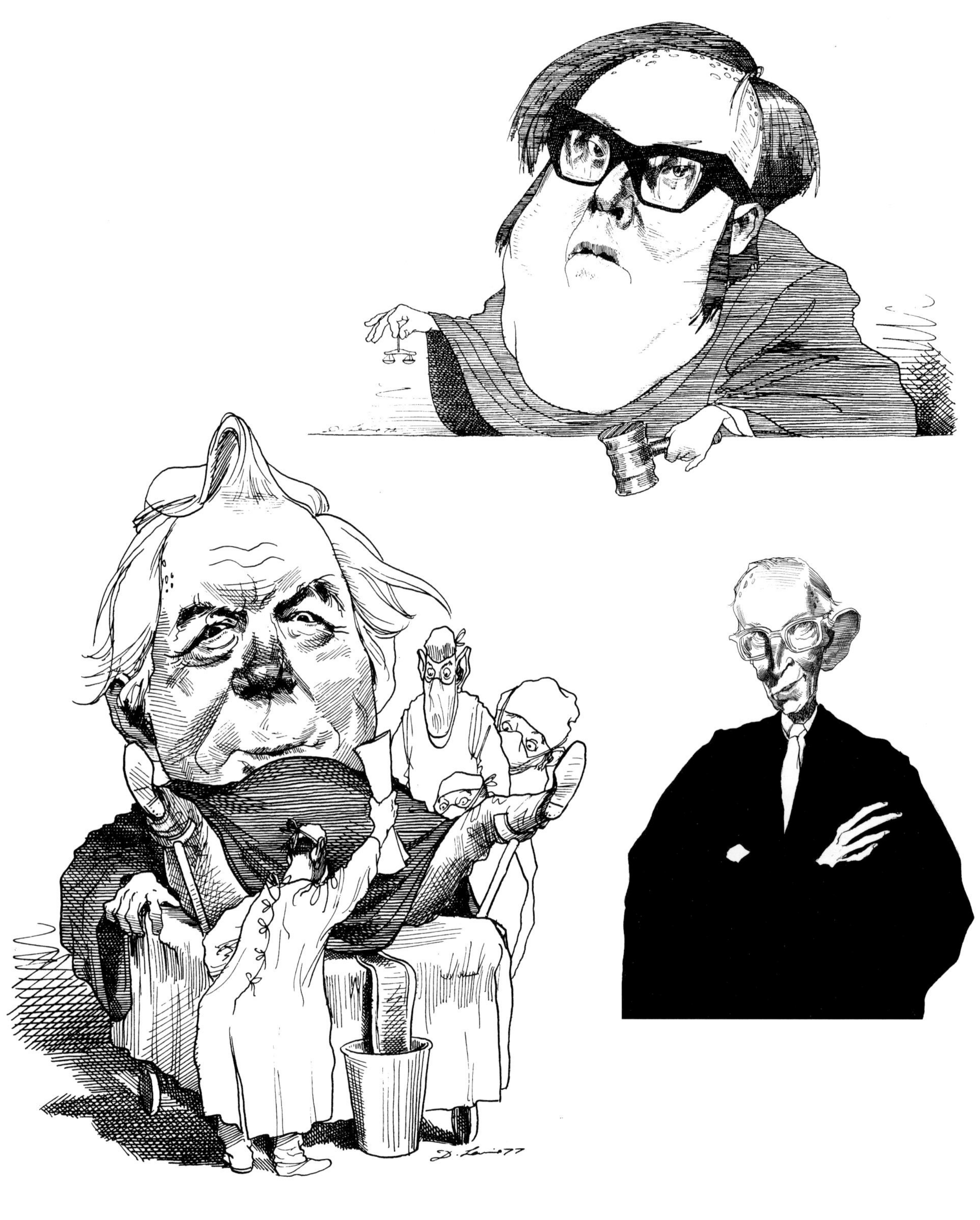

Nixon's Supreme Court nominees (CLOCKWISE FROM TOP):
WILLIAM REHNQUIST, **LEWIS POWELL, JR.**, Chief Justice **WARREN BURGER**

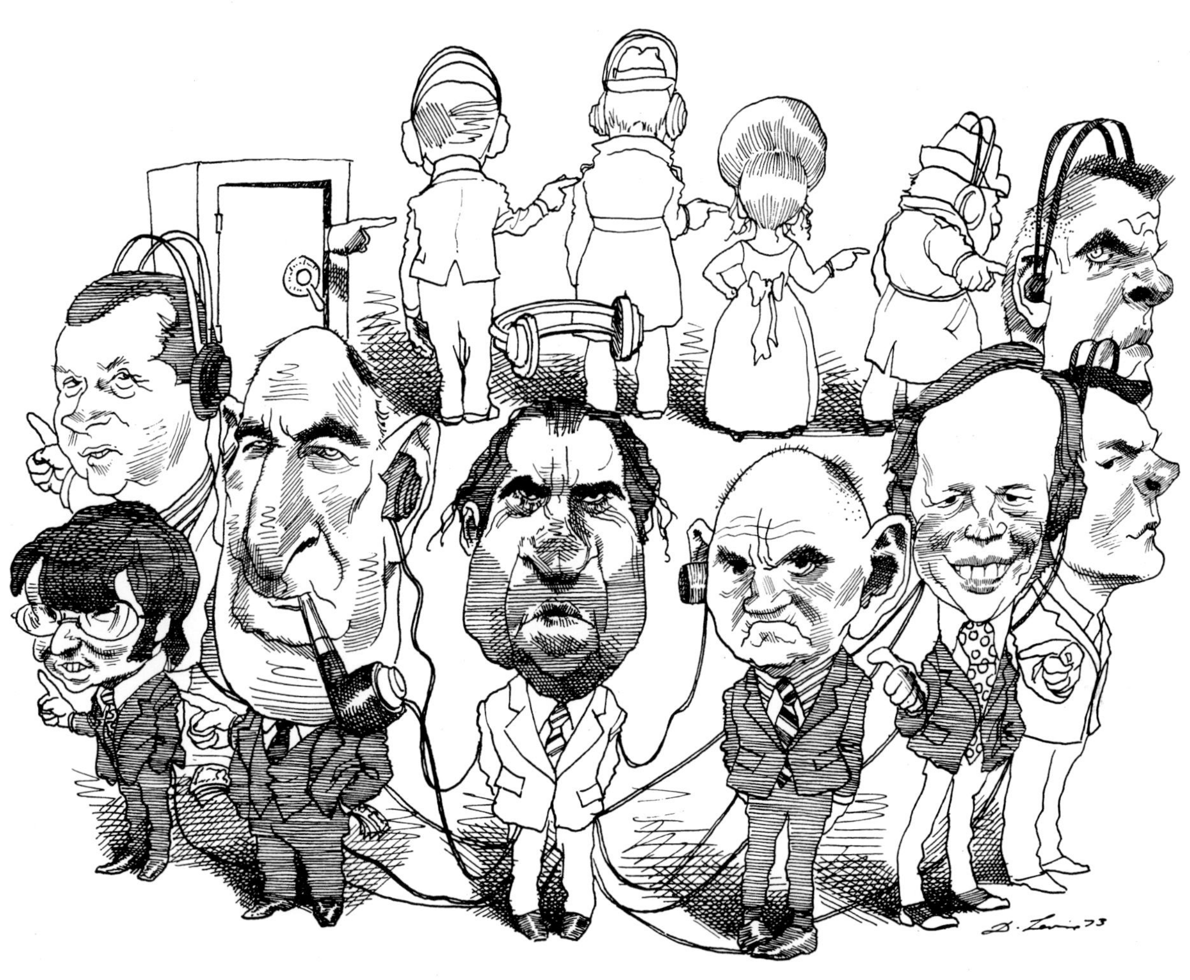

The Nixon Administration

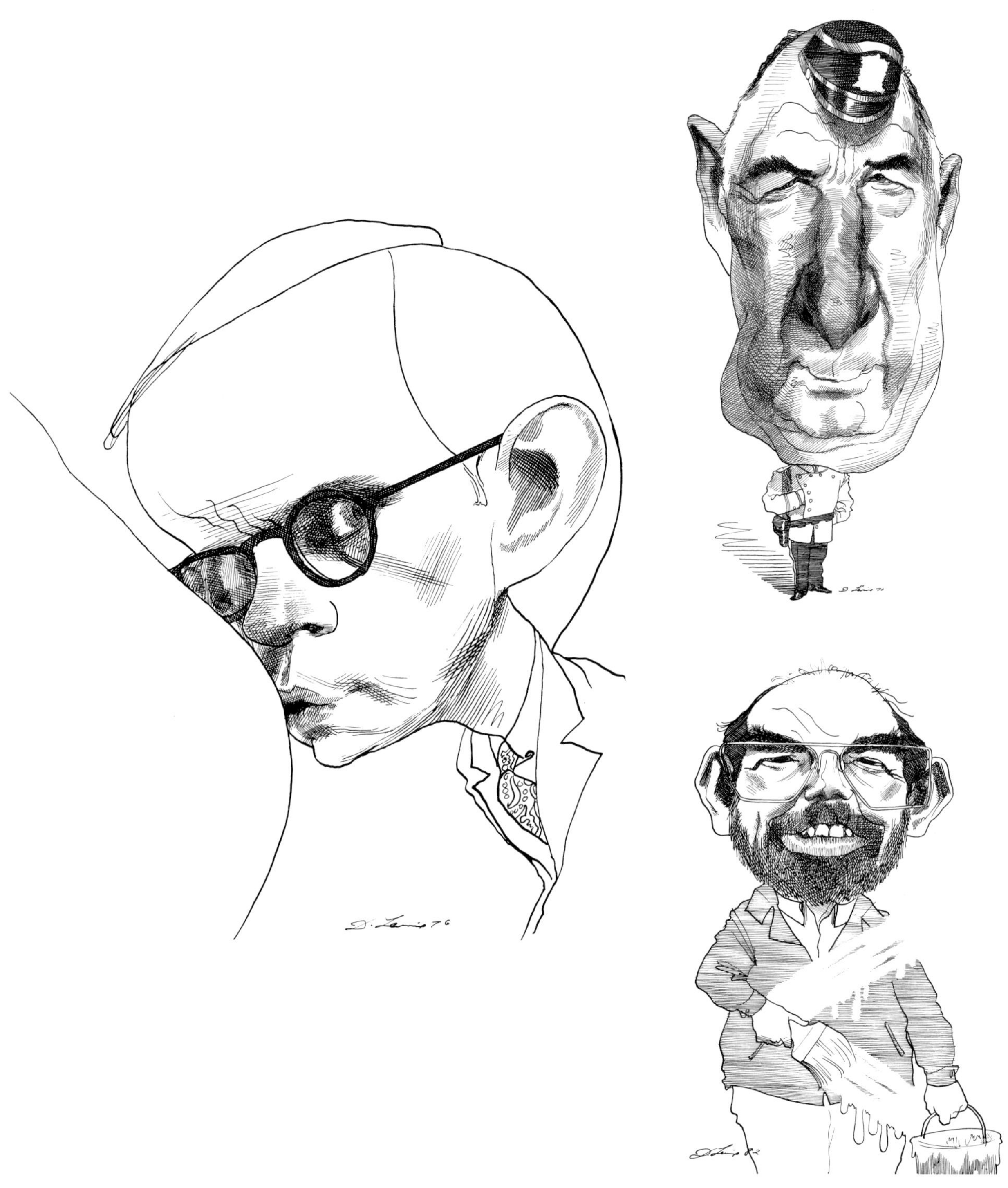

Nixon Legal Team (clockwise from left): White House Counsel **JOHN DEAN** was the "master manipulator of the cover up," of Watergate according to the FBI, and was convicted of multiple felonies and imprisoned; **JOHN MITCHELL** was the first Attorney General to be convicted and imprisoned, for his work as Nixon's campaign director, where he engineered the Watergate break-in; White House Counsel and Domestic Policy Advisor JOHN **EHRLICHMAN** was convicted of conspiracy, obstruction of justice and perjury for his role in Watergate and was imprisoned.

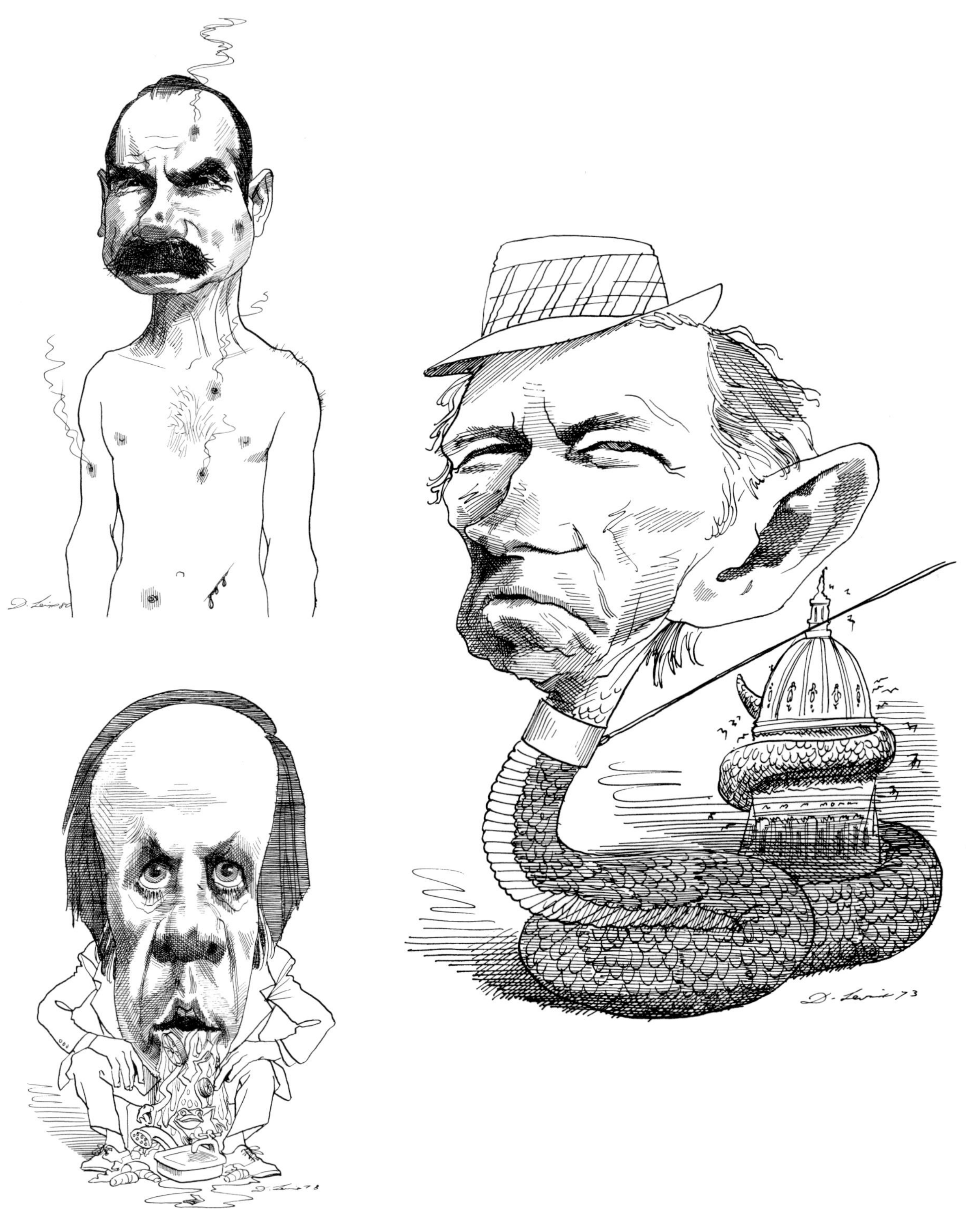

...Or "Back On the Chain Gang" (CLOCKWISE FROM TOP): **G. GORDON LIDDY** and **E. HOWARD HUNT** ran the White House Plumbers Unit to fix any "news" leaks, and for their roles in coordinating the Watergate break-in, they were convicted of conspiracy, burglary and illegal wiretapping, and imprisoned; Chief of Staff **H.R. HALDEMAN** was found guilty of conspiracy and obstruction of justice and imprisoned for his participation in the cover-up.

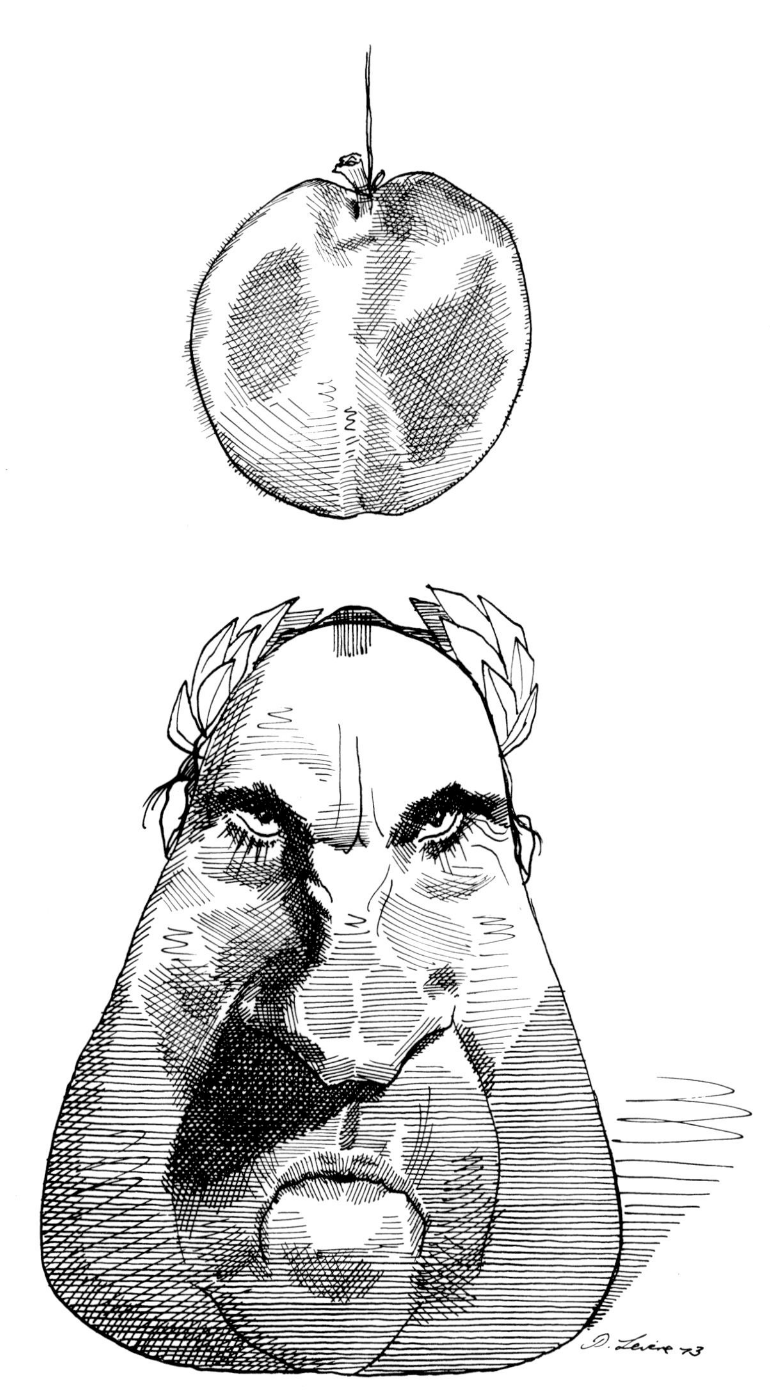

"IMPEACHMENT." Here I quote Daumier's classic caricature of King Louis-Philippe to suggest the end of Nixon's reign.

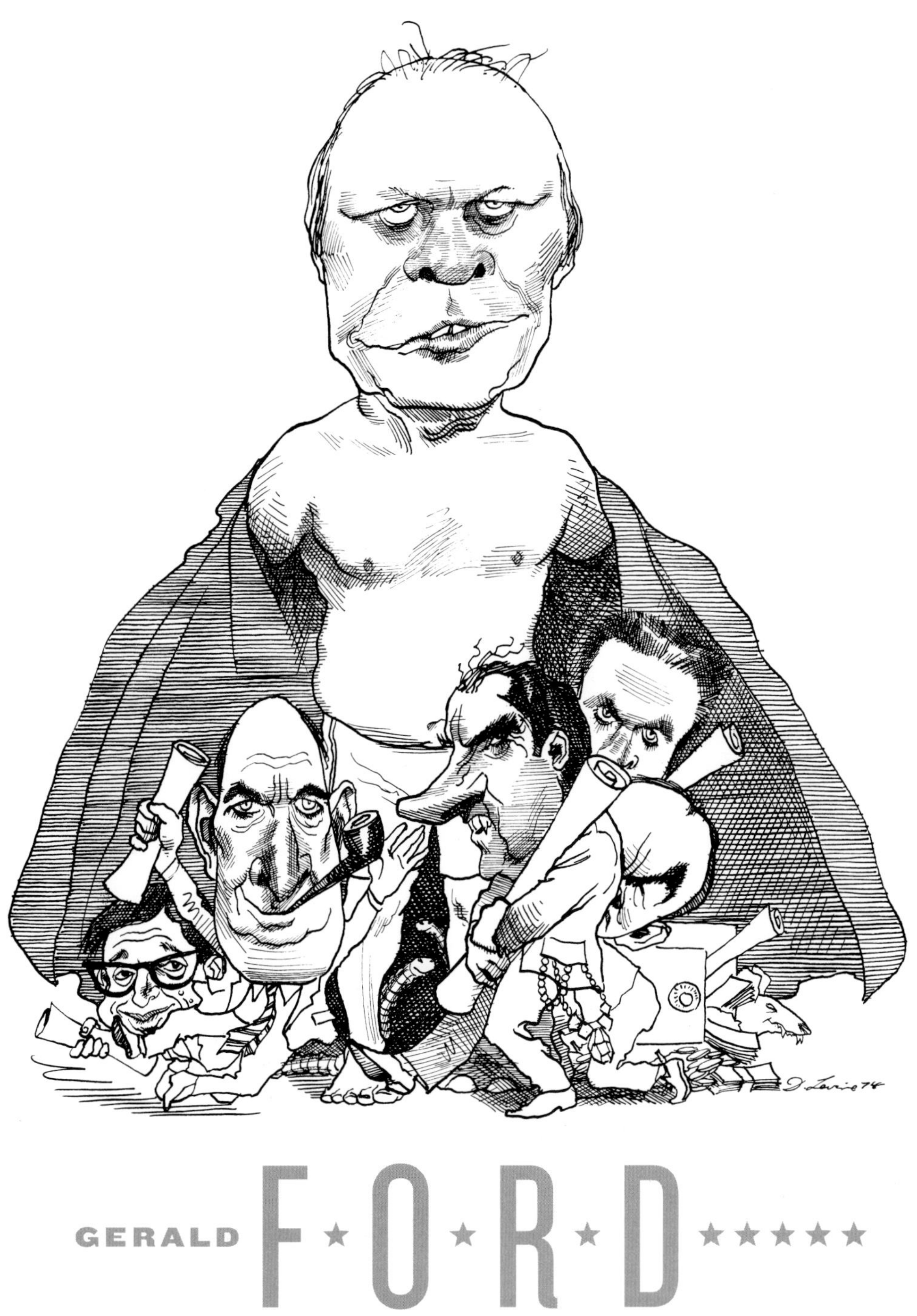

GERALD F★O★R★D ★★★★★★

➡ Ford was a letdown to draw after Nixon. Every other administration was getting caught in irregularities and criminal acts, and along comes Ford and does very little. It was almost as if he didn't believe he had the power. Yet Kissinger remained. We couldn't get rid of him.

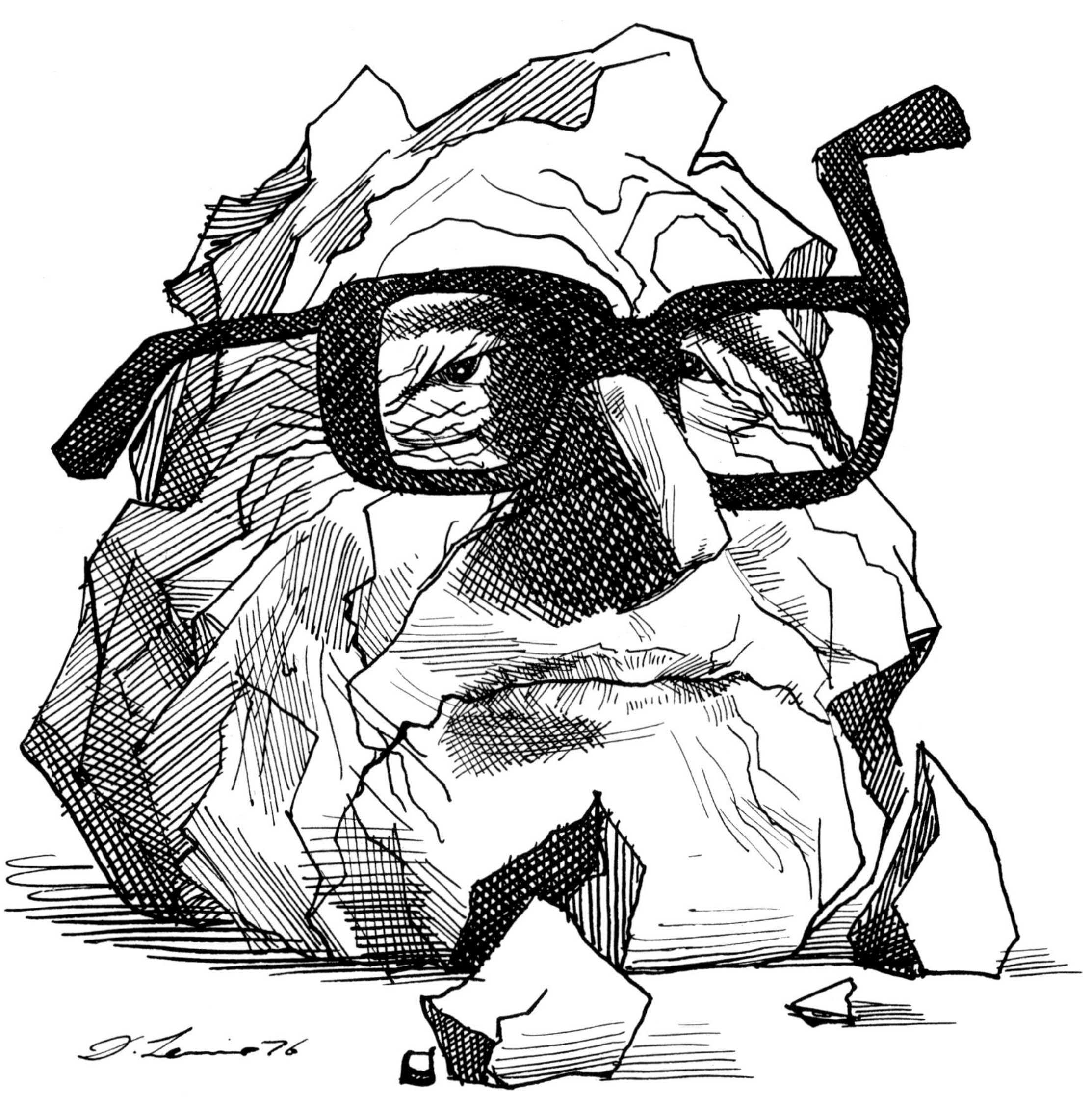

Nelson Rockefeller was a frequent candidate for president before being appointed Ford's vice president.

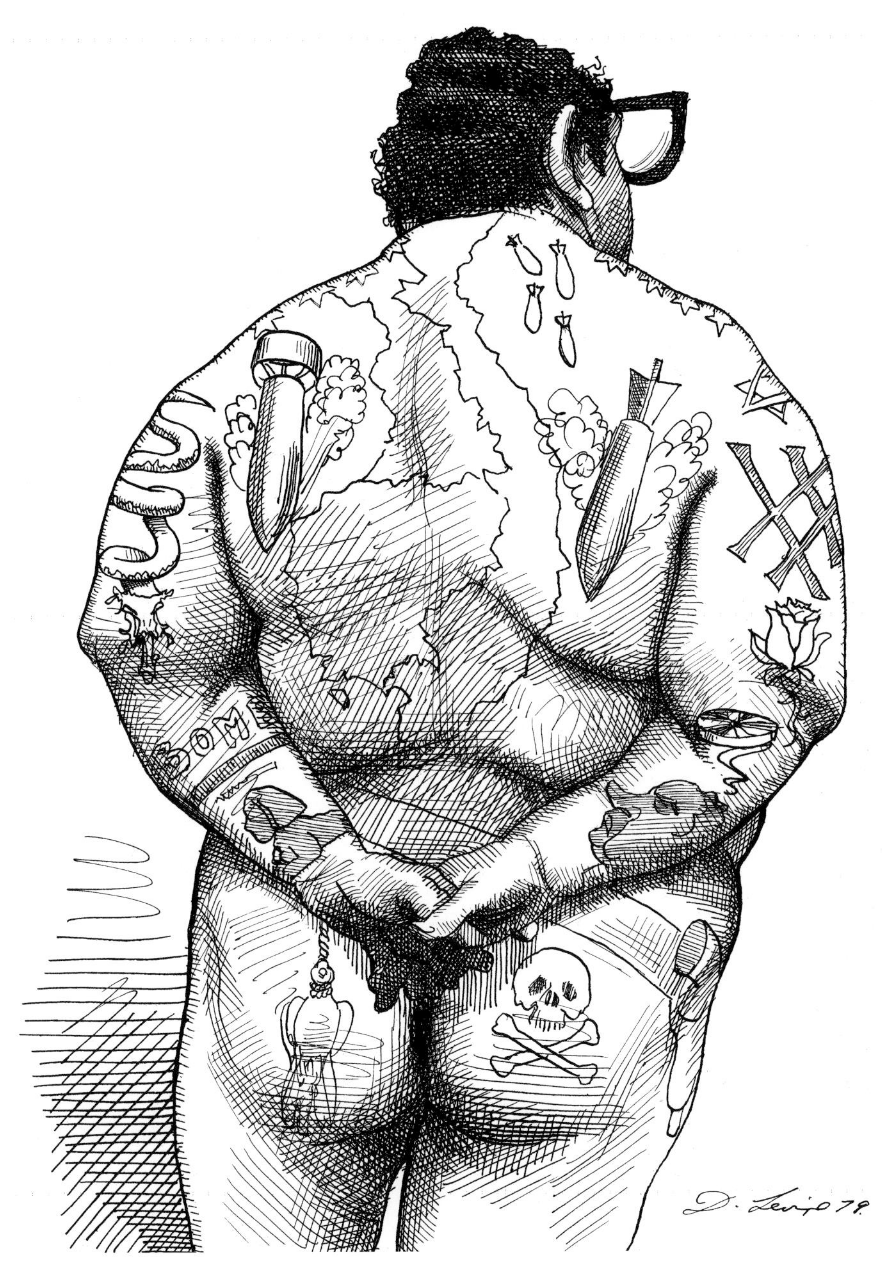

Secretary of State **HENRY KISSINGER**. This drawing was rejected by *The New York Times* as too controversial, before being published in another publication.

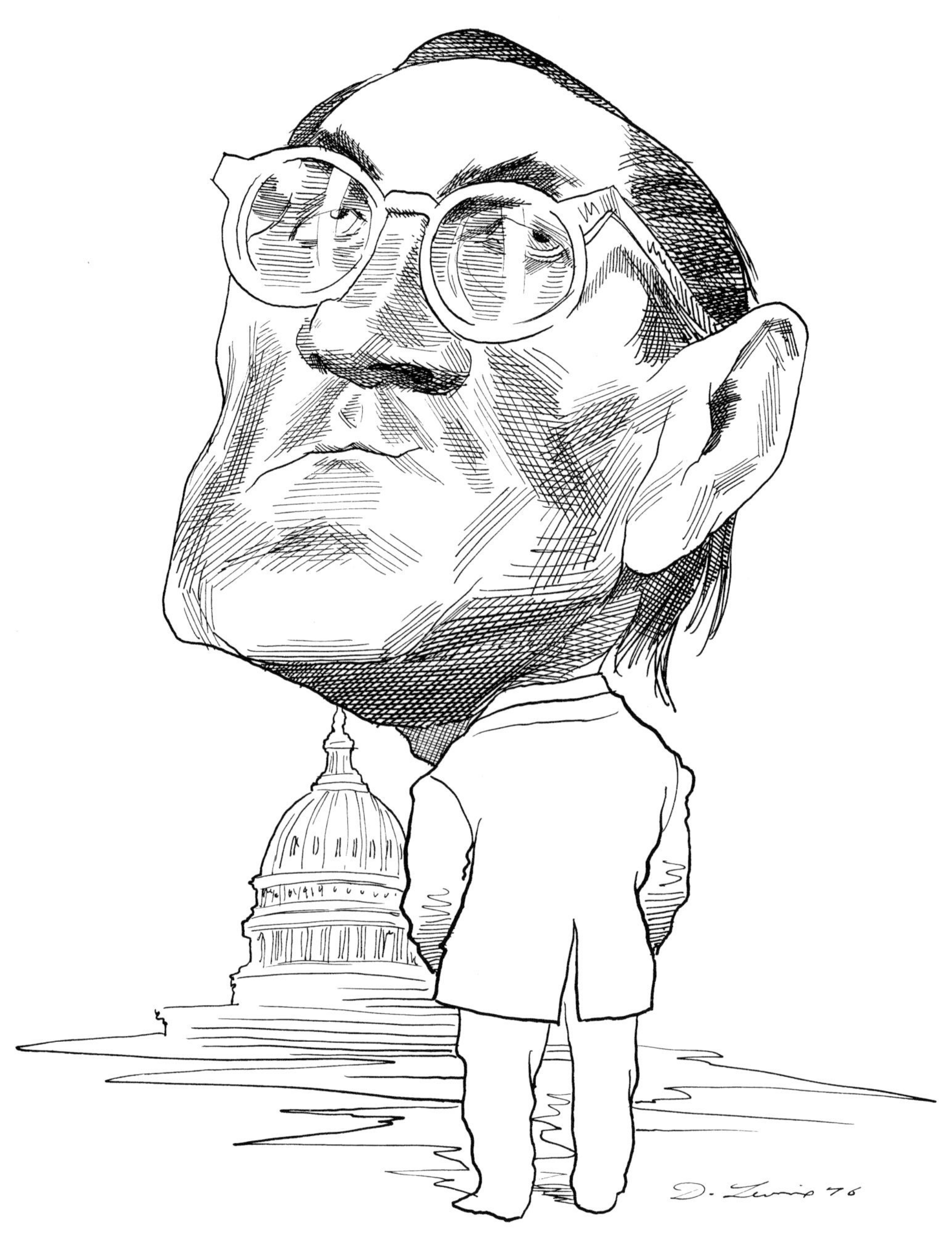

Director of Central Intelligence **William Colby**

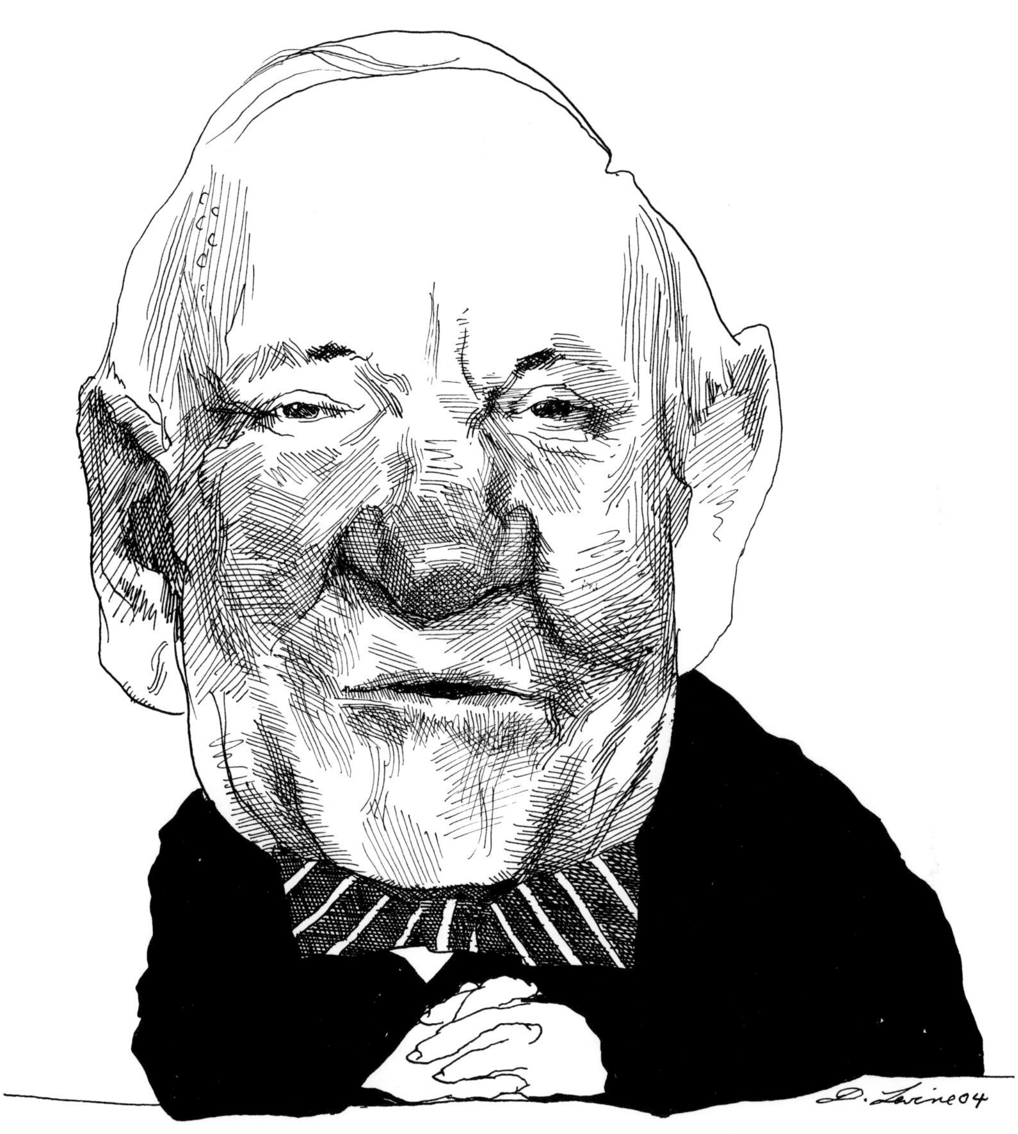

Justice **JOHN PAUL STEVENS**. Nominated to replace Justice William O. Douglas.

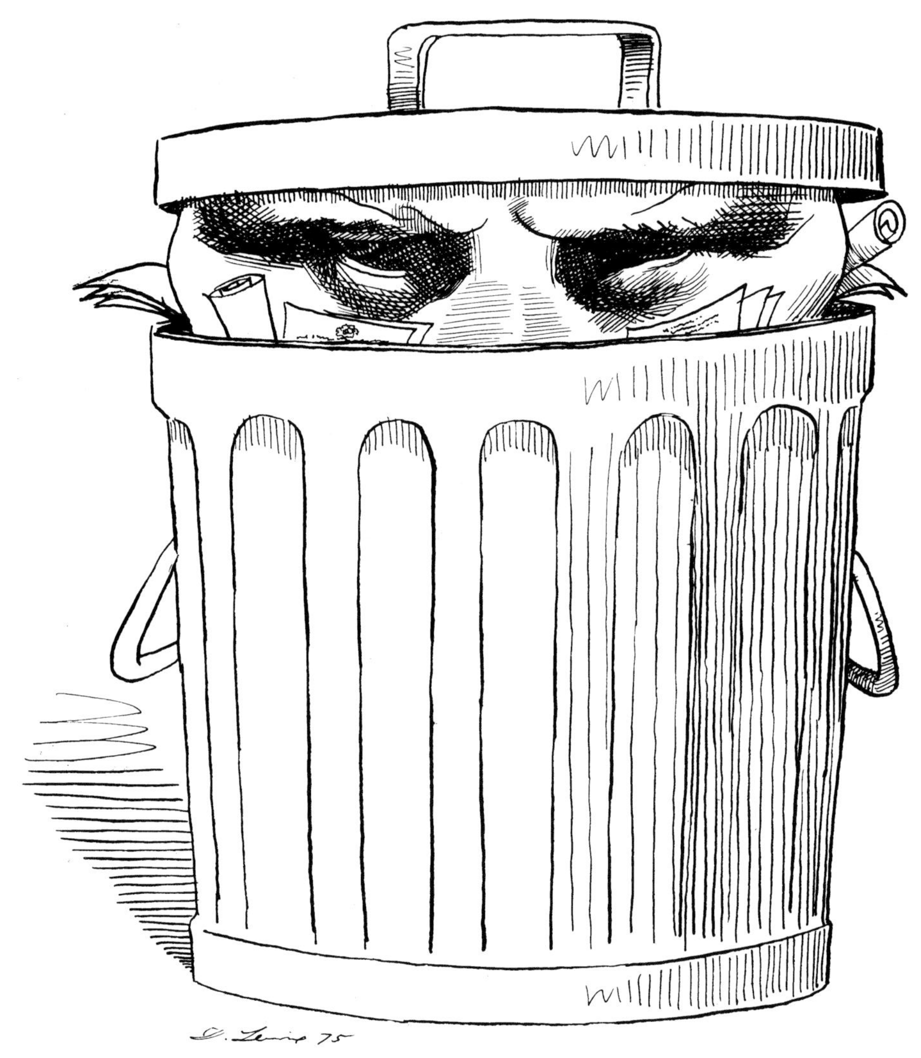

Gerald Ford

JIMMY CARTER★

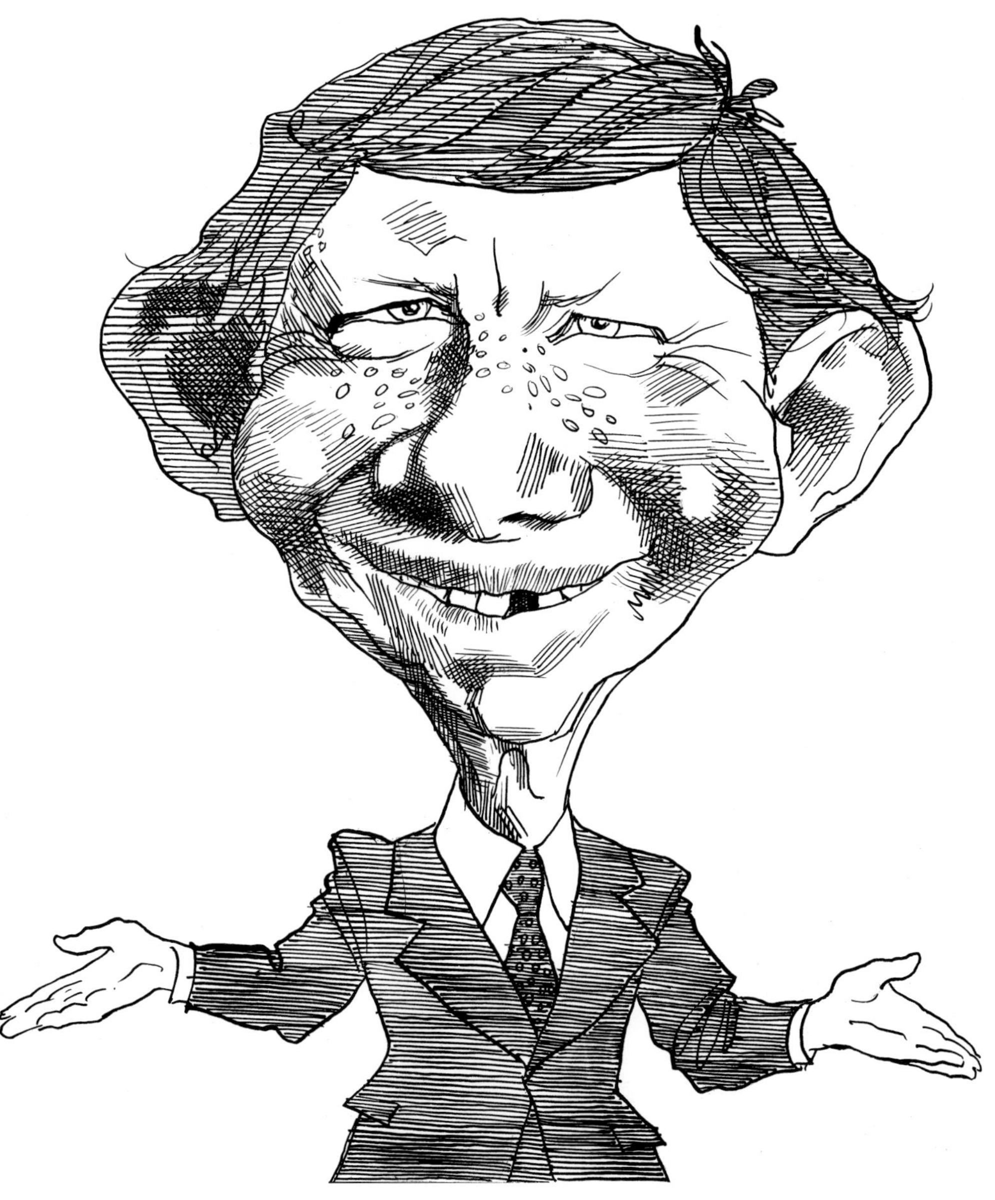

➡ I saw this idea on the *Nation*'s cover. By whom? To coin a phrase on Capital Hill, I don't remember. But I don't think this went far enough. He was better than Nixon. His mother had a more radical point of view, but he was a businessman who sold peanuts. And then there was his brother. It took on aspects of Gilbert and Sullivan. Carter play-acted, carrying empty bags off a plane. I wasn't surprised by the Camp David Accords, but I didn't believe it either. It was bubblegum, not glue. But he got further than anyone else in the Middle East.

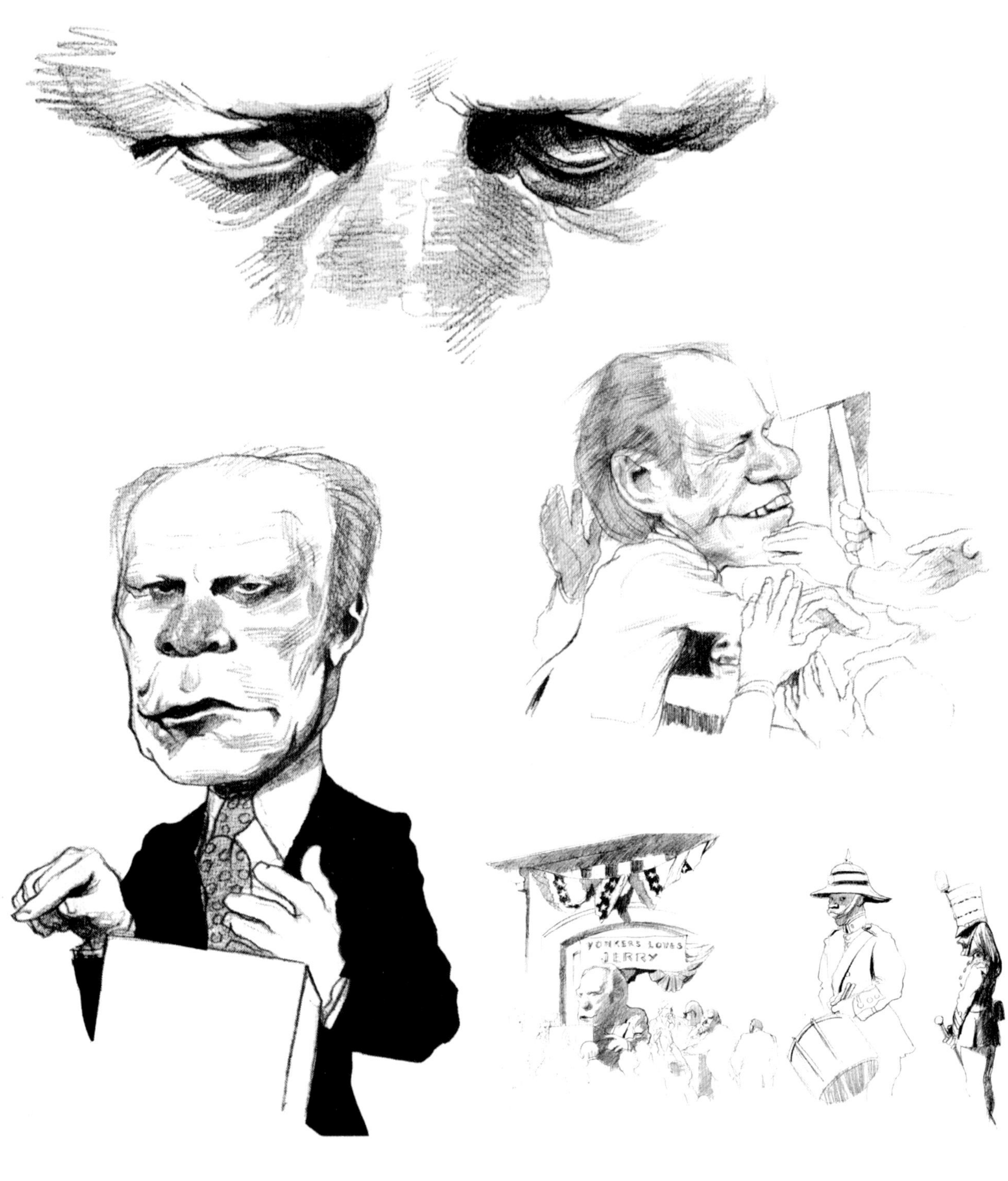

Gerald Ford Campaigning. *Time* commissioned me to cover the 1976 contest. Pages from my sketchbook show Ford pressing flesh; police in New City, NY; signing a revenue-sharing bill in Yonkers; and at his only televised debate with Carter.

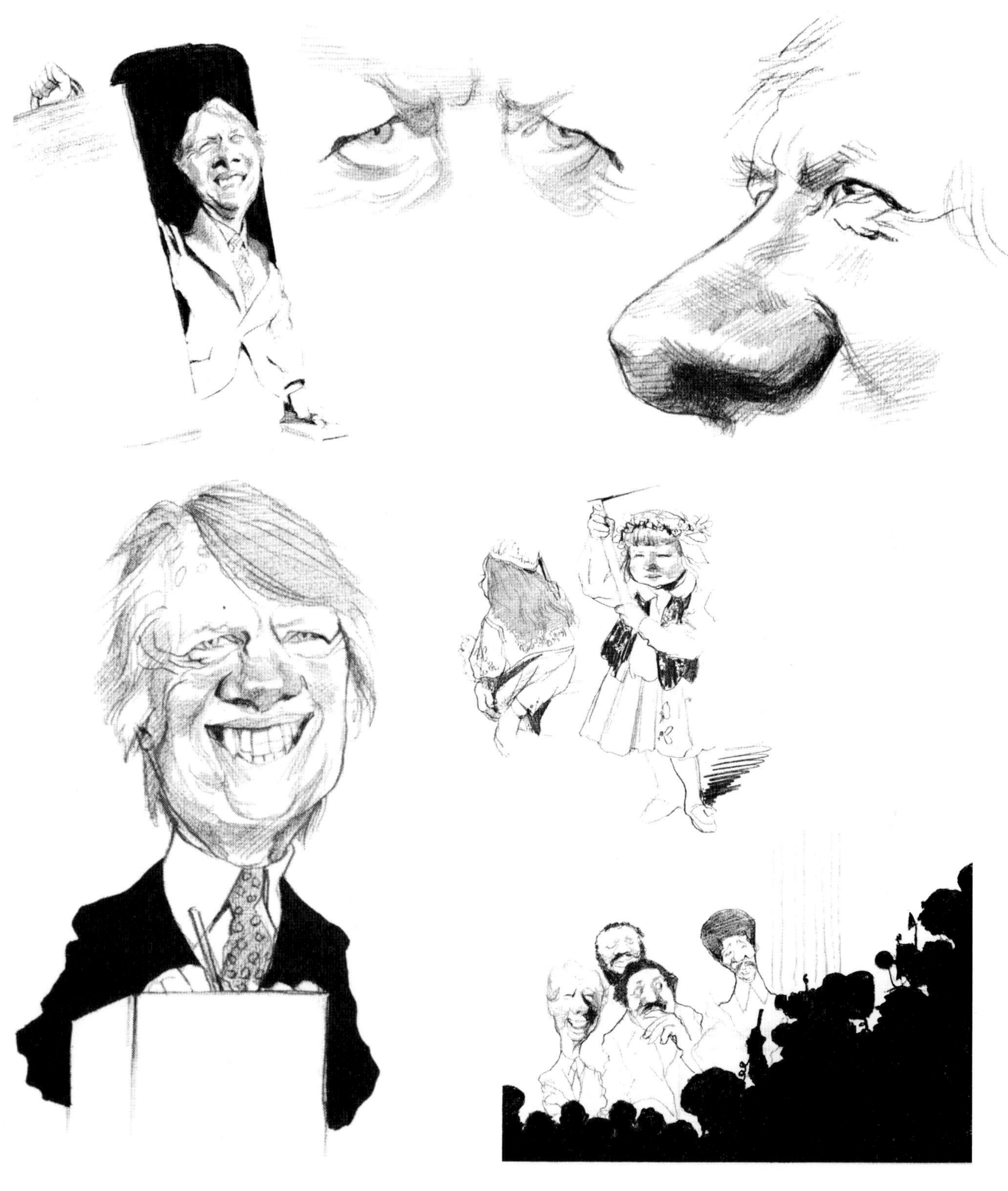

Jimmy Carter Campaigning. Carter carrying his own bags; Polish-American children at rally; Carter at an African American church; and at his debate with Ford.

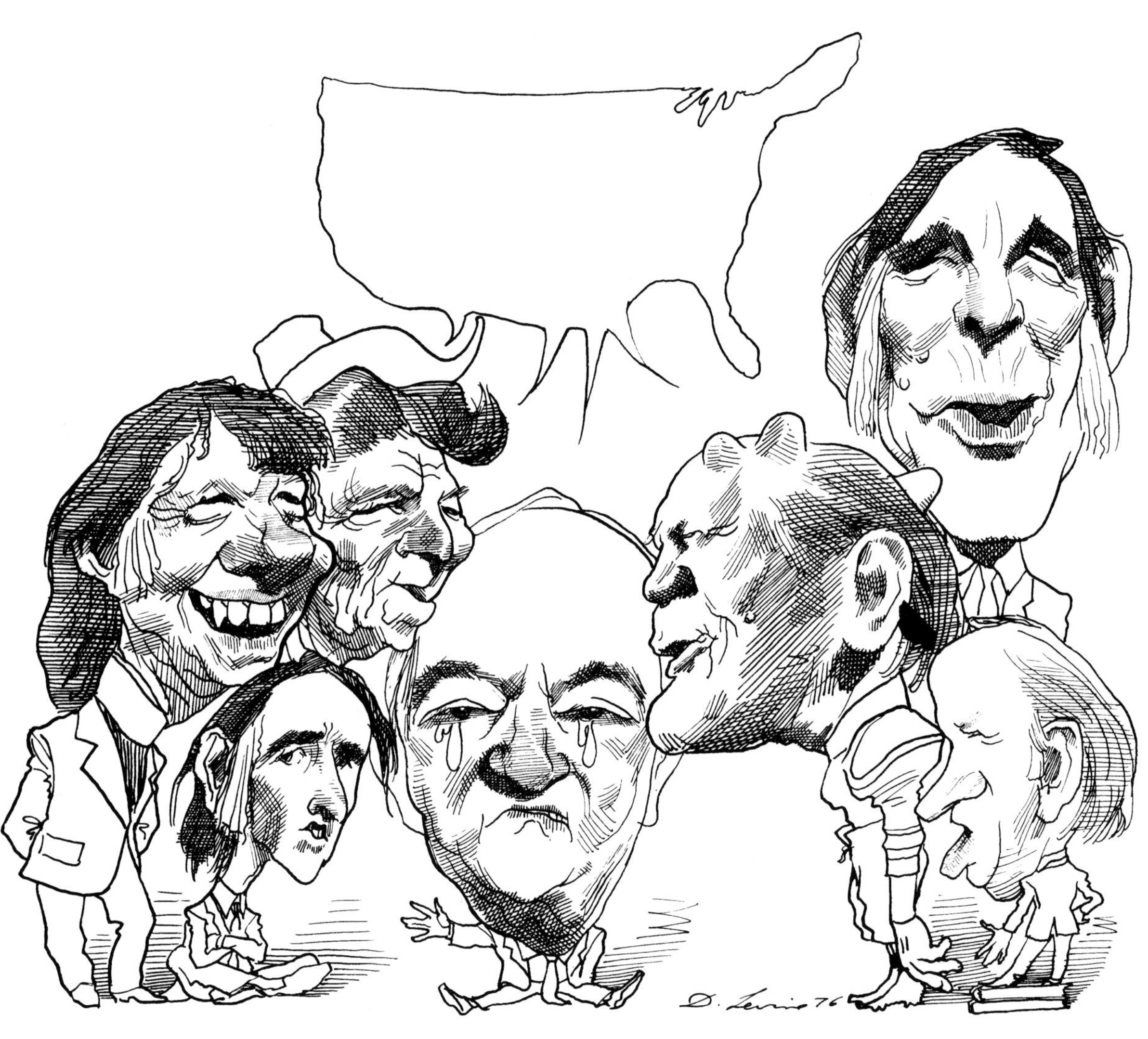

1976 Presidential Candidates (LEFT TO RIGHT): **JIMMY CARTER**, **JERRY BROWN**, **RONALD REAGAN**, **HUBERT HUMPHREY**, **GERALD FORD**, **MORRIS UDALL**, and **HENRY JACKSON**.

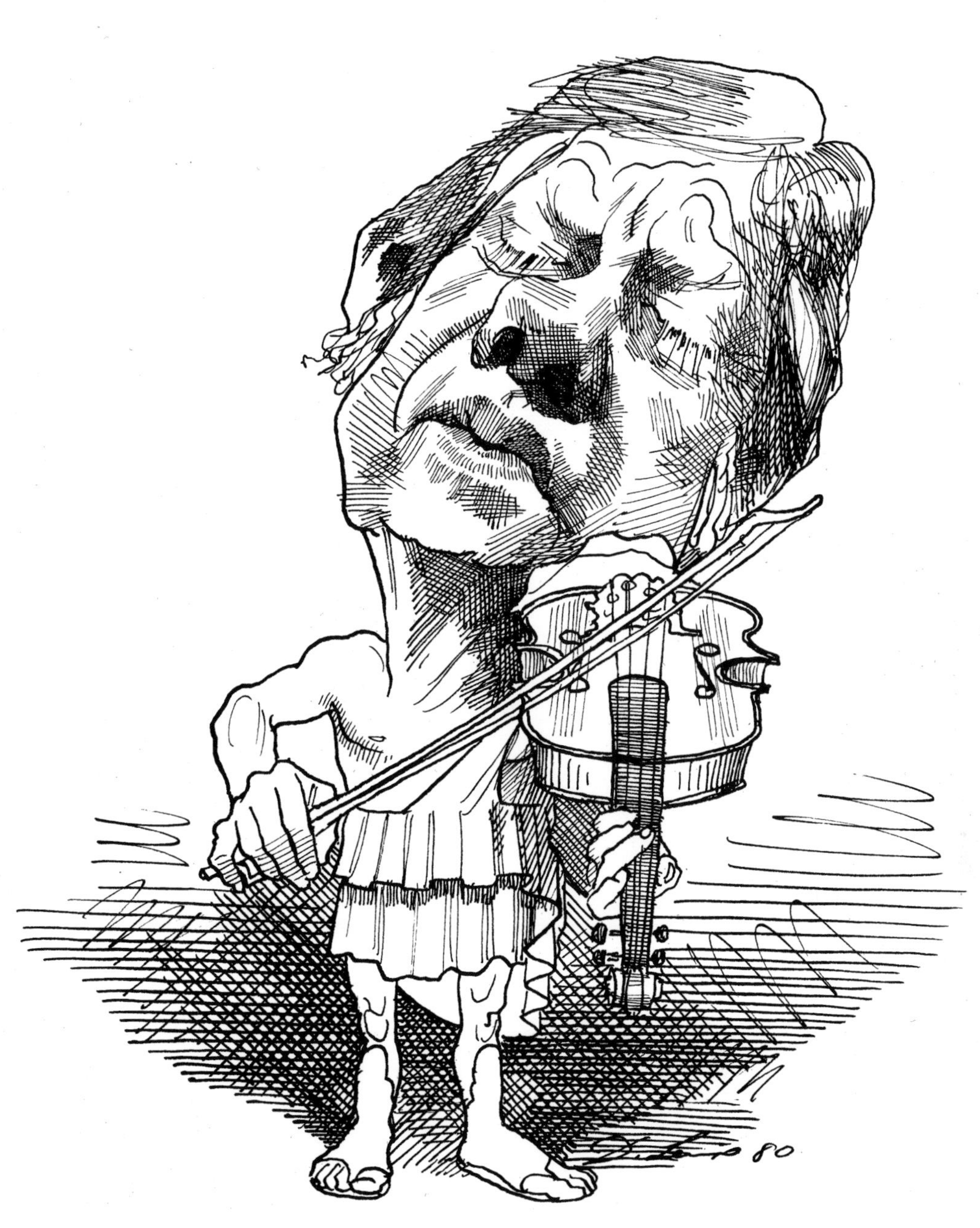

JIMMY CARTER

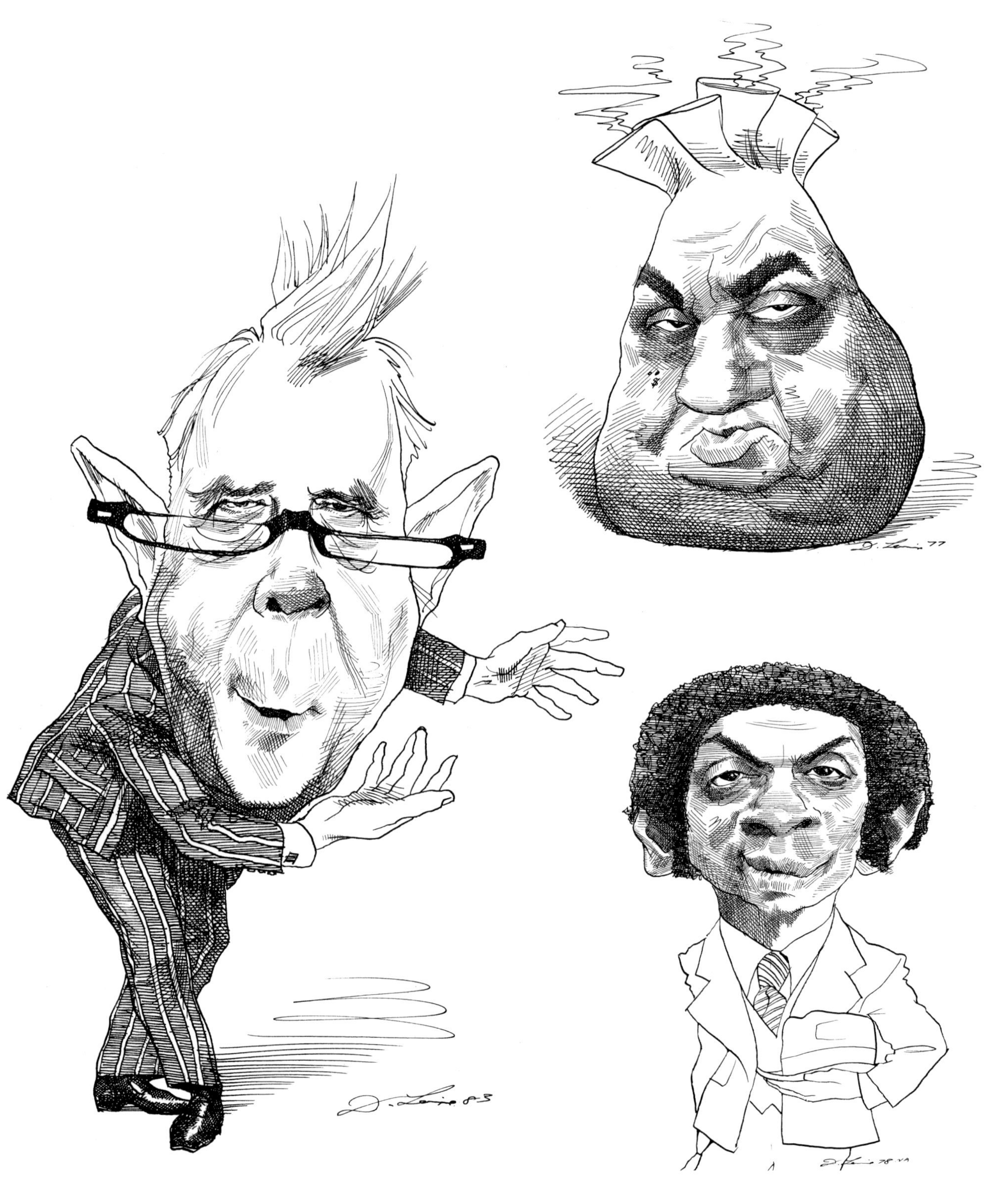

Carter Cabinet (CLOCKWISE FROM LEFT): Secretary of State **CYRUS VANCE**; Director of the Office of Management and the Budget **BERT LANCE**, who resigned in the wake of mismanagement and corruption scandal; United Nations Ambassador **ANDREW YOUNG**

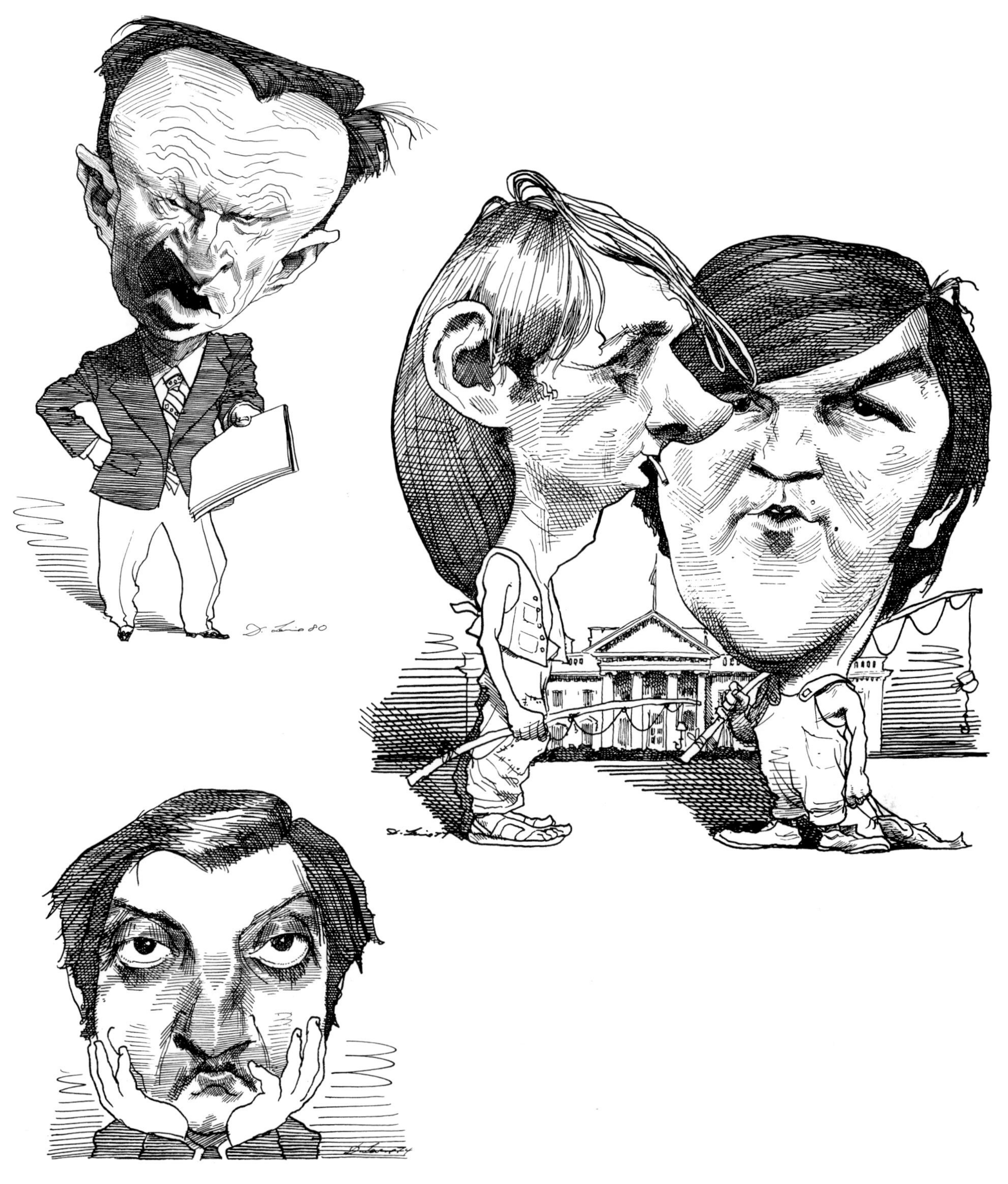

National Security Advisor **ZBIGNIEW BRZEZINSKI** (TOP); Press Secretary **JODY POWELL** (MIDDLE LEFT) and Chief of Staff **HAMILTON JORDAN** (MIDDLE RIGHT), drawn for a *Time* cover, were both members of the "Georgia Mafia," a tight knit group of aides who had come to Washington with Carter; Vice President **WALTER MONDALE** (BOTTOM)

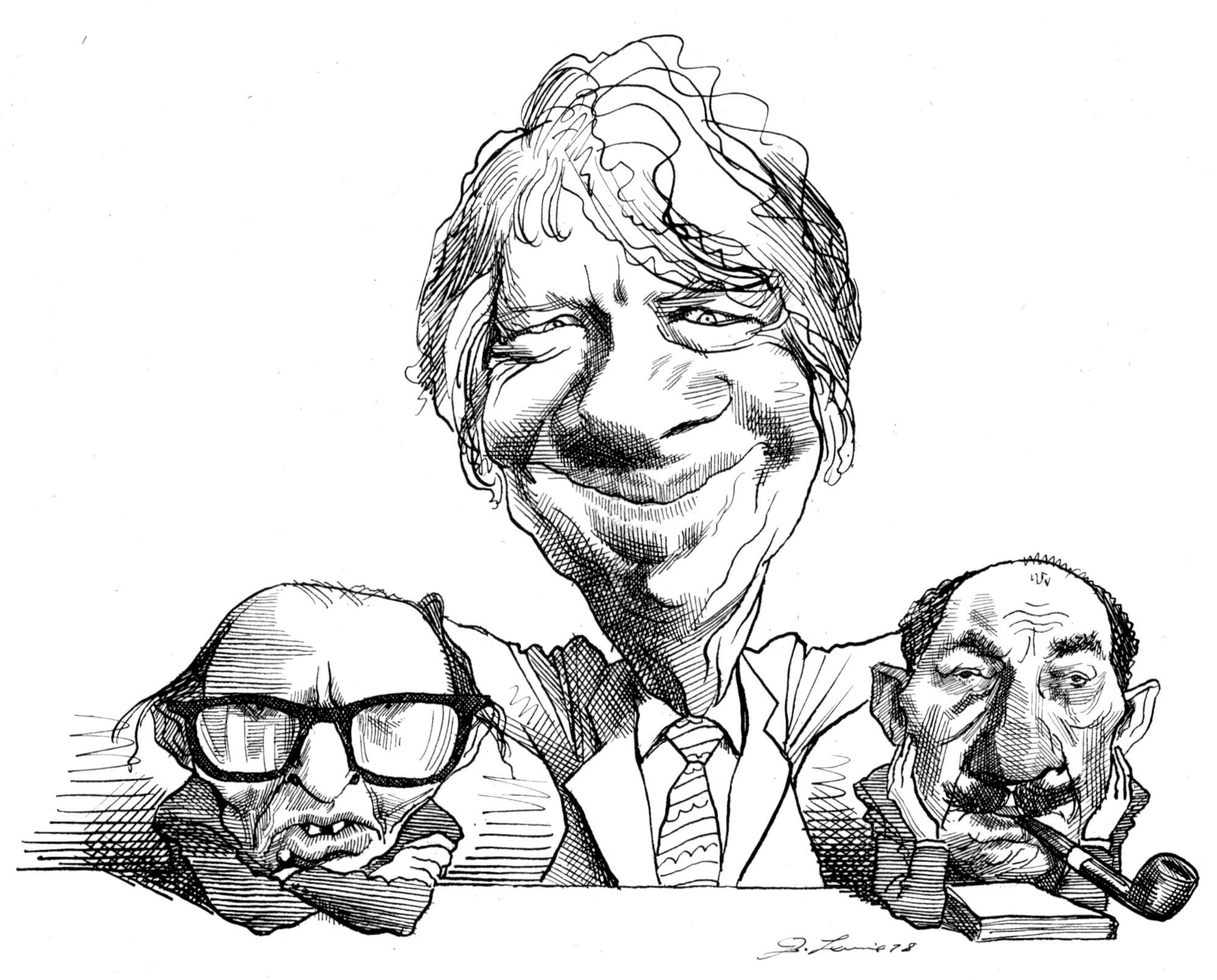

MENACHIM BEGIN, **JIMMY CARTER**, and **ANWAR SADAT**. Undoubtedly, Carter's greatest achievement is the Camp David Accords which initiated the first peace treaty between Israel and one of its Arab neighbors, Egypt.

★ ★ RONALD ★ ★ ★ ★ ★ ★ ★ ★

REAGAN

➽ The Actor, dressed in a certain way, the smile was always there. He was carrying on a classic right wing agenda. I generally thought there was no hope when he was elected. We were just going from one to another. I created my own tool for Reagan which was his hair and the linear breakdown of his facial muscles, and it enabled me to do him over and over. He made it easy for artists like me.

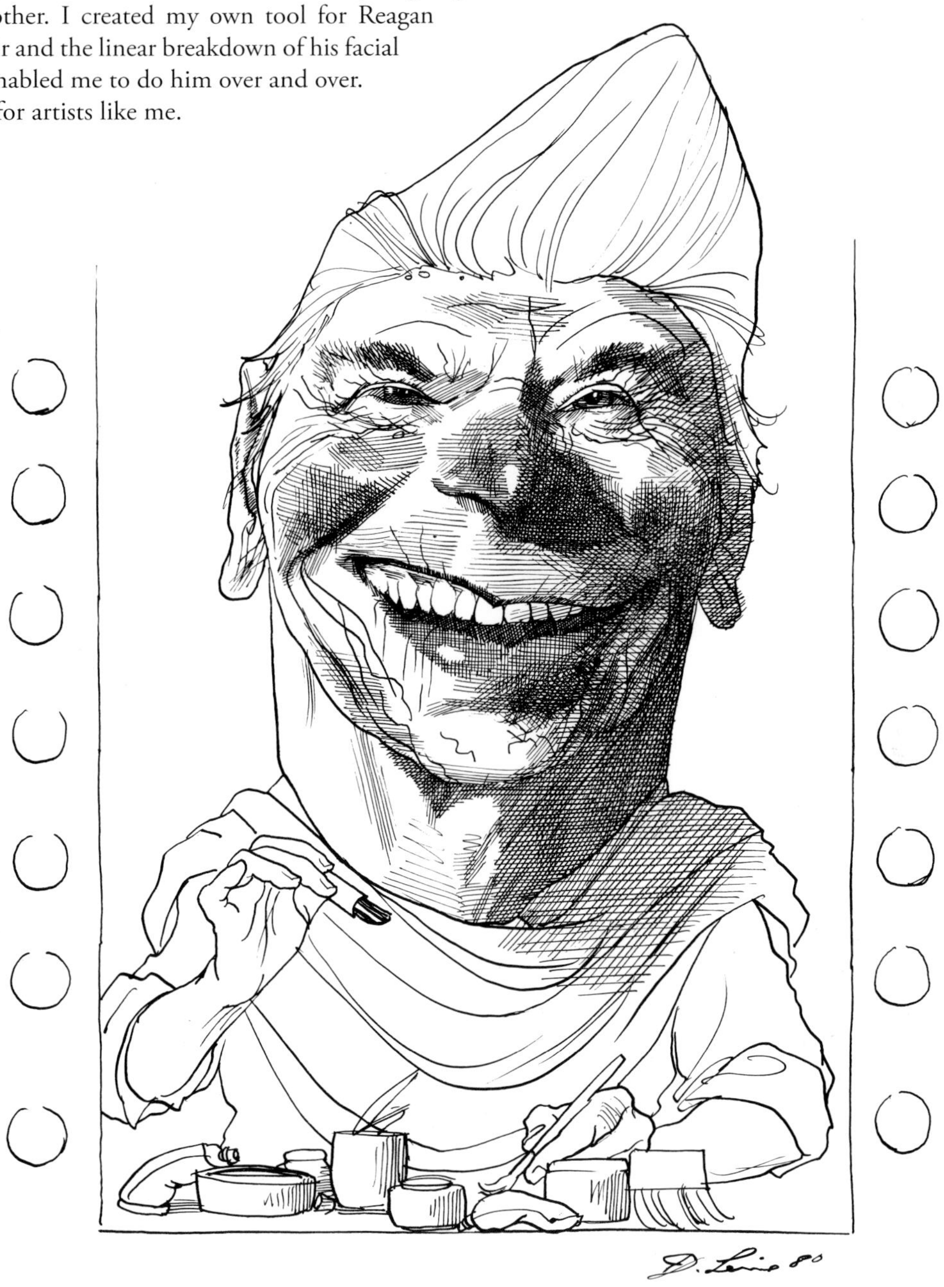

D. Levine 80

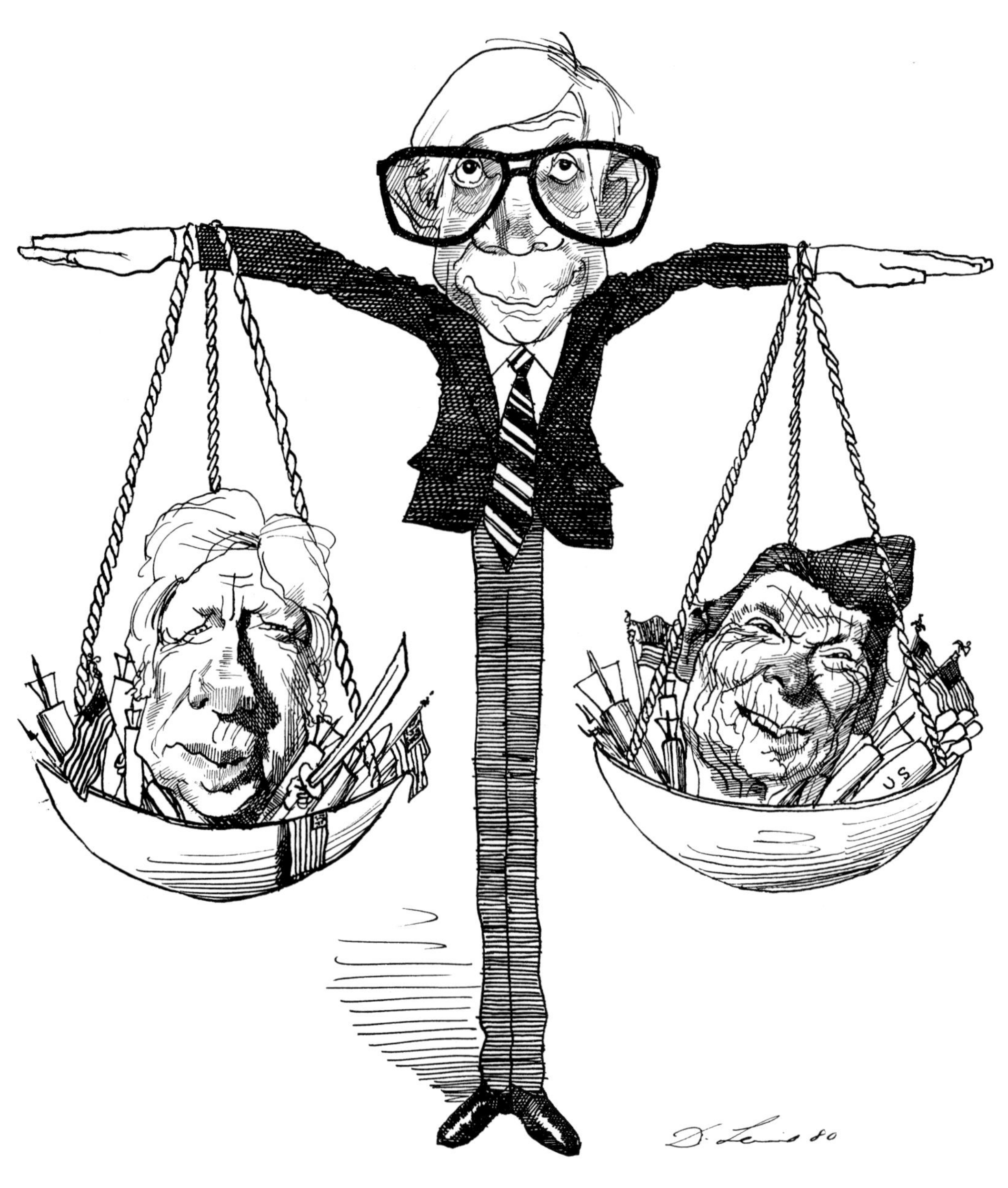

JIMMY CARTER, **JOHN ANDERSON**, and **RONALD REAGAN**. Anderson was a prominent third party candidate who garnered six percent of the national vote.

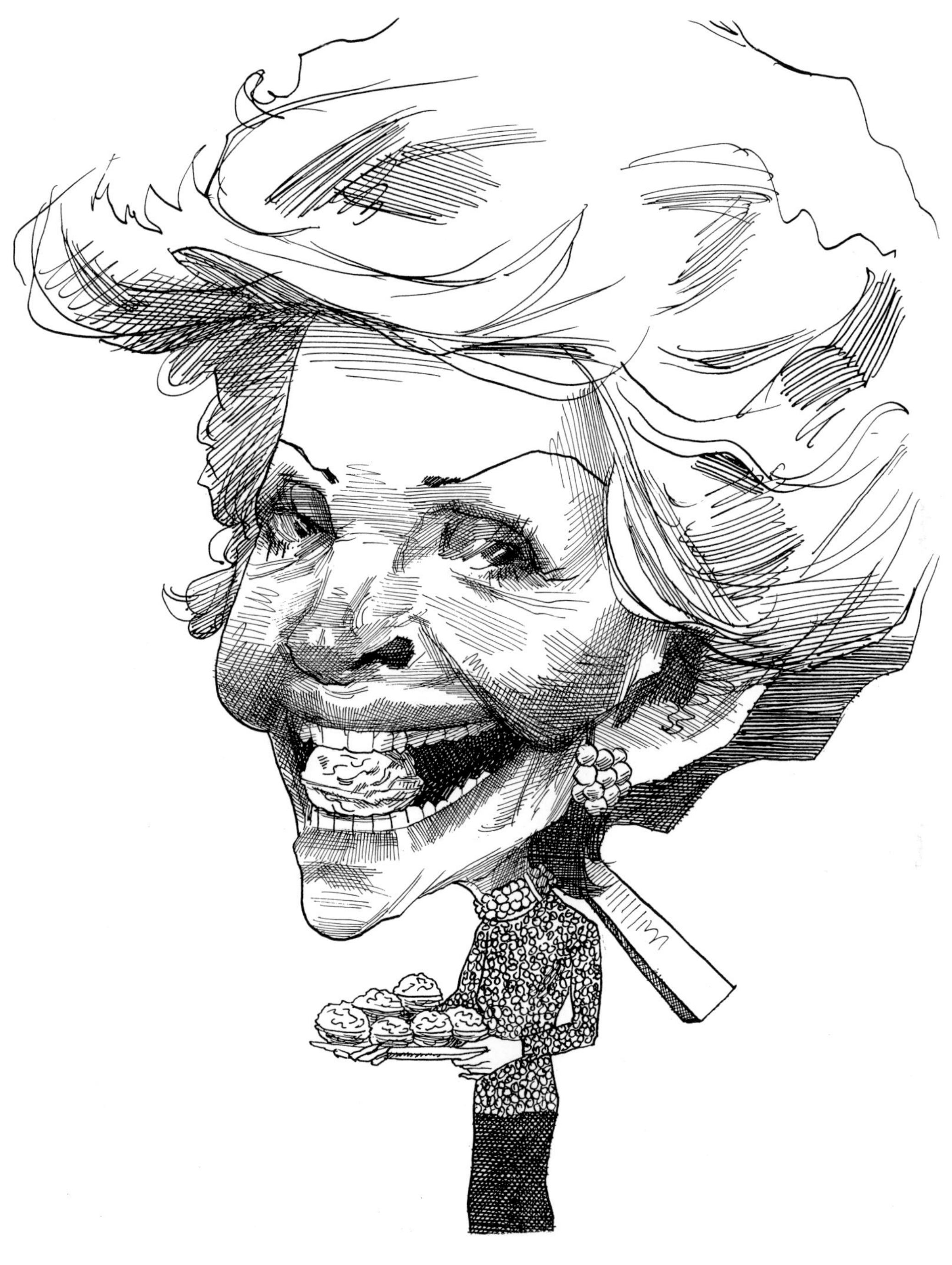

NANCY REAGAN

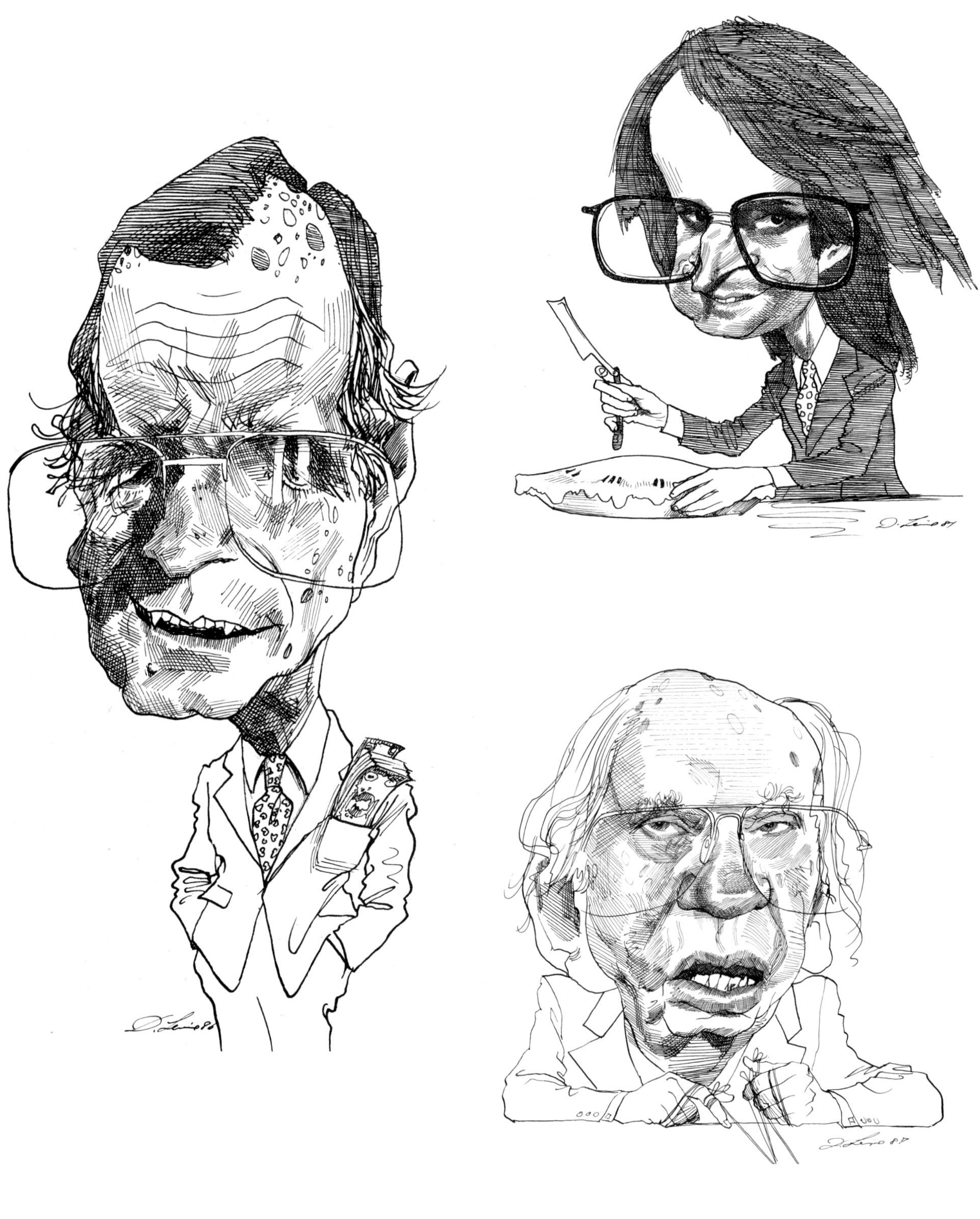

(clockwise from left) Vice president **George Bush**; Director of the Office of Management and Budget **David Stockman**, who was committed to the "supply–side" economics; director of the CIA **William Casey**.

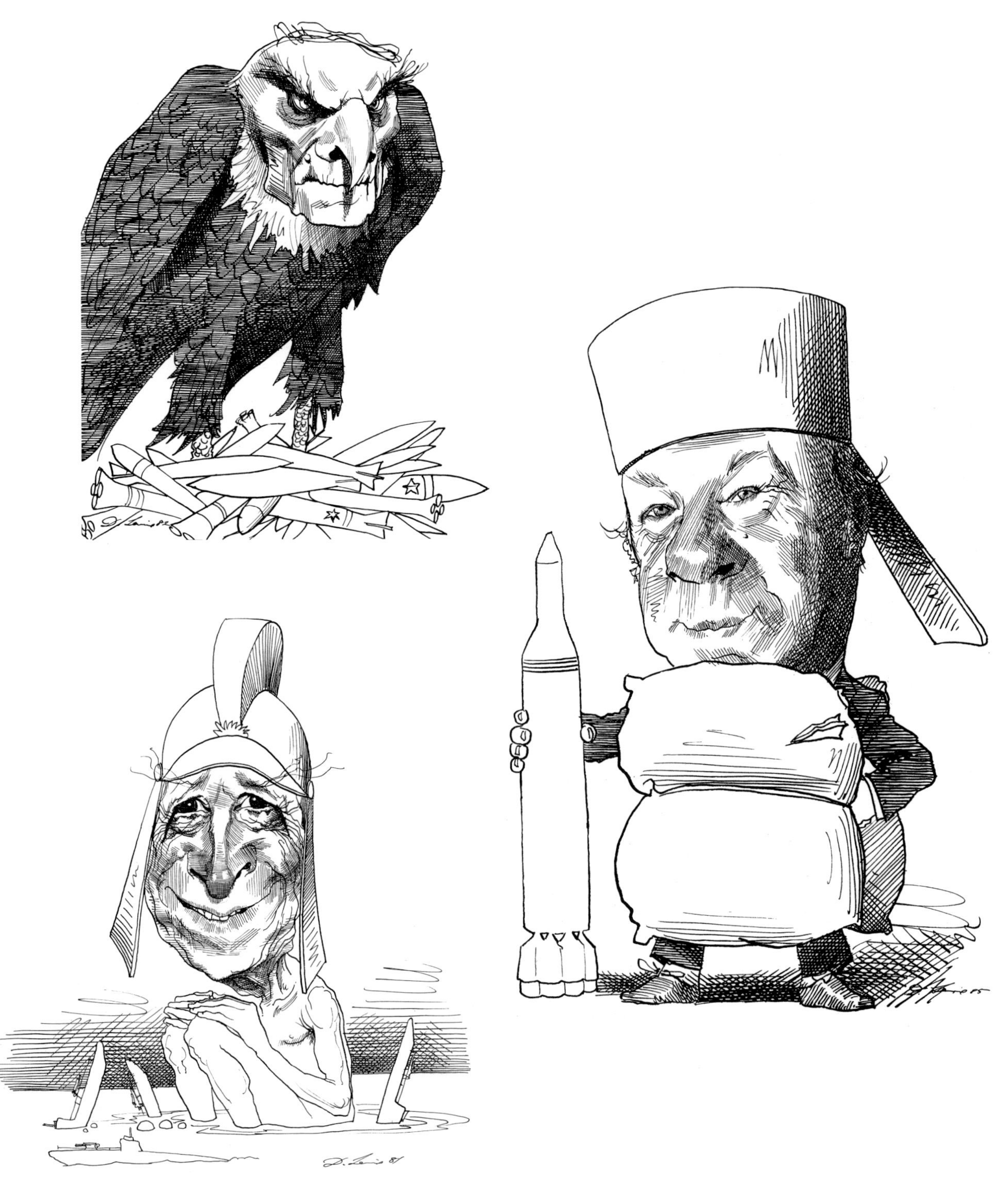

(clockwise from top) Secretaries of State **ALEXANDER HAIG** and **GEORGE SHULTZ**; Secretary of Defense **CASPAR WEINBERGER**.

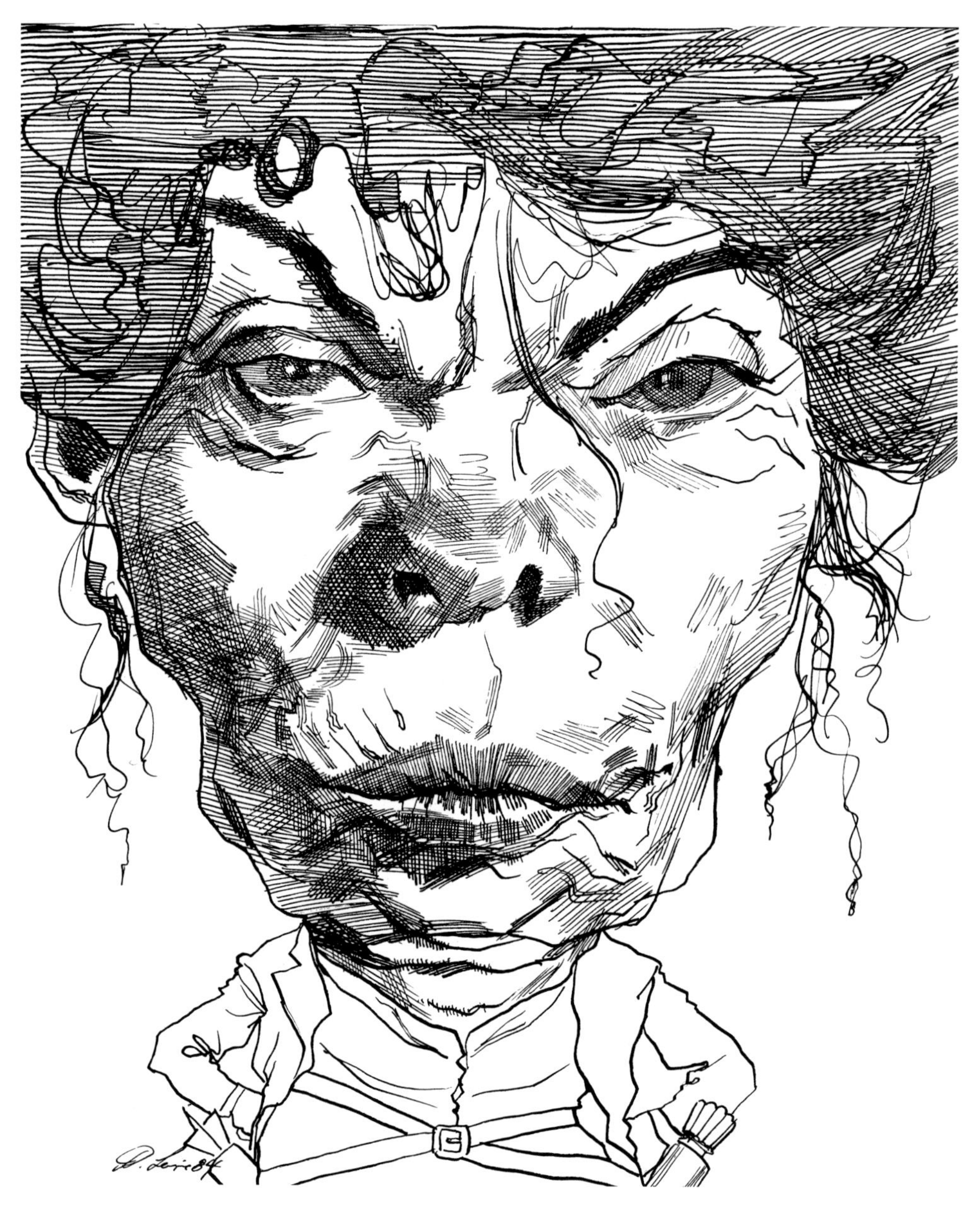

United Nations Ambassador **Jeanne Kirkpatrick**'s philosophy: "Traditional authoritarian governments are less repressive than revolutionary autocracies."

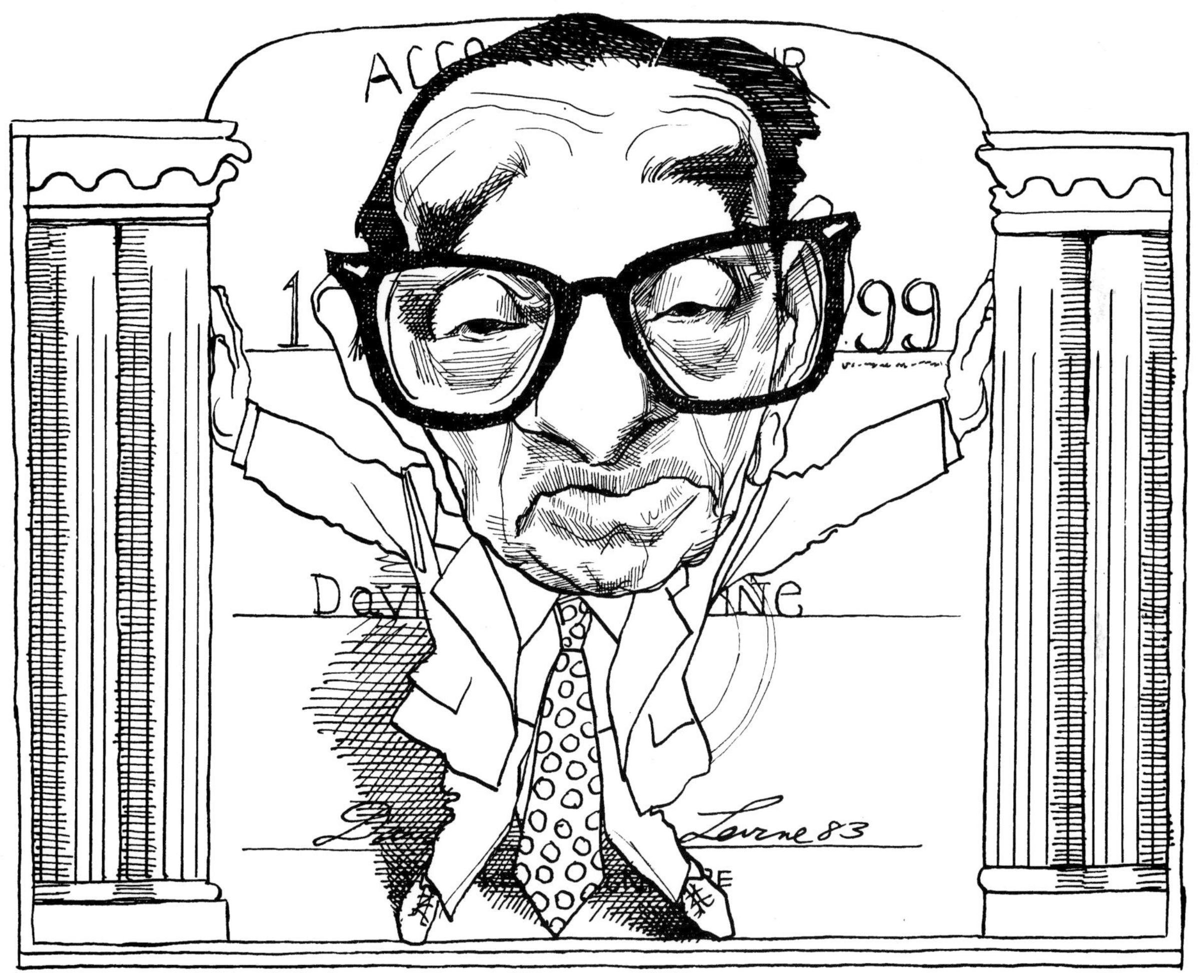

Chairman of the Federal Reserve **ALAN GREENSPAN**.

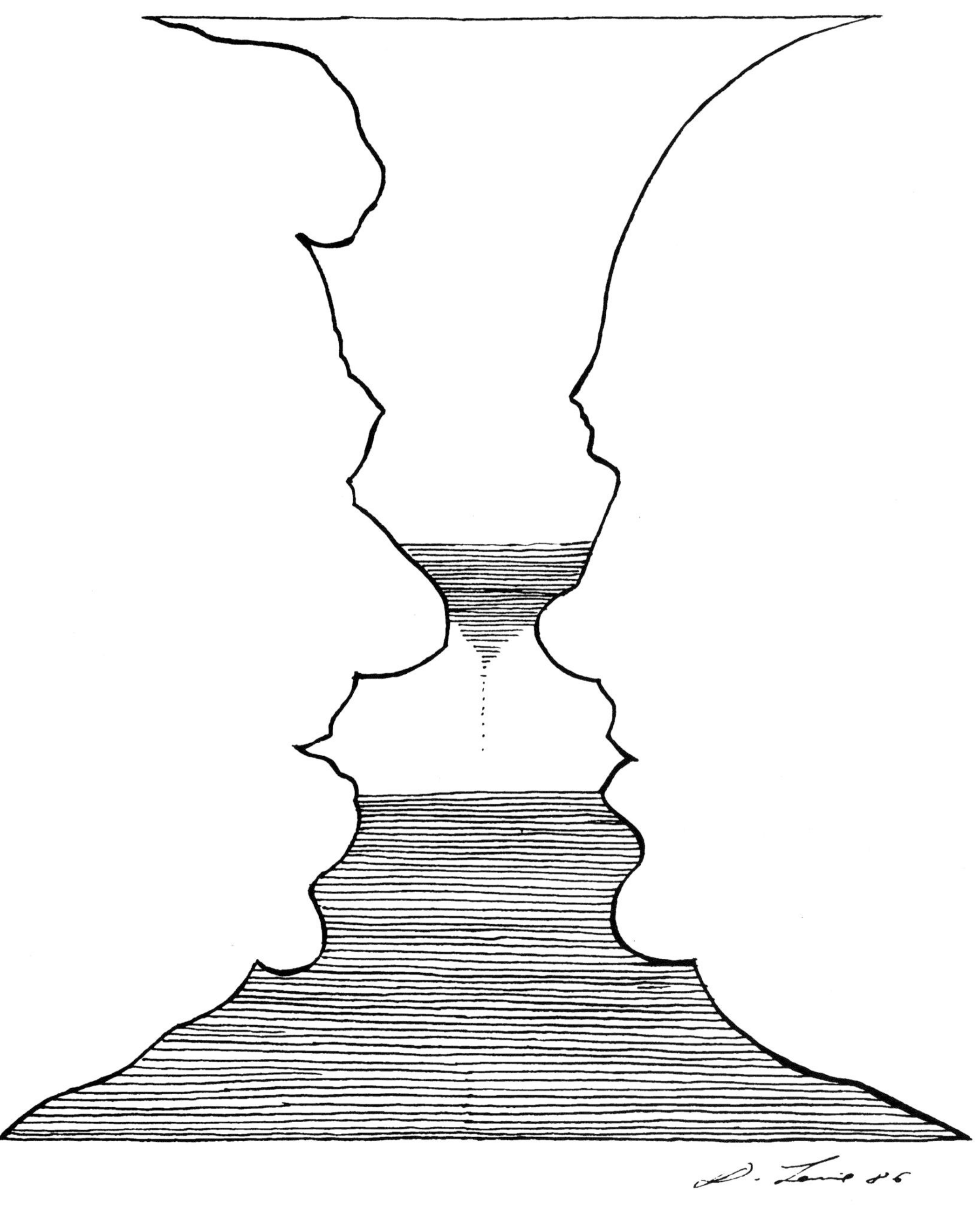

Reagan and Gorbachev. The hourglass silhouette of the leaders' heads shows time slipping away from weapons treaties between the U.S. and the Soviet Union.

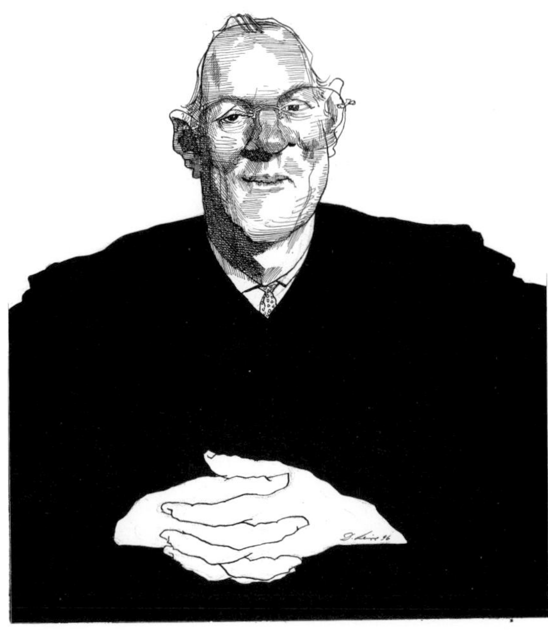

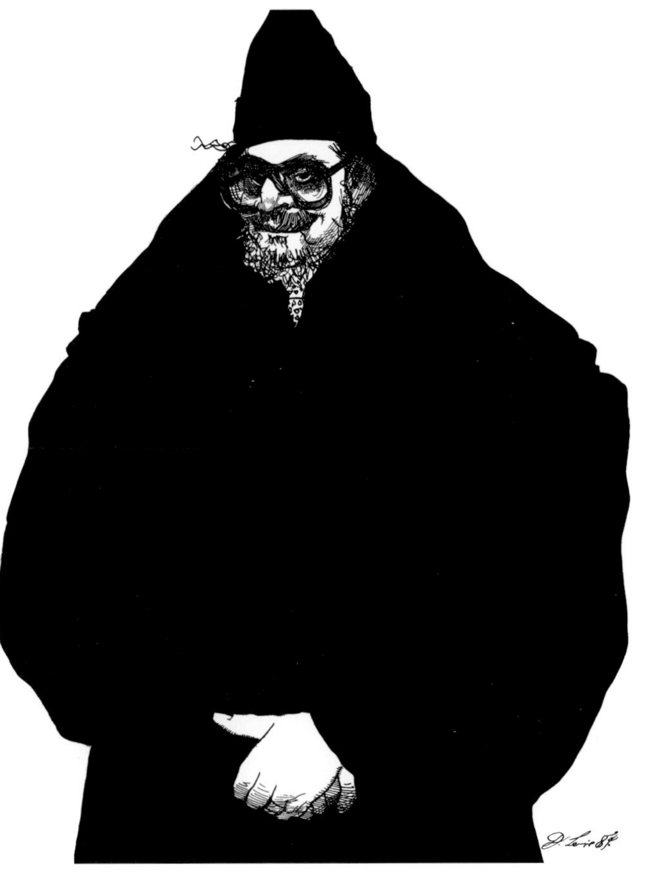

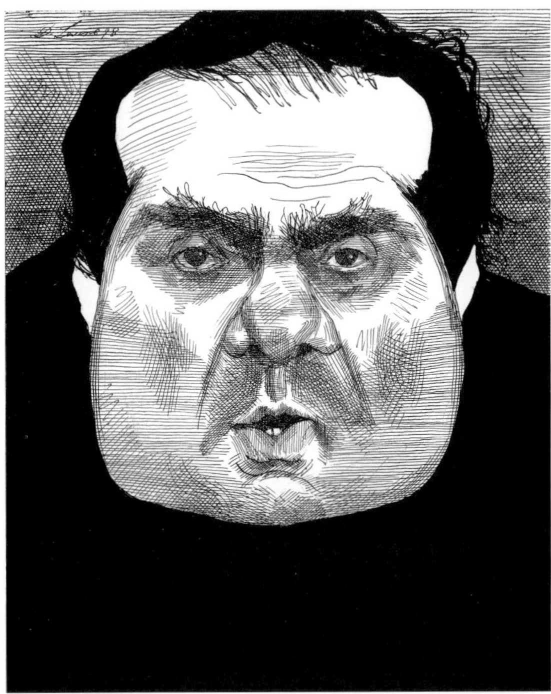

Supreme Court Nominees (CLOCKWISE FROM TOP LEFT): **ANTHONY KENNEDY**; **ROBERT BORK** was nominated but rejected by the Senate for extreme conservative ideology; yet **ANTONIN SCALIA** was approved despite his extreme conservative philosophy.

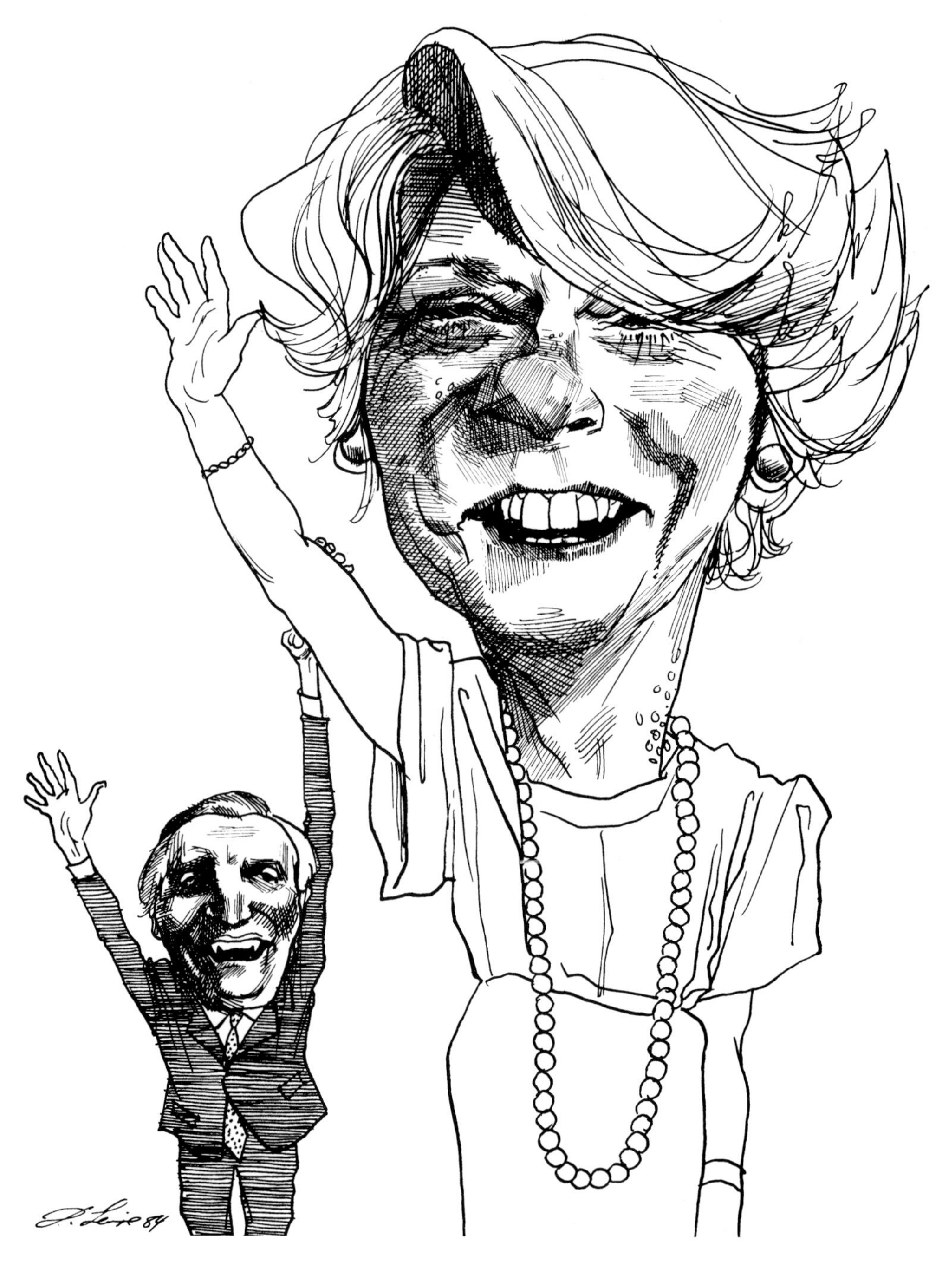

WALTER MONDALE and **GERALDINE FERRARO**. The 1984 Democratic presidential ticket, despite having the first woman on a major party slate, lost in a landslide.

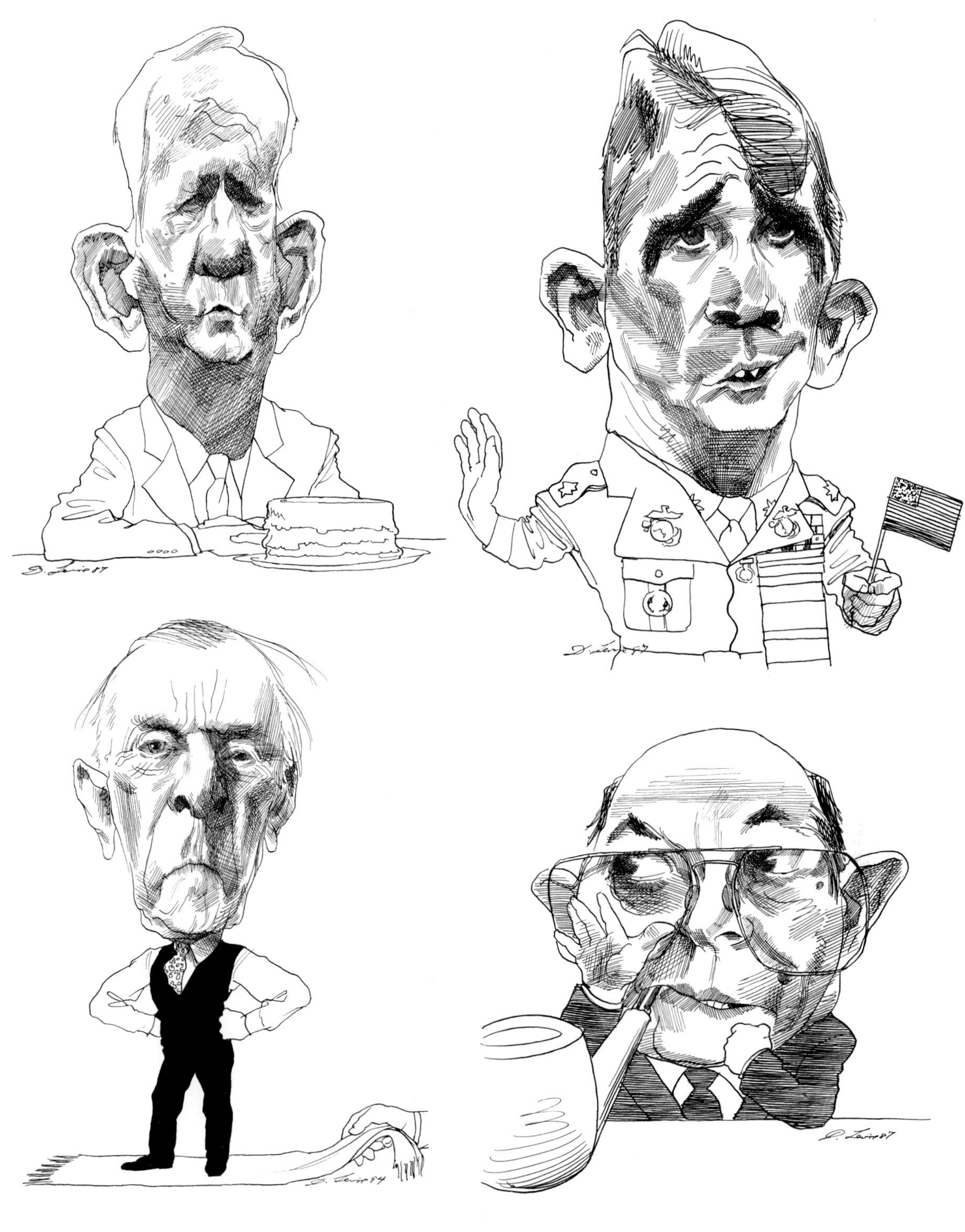

The Iran-Contra scandal resulted from selling weapons to Iran and diverting the proceeds to Contras in Nicaragua, despite a Congressional ban against such funding. The players (CLOCKWISE FROM TOP LEFT): former NSA Advisor **ROBERT McFARLANE**, who took a cake and Bible with the first Iran arms shipment; **OLIVER NORTH**, the National Security official who coordinated the illegal activity; National Security Advisor **JOHN POINDEXTER**, who was convicted of multiple felonies for his role; Independent Counsel **LAWRENCE WALSH**, who investigated the matter.

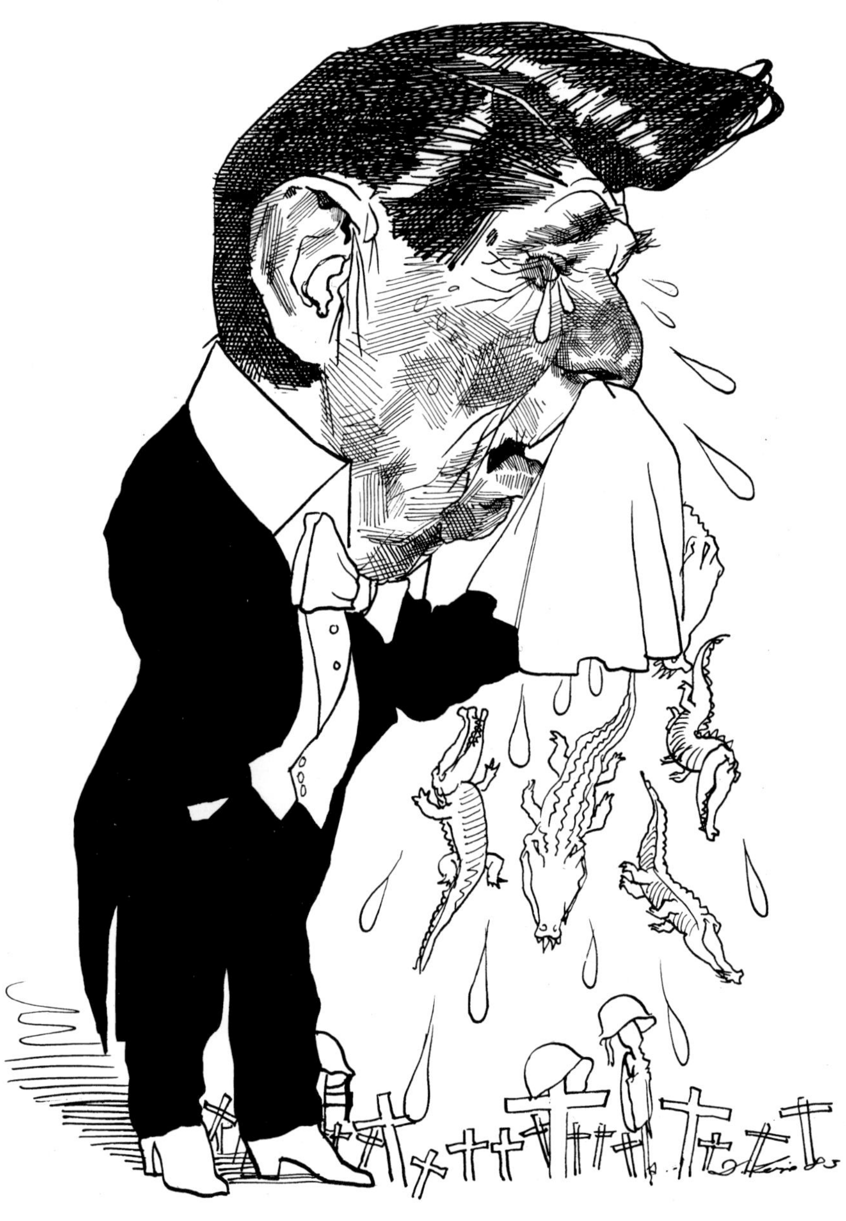

Ronald Reagan. In 1985, Reagan visited a German military cemetery in Bitburg which held the graves of 49 members of the Waffen-SS. Reagan issued a statement that called the Nazi soldiers buried in that cemetery "victims," implicitly comparing their deaths to those of Holocaust victims.

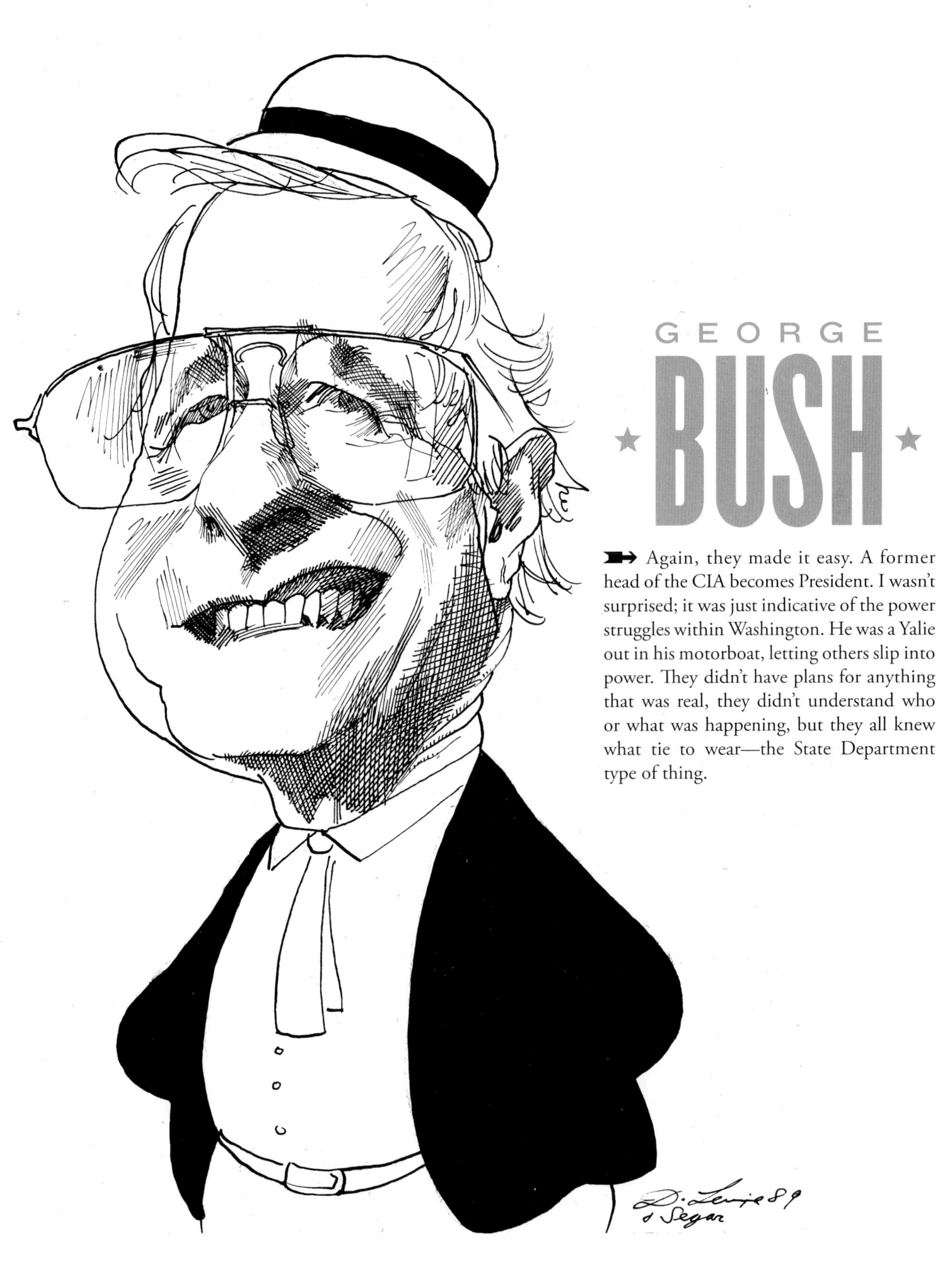

GEORGE BUSH

Again, they made it easy. A former head of the CIA becomes President. I wasn't surprised; it was just indicative of the power struggles within Washington. He was a Yalie out in his motorboat, letting others slip into power. They didn't have plans for anything that was real, they didn't understand who or what was happening, but they all knew what tie to wear—the State Department type of thing.

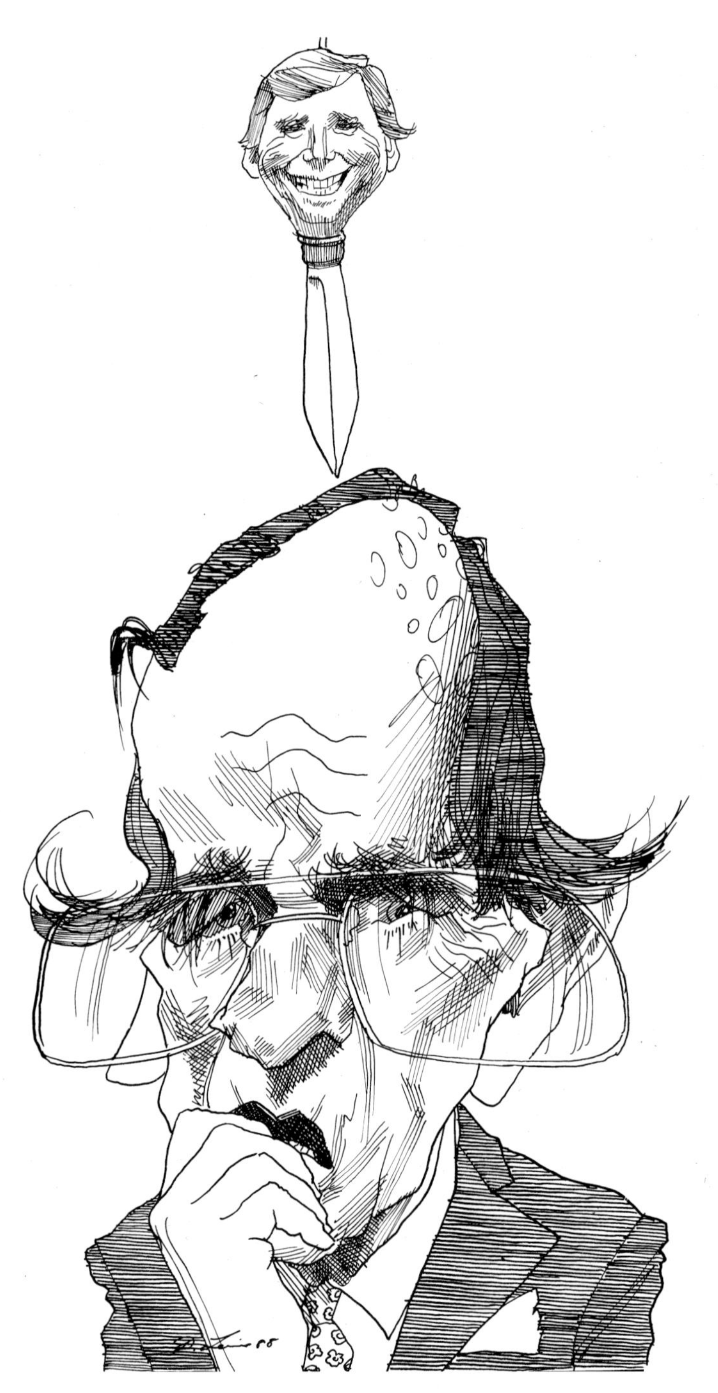

George Bush and Vice President **Dan Quayle**

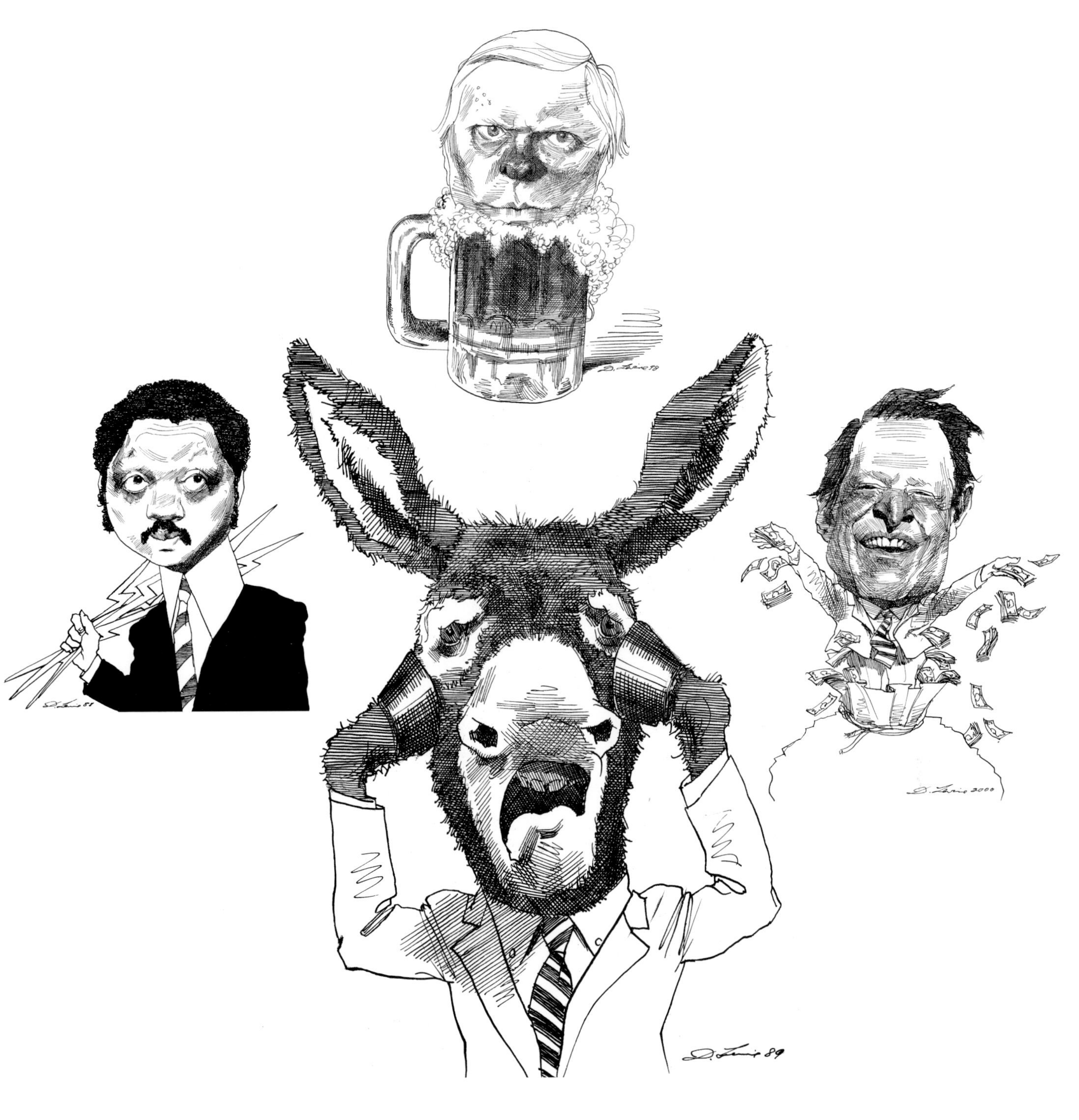

Democratic Presidential Candidates (CLOCKWISE FROM LEFT) **JESSE JACKSON**, **RICHARD GEPHARDT**, and **AL GORE**.

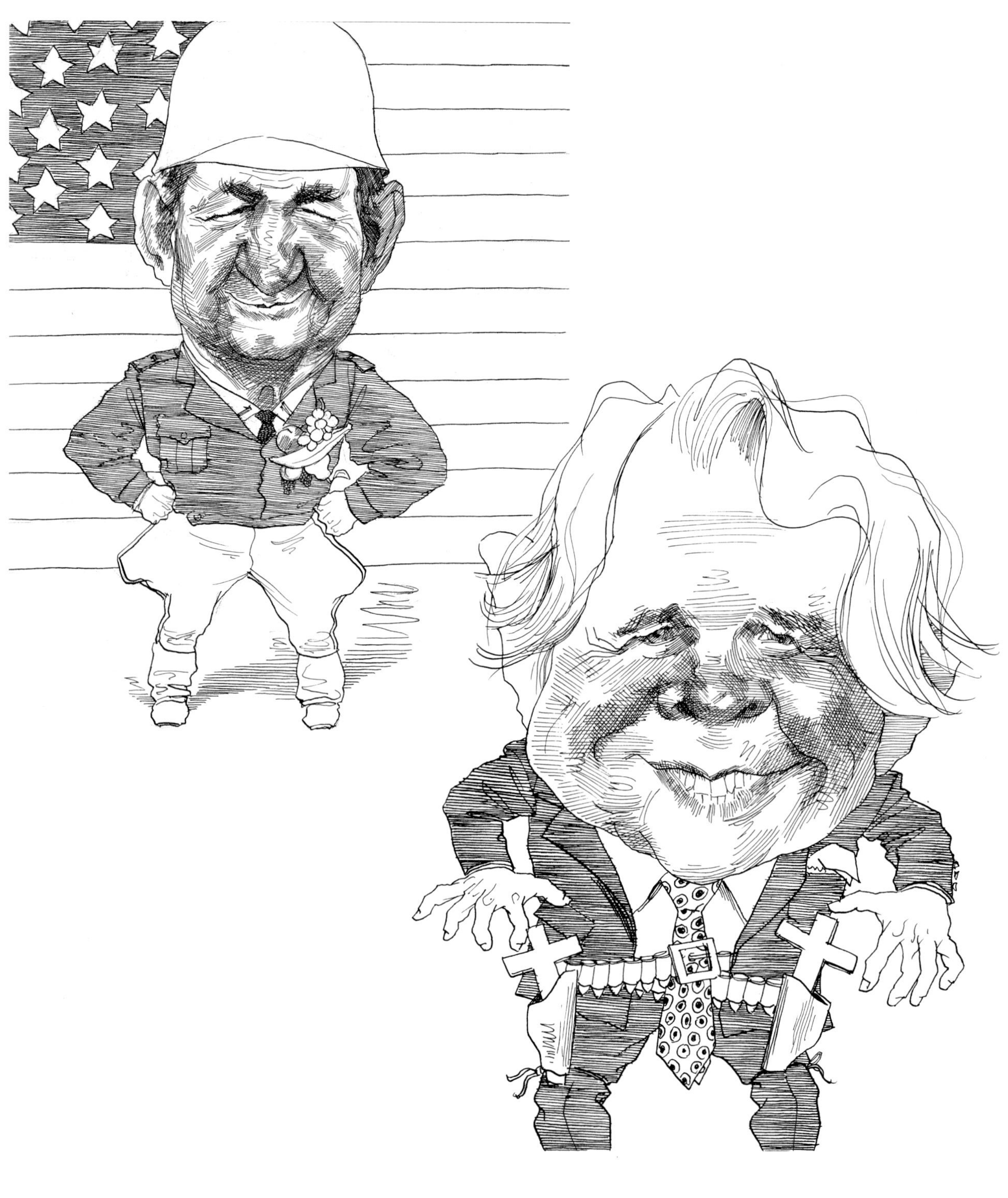

Republican challengers: Right wing demagogue **PATRICK BUCHANAN** (TOP) in 1992;
Evangelist **PAT ROBERTSON** (BOTTOM) in 1988

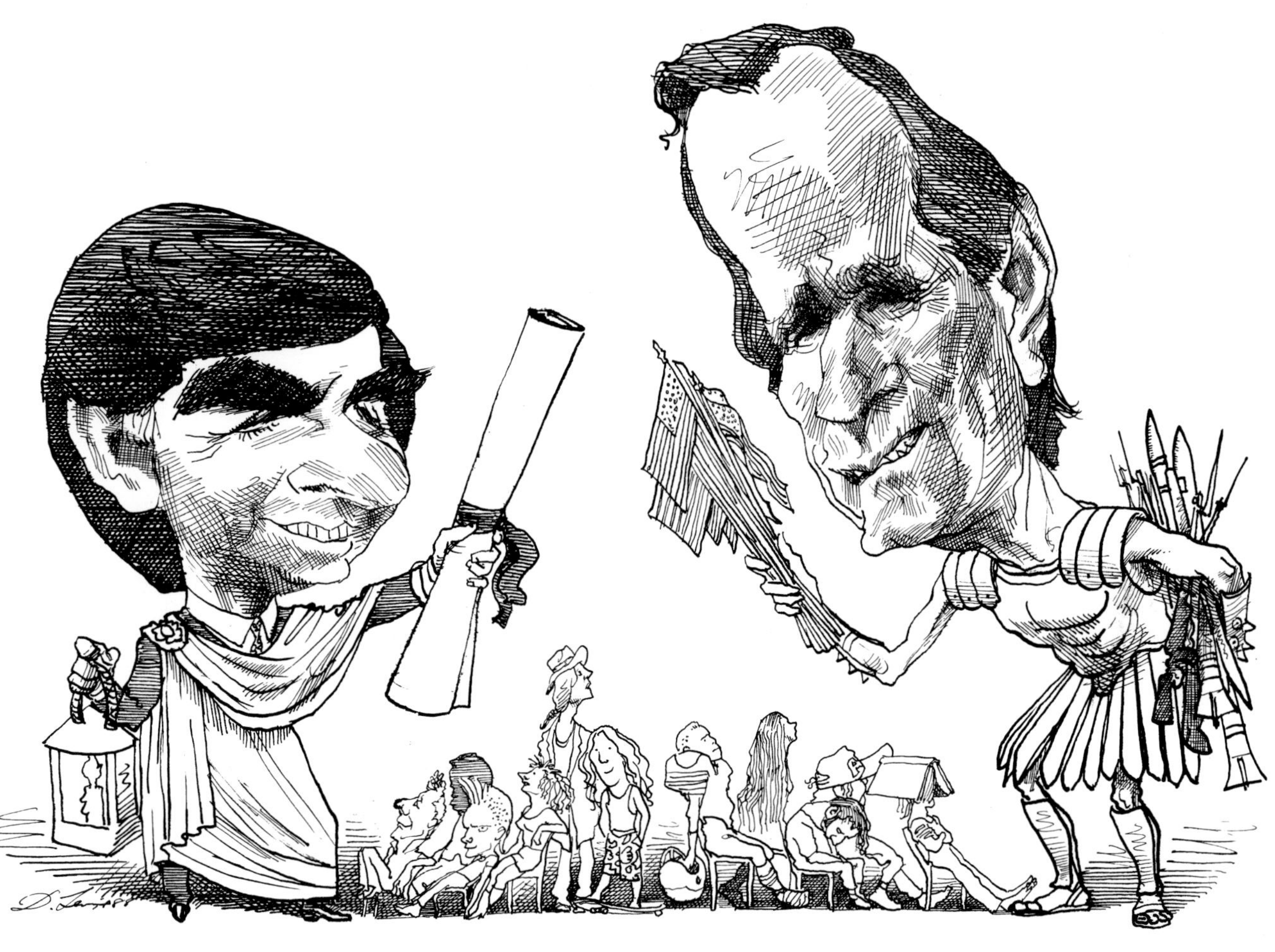

Michael Dukakis and **George Bush**. Dukakis was effectively portrayed as an effete intellectual while Bush played the unlikely role (for him) of noble warrior. Bush won in a landslide.

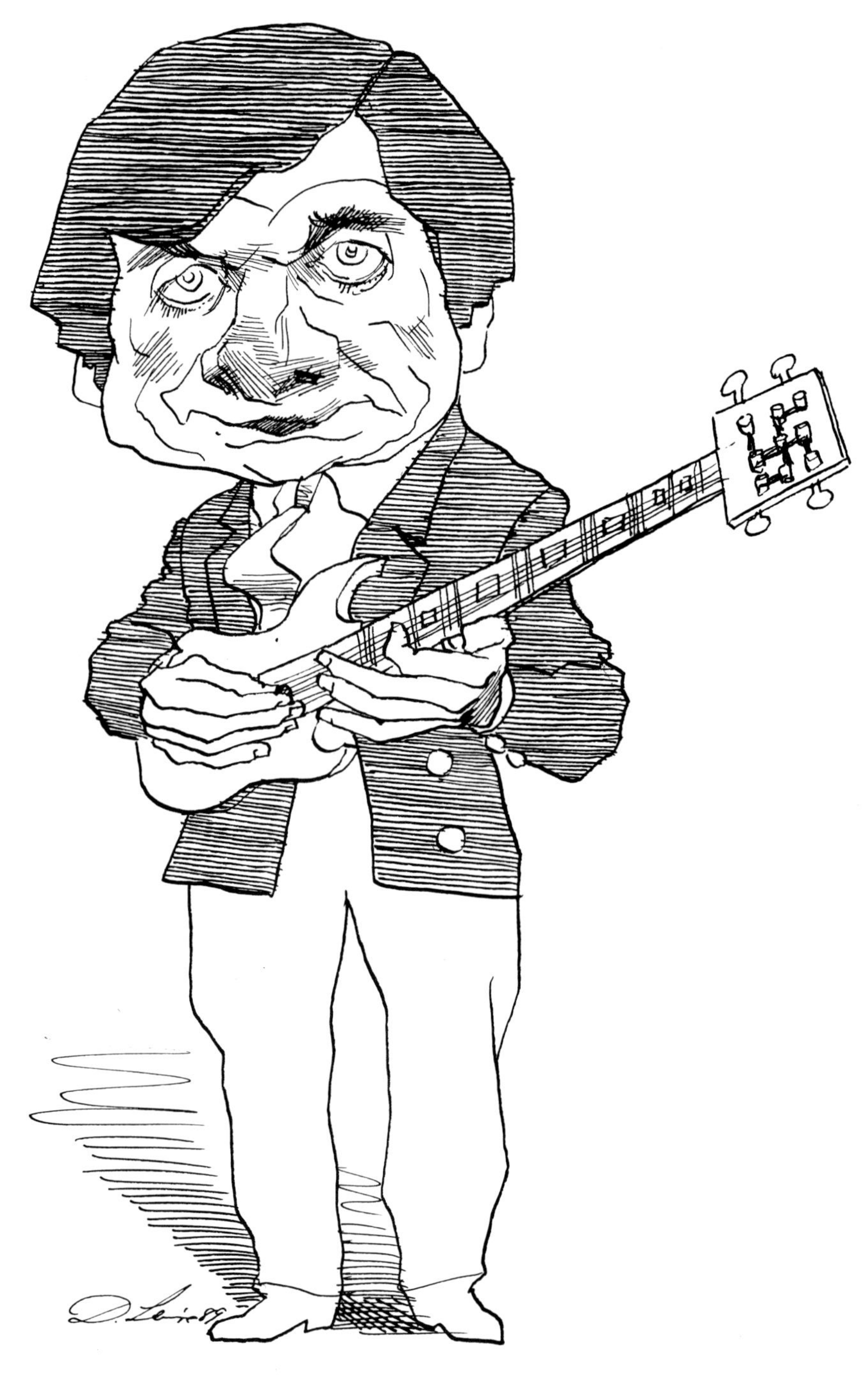

Lee Atwater. Bush's aggressive campaign manager whose ruthless tactics initiated a new level of attack politics. His racists slurs belied his affection for blues music.

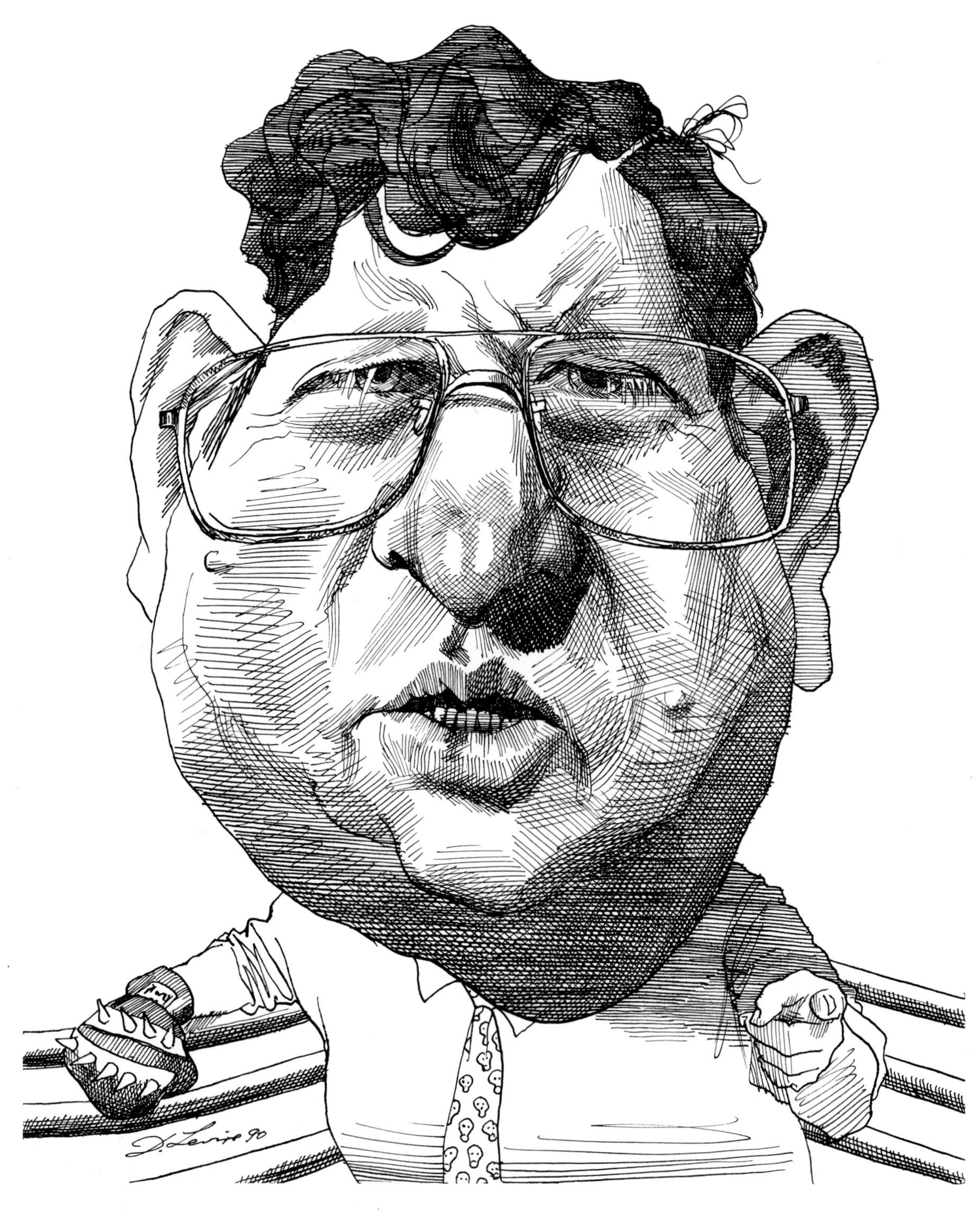

Chief of Staff **JOHN SUNUNU**. Bush's bad cop, he was forced to resign over his personal use of government military aircraft.

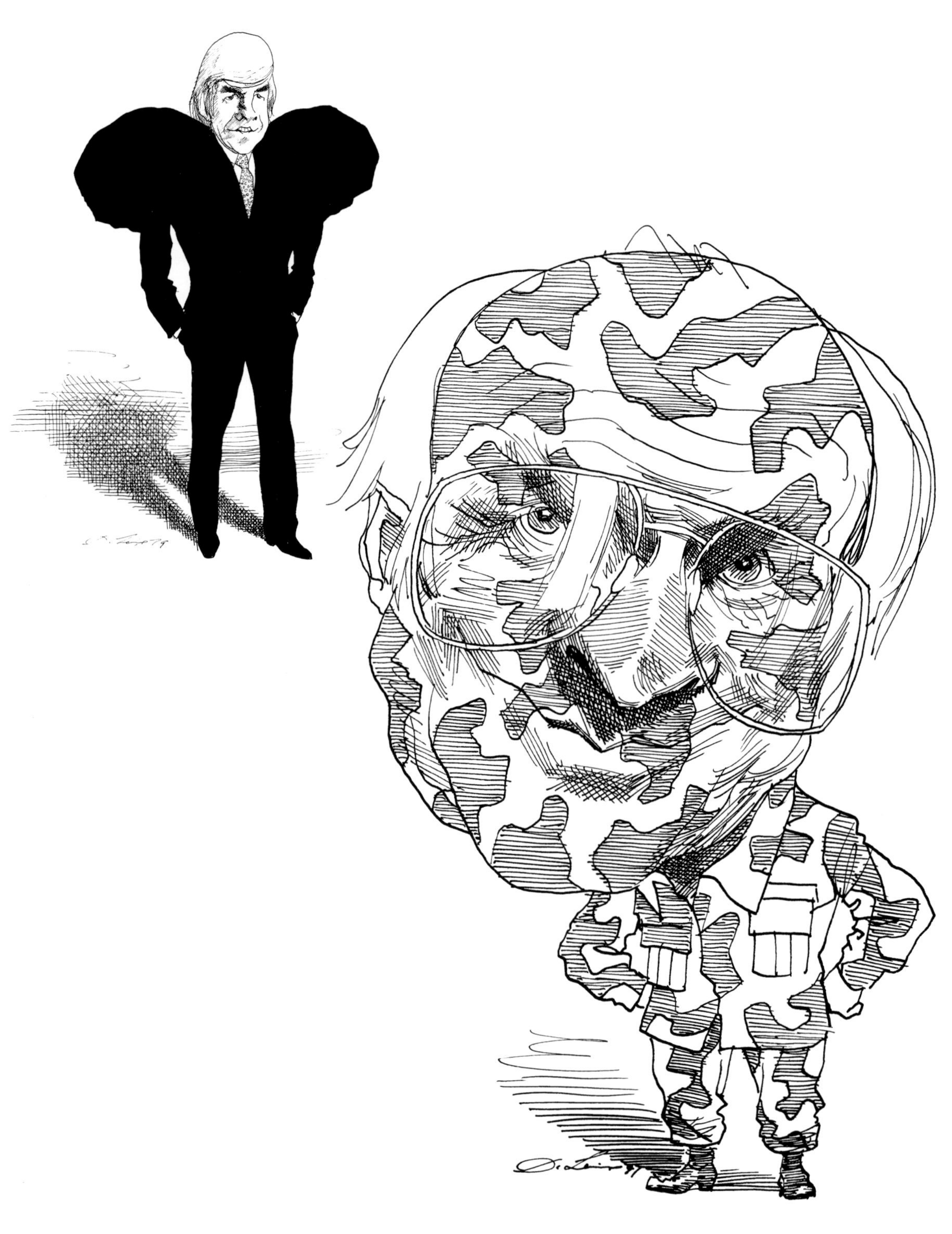

Secretary of Housing and Urban Development **JACK KEMP** (TOP), a former football player, ran for President in 1988 and vice president in 1996. He fared better on the football field. Secretary of Defense **DICK CHENEY** (BOTTOM), "who had other priorities in the '60s than military service" (although he supported the Vietnam War), oversaw the invasion of Panama and Operation Desert Storm

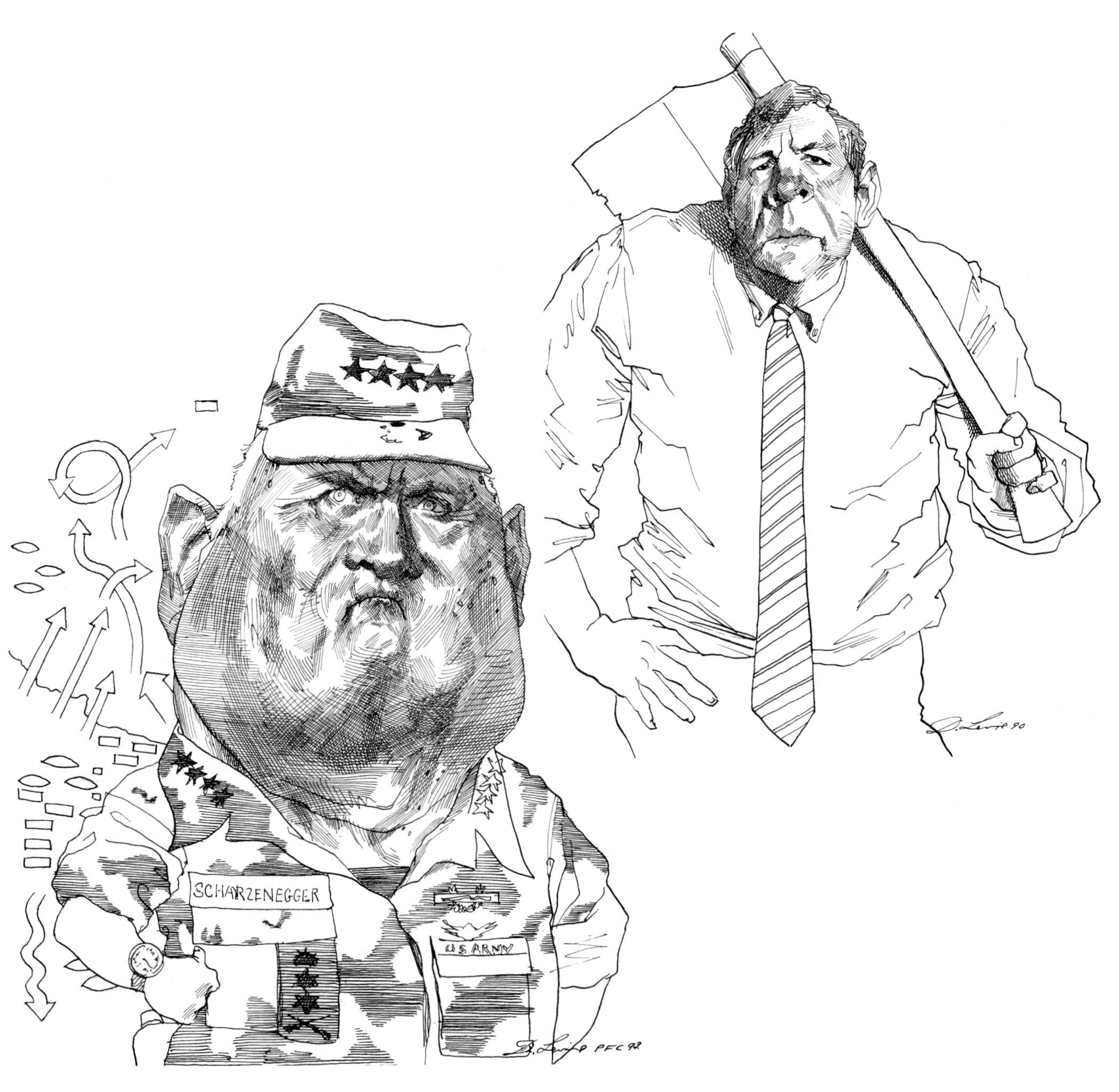

General **NORMAN SCHWARZKOPF** (LEFT) was commander of the Coalition Forces in the Gulf War of 1991; "Drug Czar" **WILLIAM BENNETT** (RIGHT) liked to get tough with addiction, just not his own gambling problem.

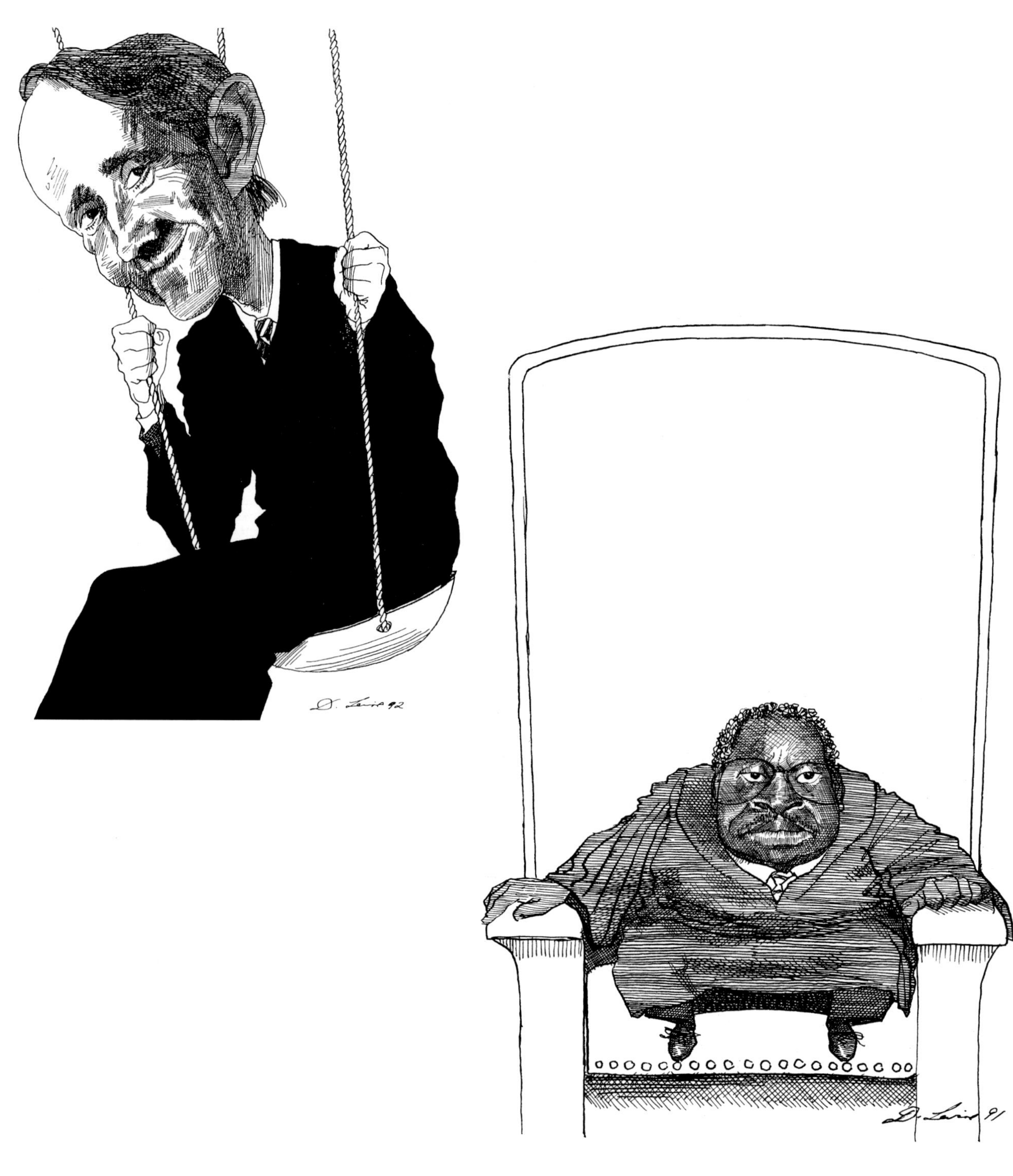

Supreme Court nominees: **DAVID SOUTER** (TOP) and **CLARENCE THOMAS** (BOTTOM)

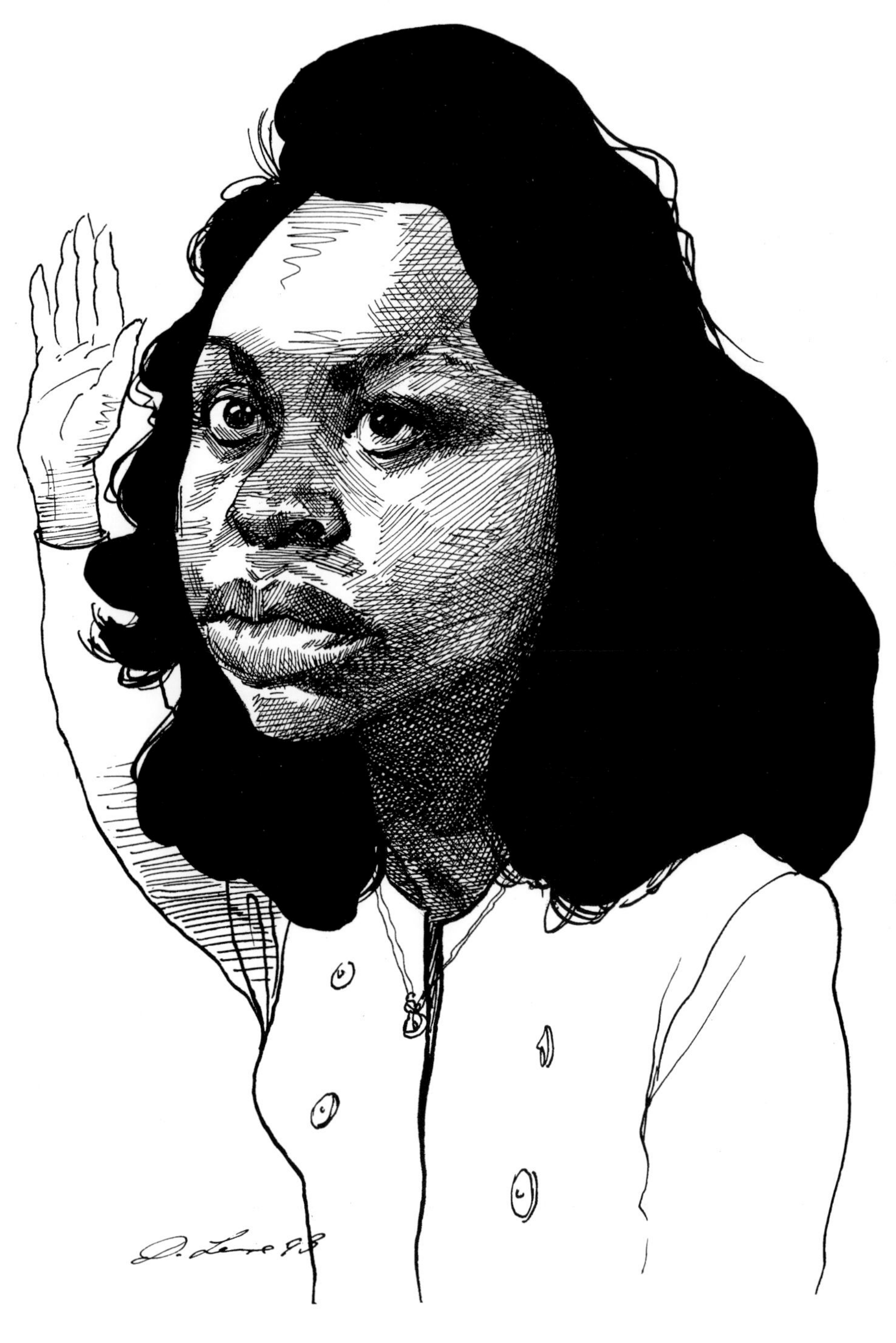

Anita Hill's testimony at Clarence Thomas' nomination hearings almost derailed his appointment when she testified to his repeated sexually provocative statements.

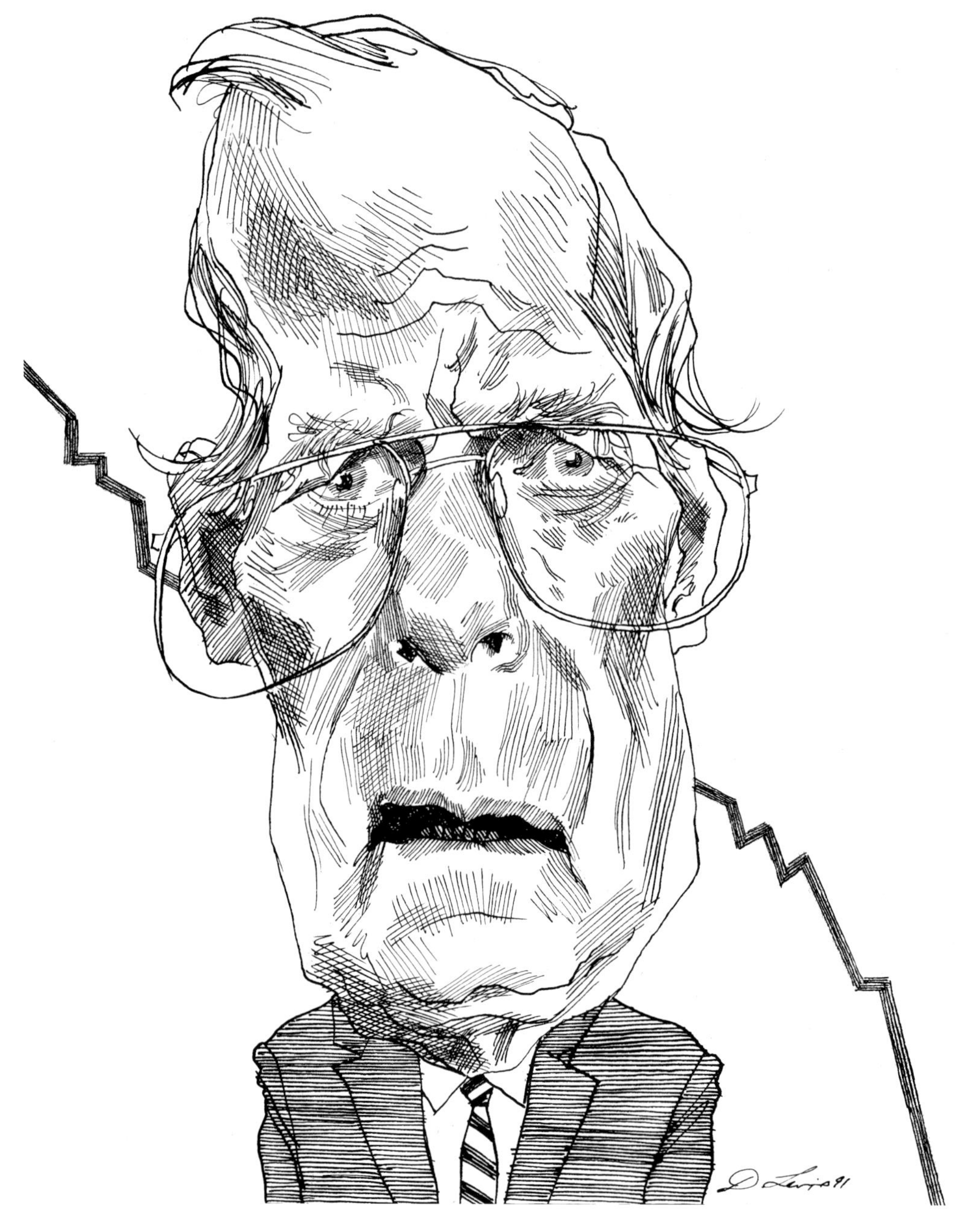

"Depressed Bush"

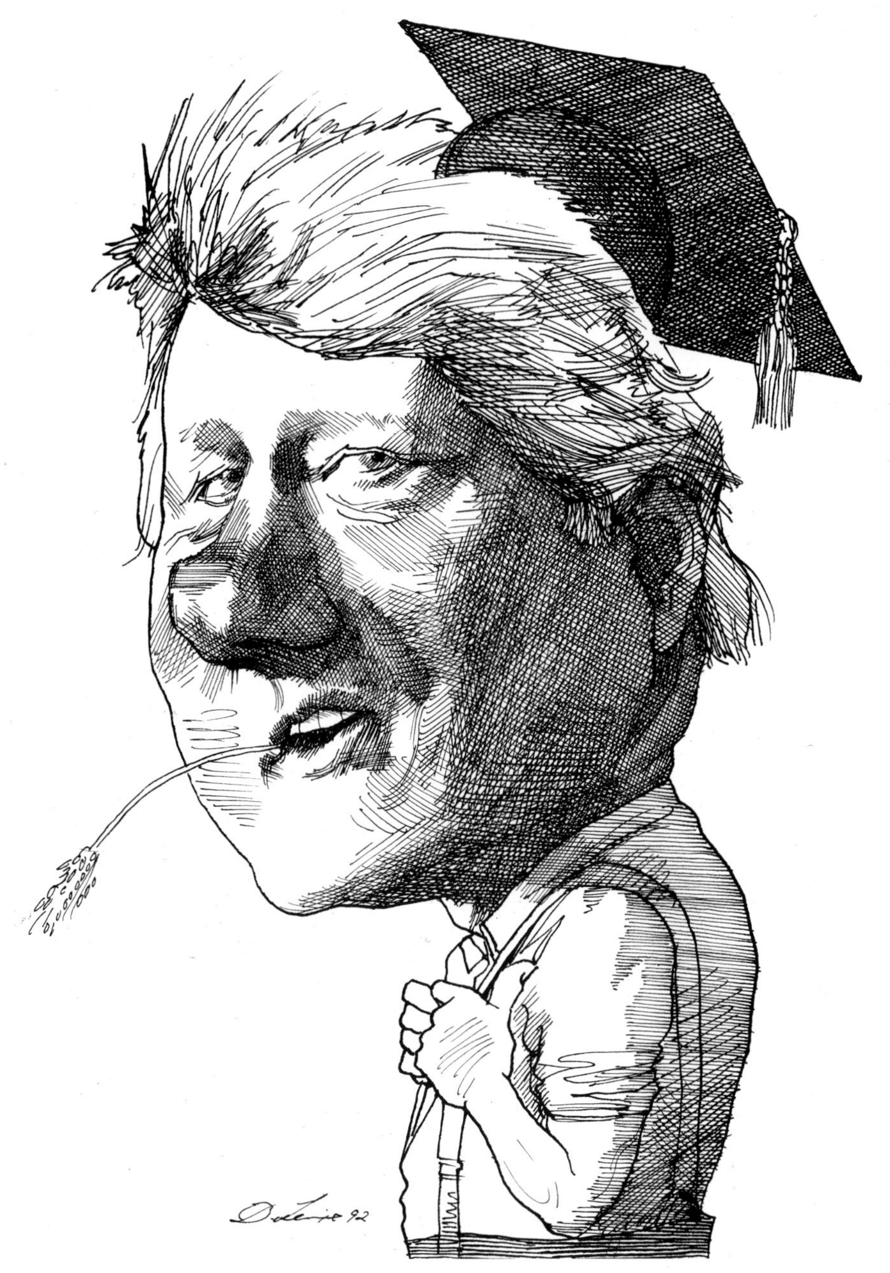

BILL ★CLINTON★

My reading of Clinton and his acts was that sex and writing a bill come from the same place. It is fun and play. It wasn't like he was the first president to fool around. For a so-called socially aware administration, in area after area, very little really was done. The labor movement got nowhere, and Congressional bills actually broke down the union movement. He may be the first president who didn't want to leave office. The others were probably happy to leave because they messed up so many things. But he wasn't. He still sees himself as the President.

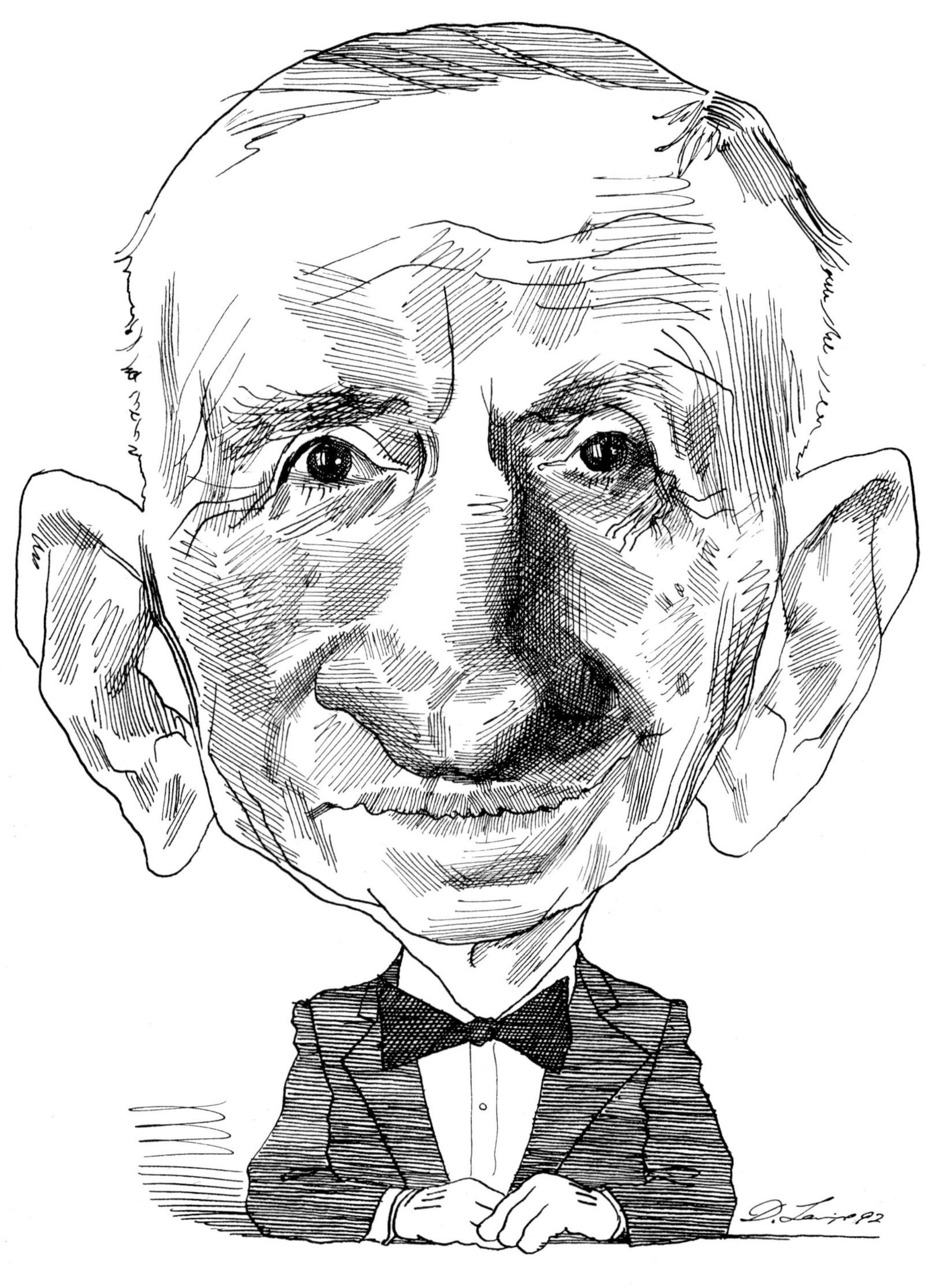

Ross Perot. The Texas businessman pulled nearly 19% of the vote in 1992 despite his on again-off again campaign.

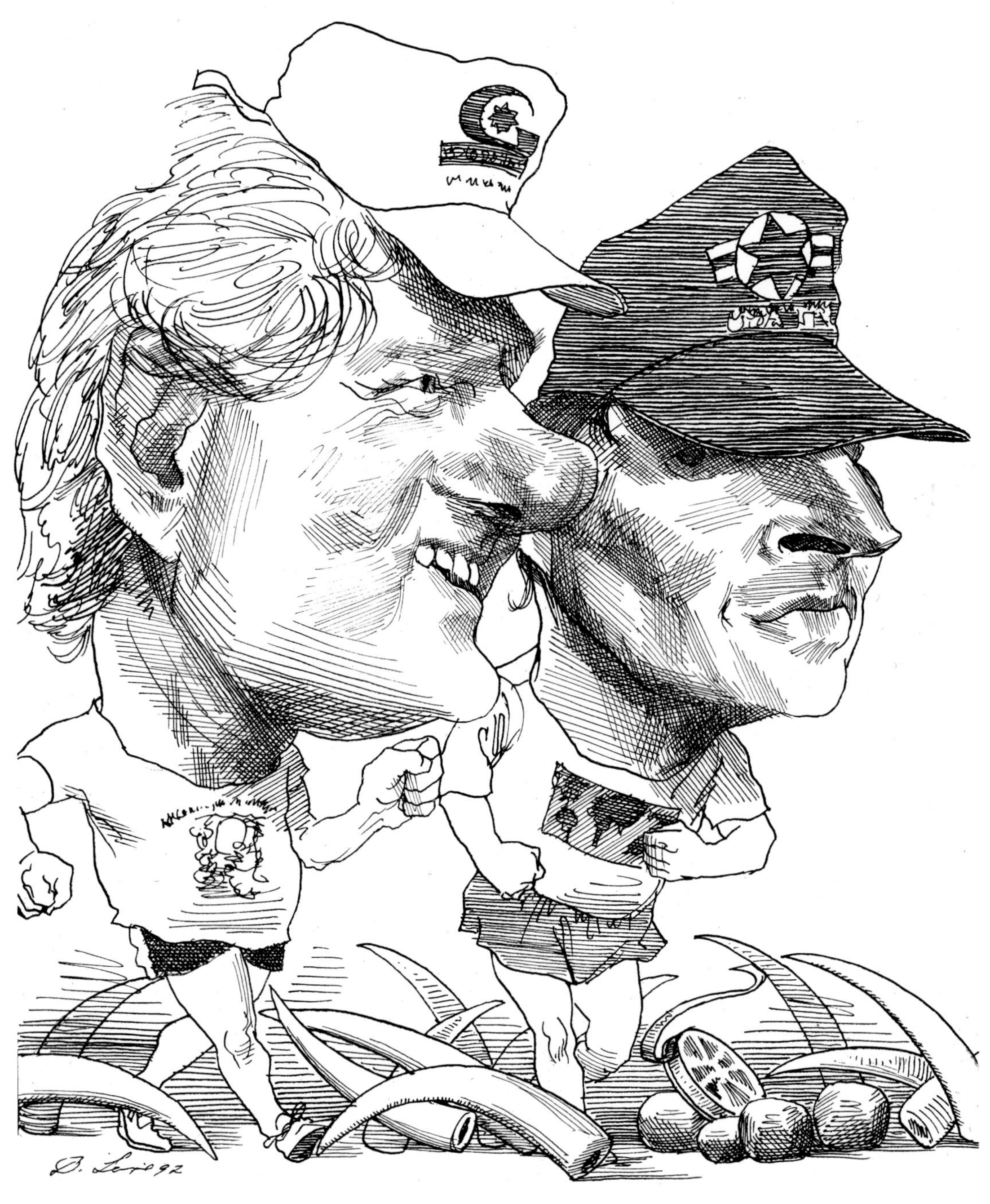

BILL CLINTON and **AL GORE**

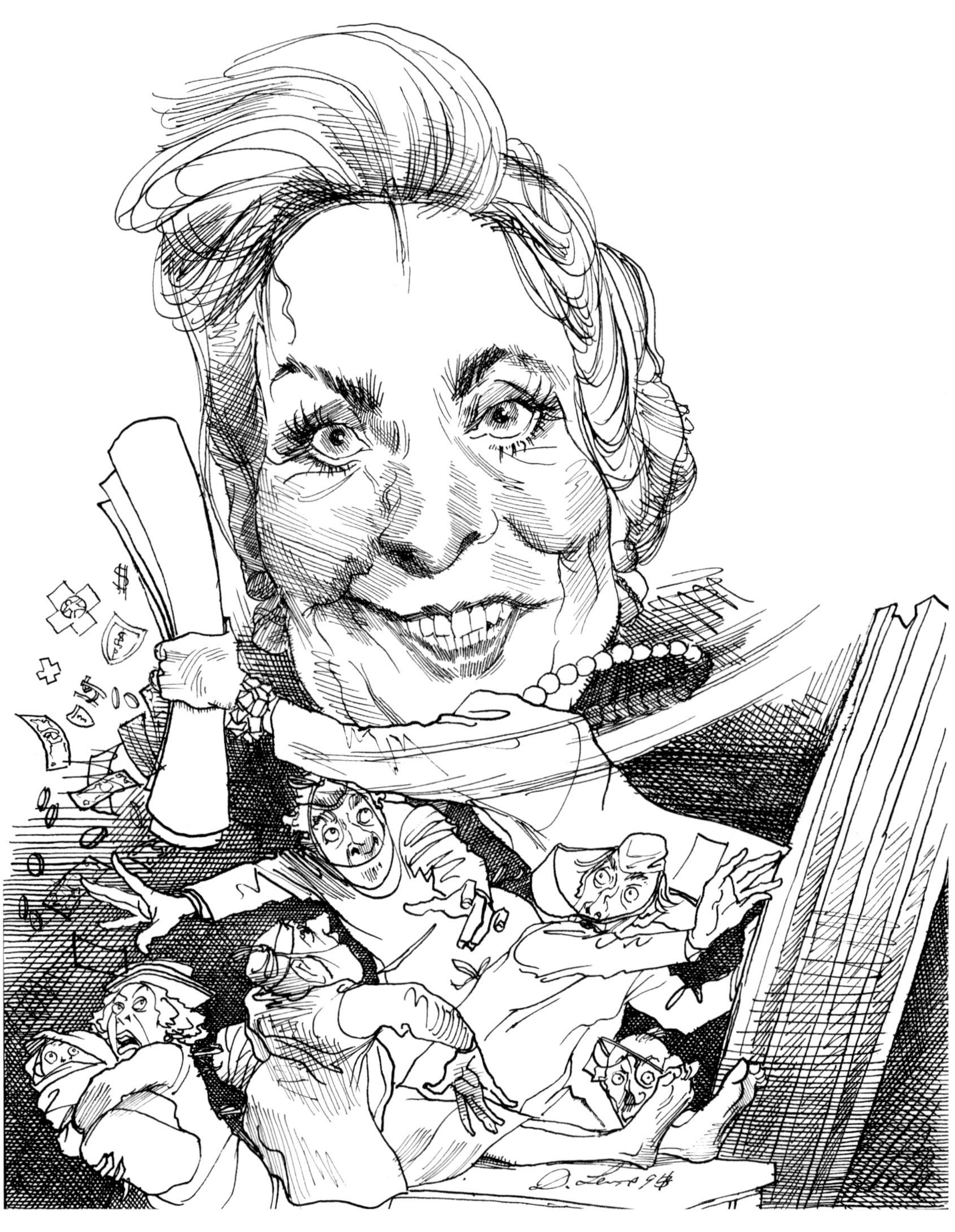

Hillary Clinton

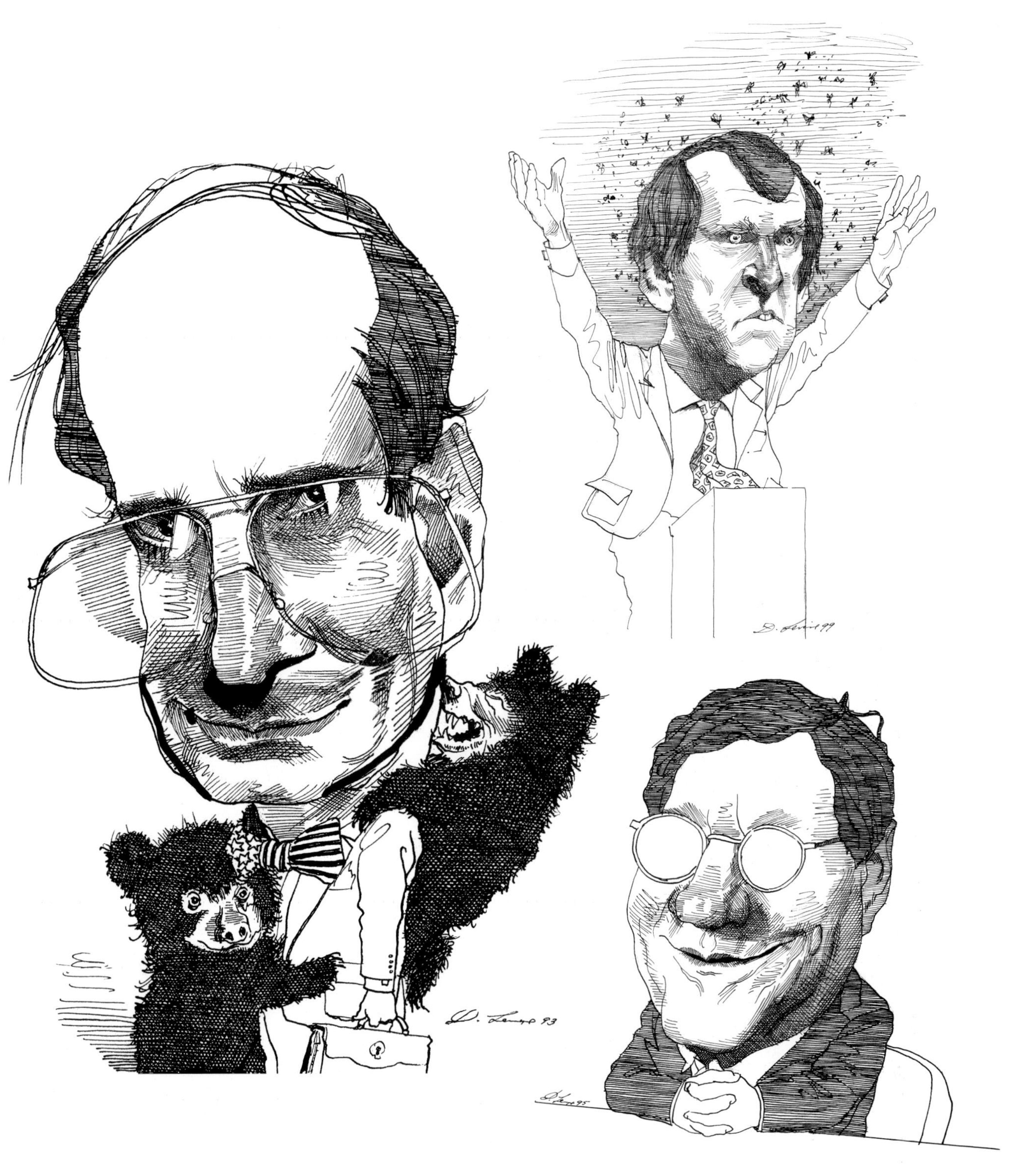

Clinton cabinet (CLOCKWISE FROM LEFT): Journalist turned deputy Secretary of State **STROBE TALBOTT**; Secretary of Defense **WILLIAM COHEN**, a Republican appointee in a Democratic cabinet; Assistant Secretary of State **RICHARD HOLBROOKE**, who helped broker the Bosnian Peace Accords at Dayton.

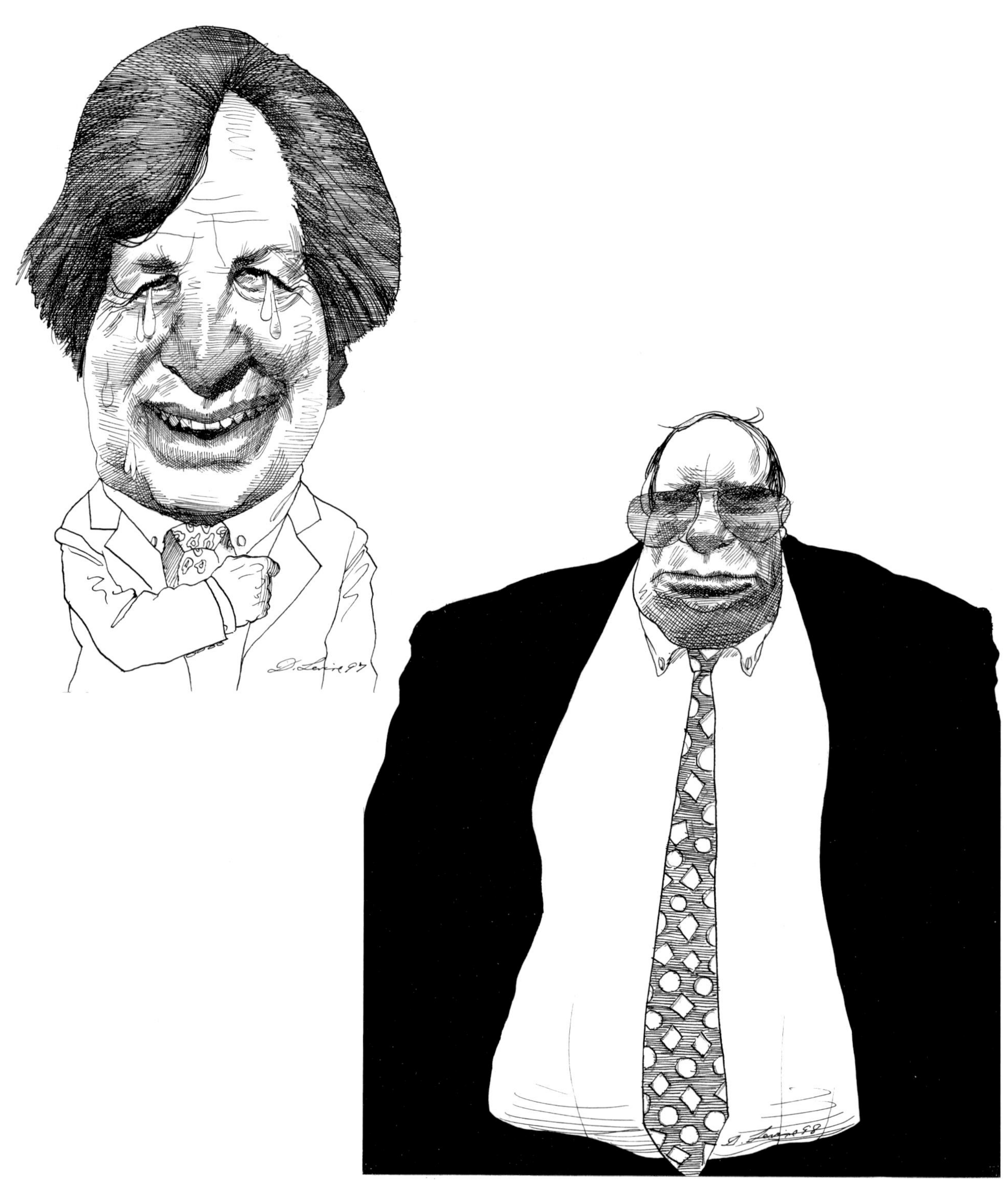

Pollster **DICK MORRIS** (TOP) helped Clinton develop his policy of triangulation and ran the 1996 re-election campaign until he was forced to resign after being discovered with a hooker; Associate Attorney General **WEBSTER HUBBELL** (BOTTOM) was forced to resign after pleading guilty to federal mail fraud and tax evasion.

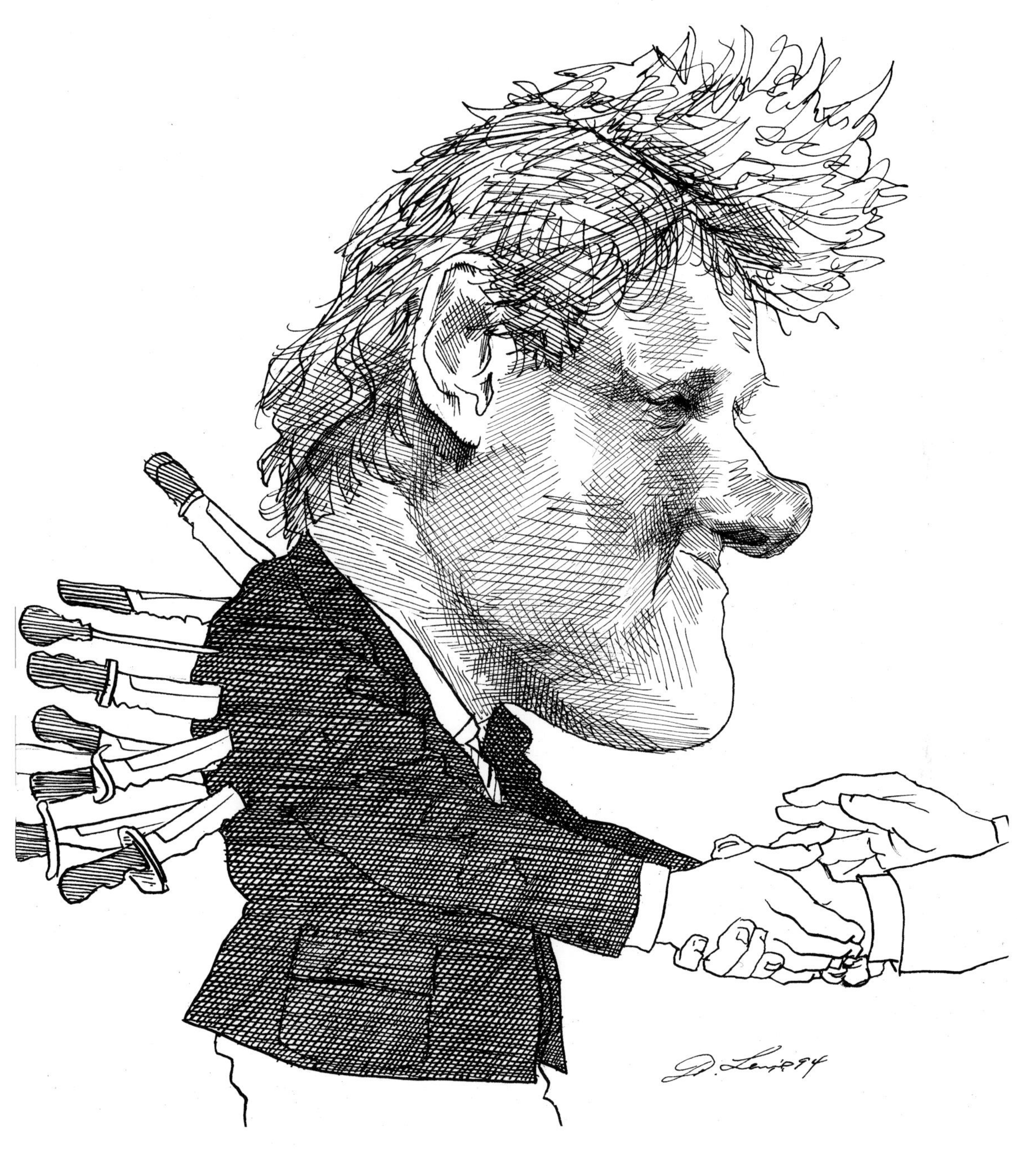

Bill Clinton

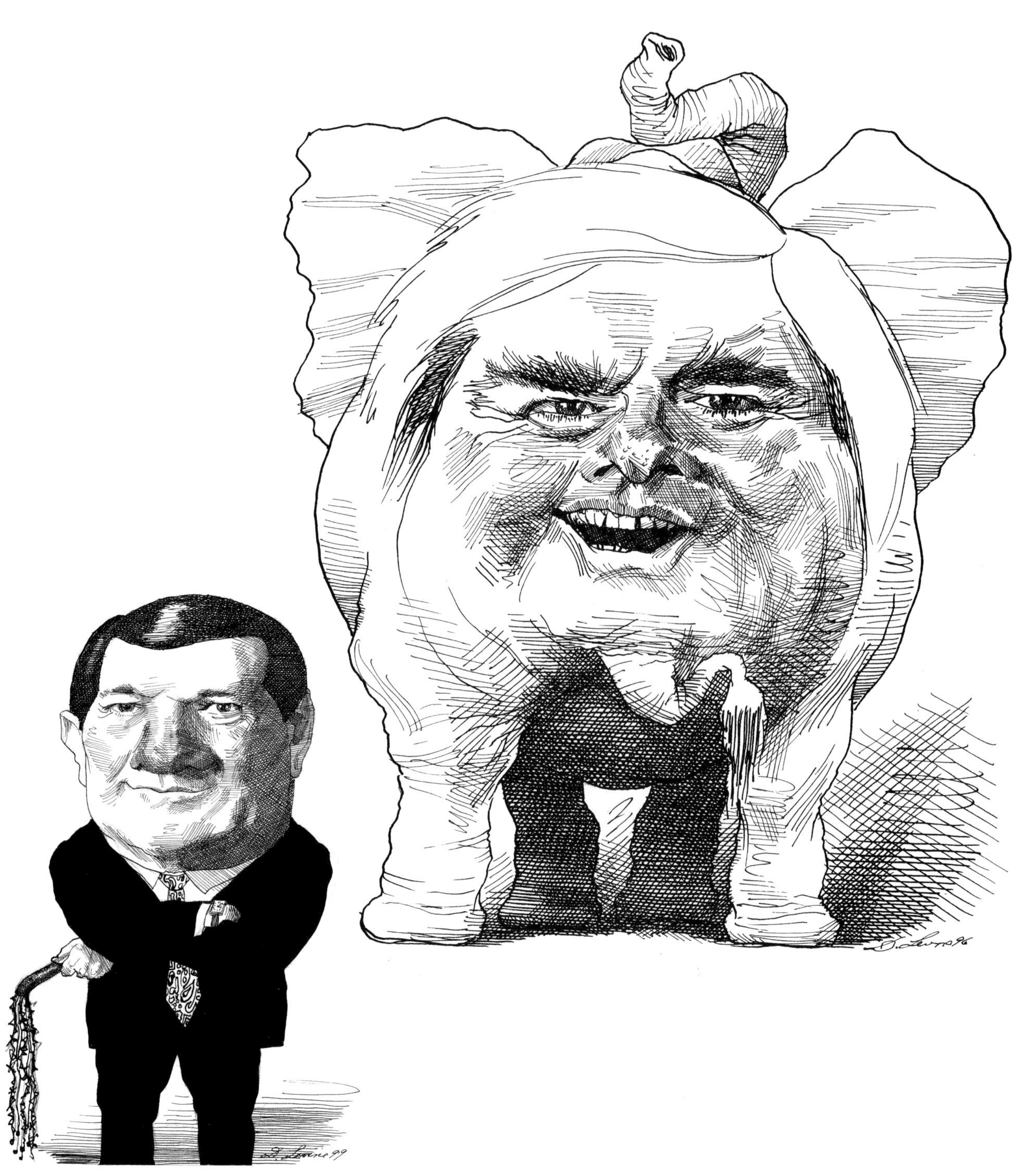

Adversaries: House Majority Whip **Tom DeLay** (left), known as "The Hammer" for his enforcement of party discipline and reputation for taking political retribution on opponents, was a driving force behind the Clinton impeachment; Speaker of the House **Newt Gingrich** (right) pioneered the Republican takeover of the Congress in 1994, but soon was so unpopular that he was forced to resign his House seat.

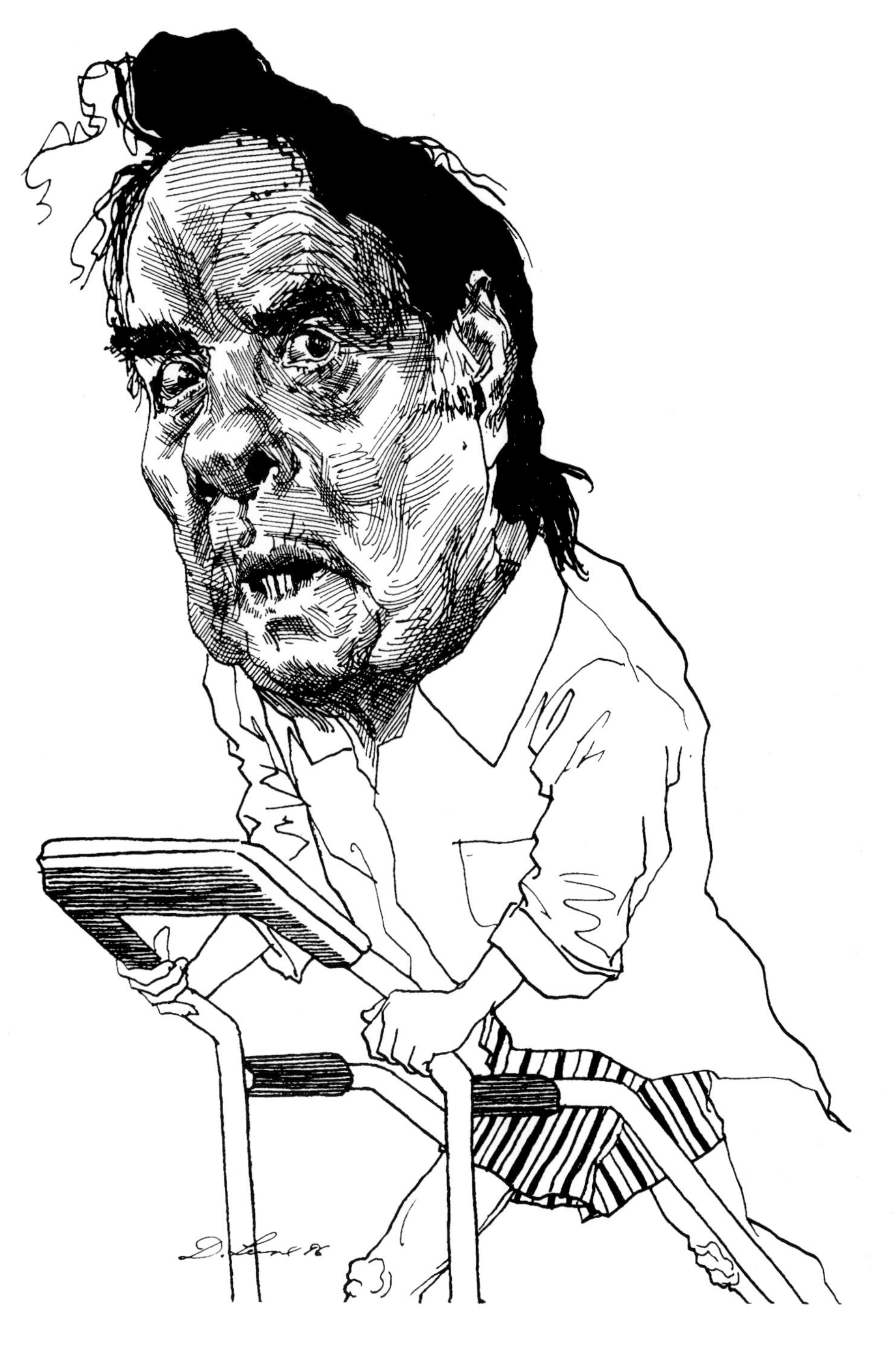

Senator **BOB DOLE** was a vice presidential candidate in 1976, ran for president in 1988, and became the Republican nominee in 1996, only to lose to Bill Clinton, who won in a landslide.

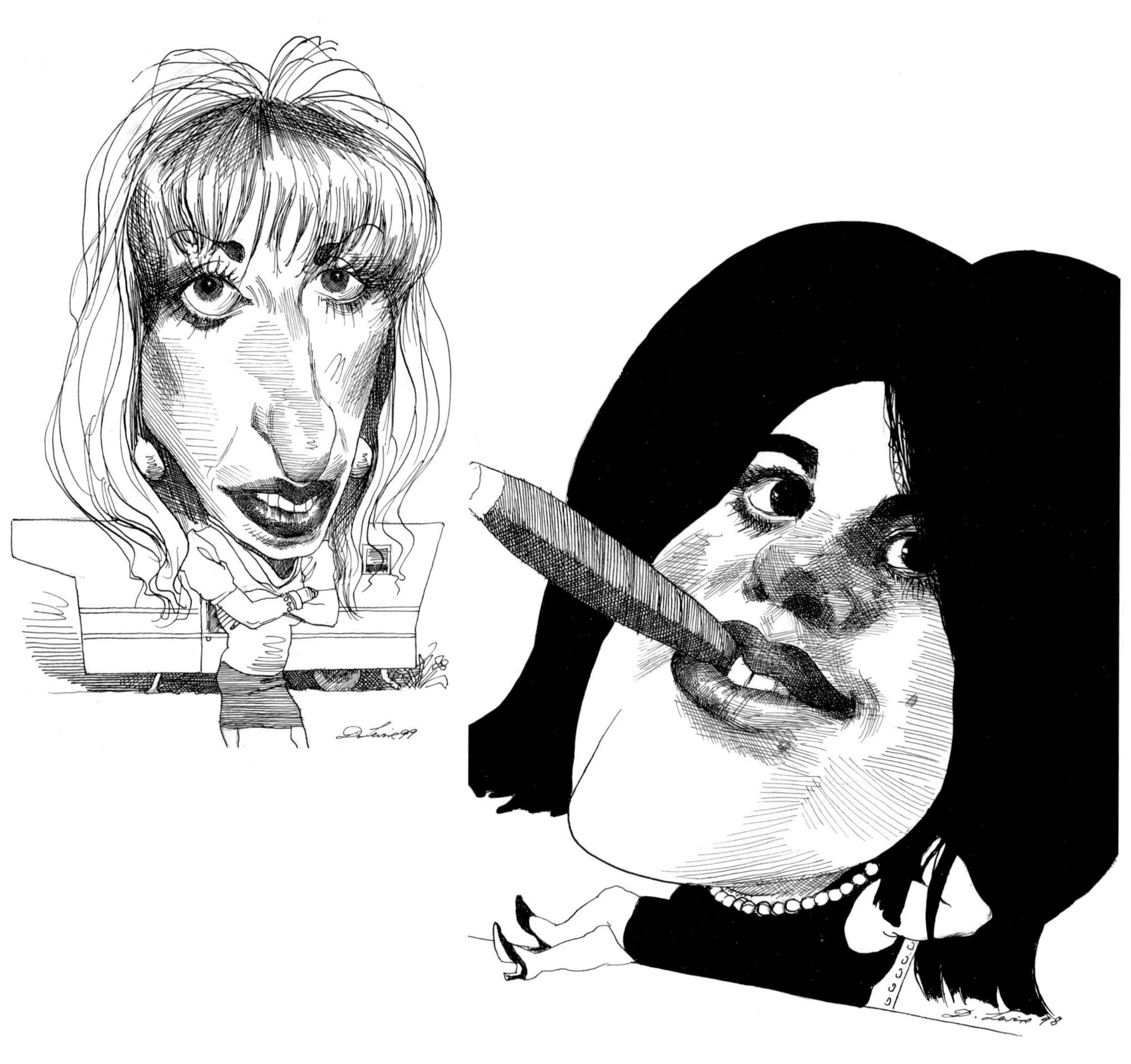

Paula Jones (left) was a former Arkansas state employee who sued Bill Clinton for sexual harassment after she claimed then Governor Clinton exposed himself to her six years earlier. Although her case was eventually dismissed, Clinton had testified that he did not have "sexual relations" with **Monica Lewinsky** (right), a young White House intern. It was this perjury that led to his impeachment trial.

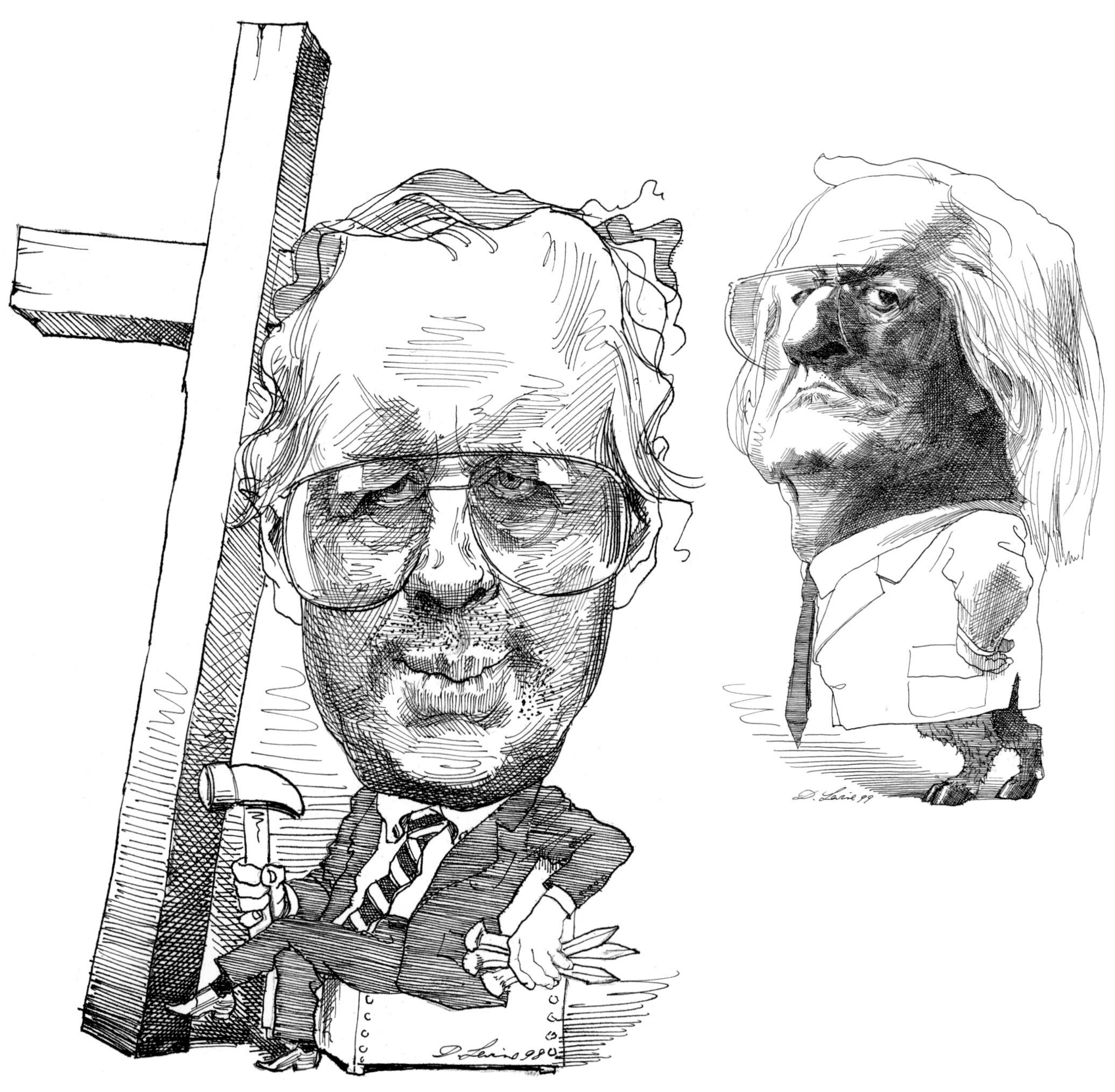

KENNETH STARR (LEFT) spent five years and 50 million dollars as Independent Counsel to discover that Bill Clinton had nothing to do with aide Vincent Foster's death or anything illegal in his Whitewater deals, but did discover that the president had lied about his relationship with Lewinsky. Rep. **HENRY HYDE** (RIGHT) spearheaded the impeachment hearings of Clinton while at the same time his own extramarital affairs were revealed.

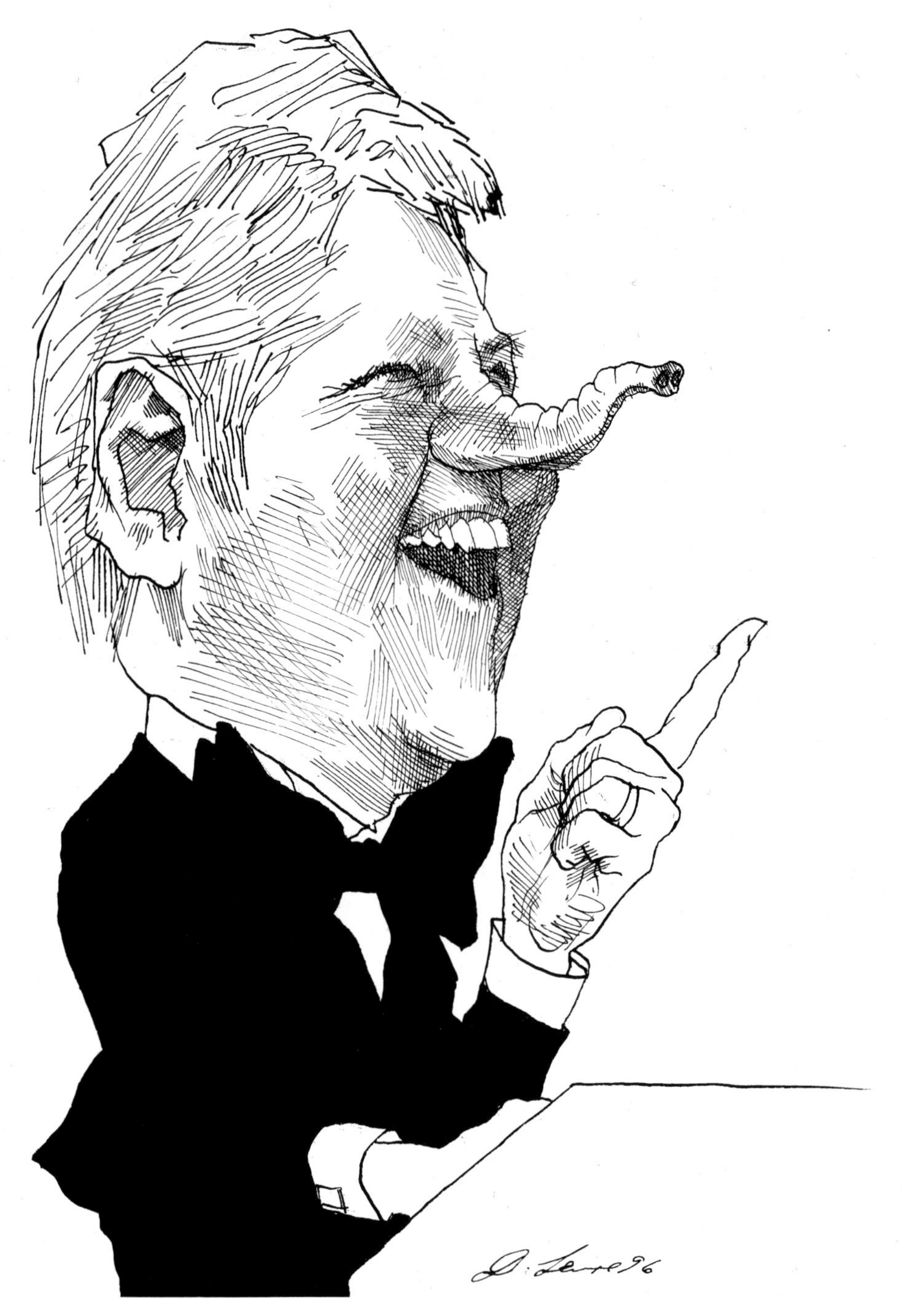

Bill Clinton

GEORGE W. BUSH

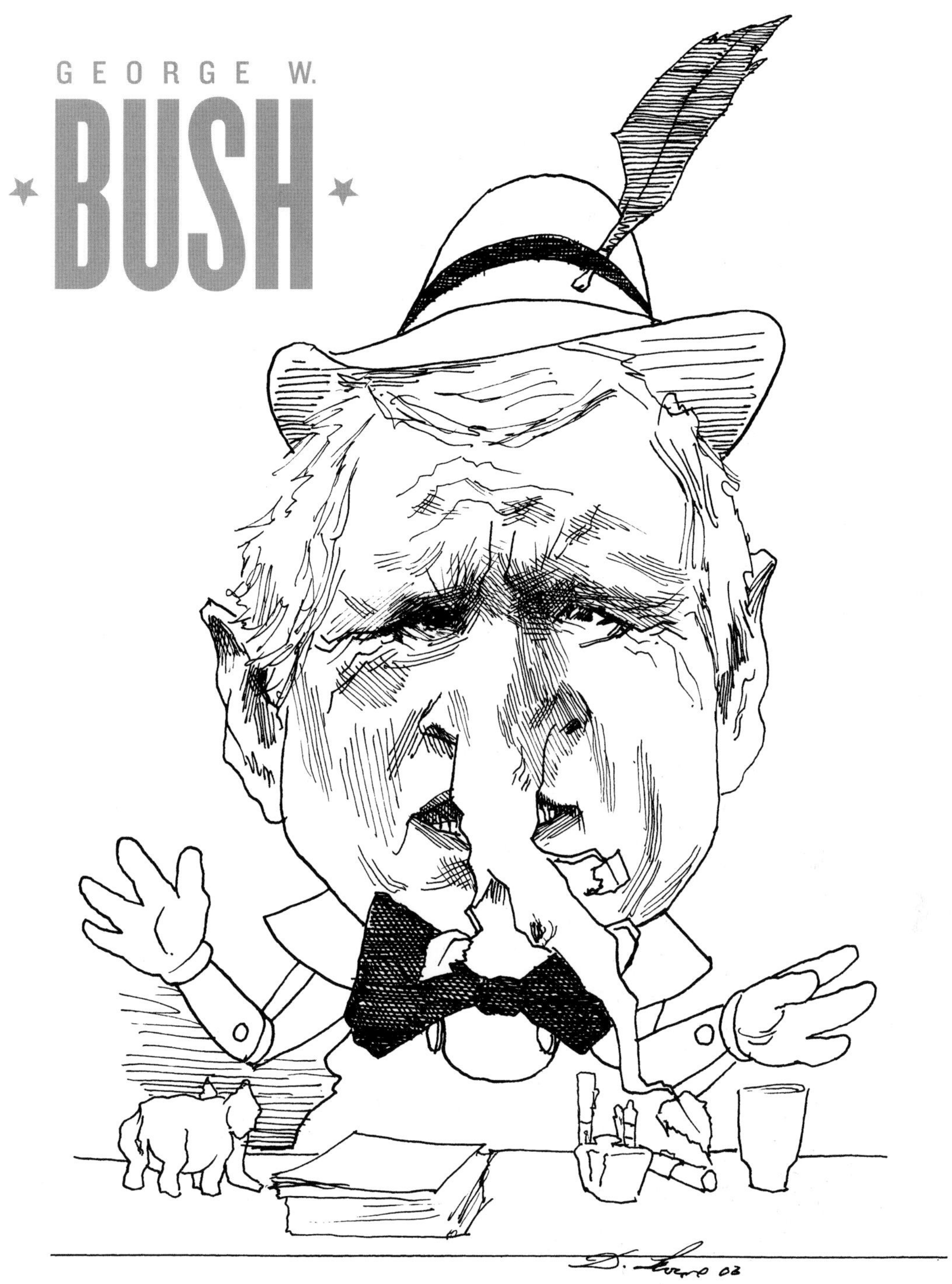

I couldn't believe that his election could be enacted in the open. It characterizes American government more than anything else. I guarantee you that at every other cabinet meeting in the world they were looking at that with amazement. Bush's accomplishment was getting us into a war. Others, even the bad ones, turned to Congress, but he thrust us right into it. History will judge him as incapable of understanding the potential of what a government could do for its people.

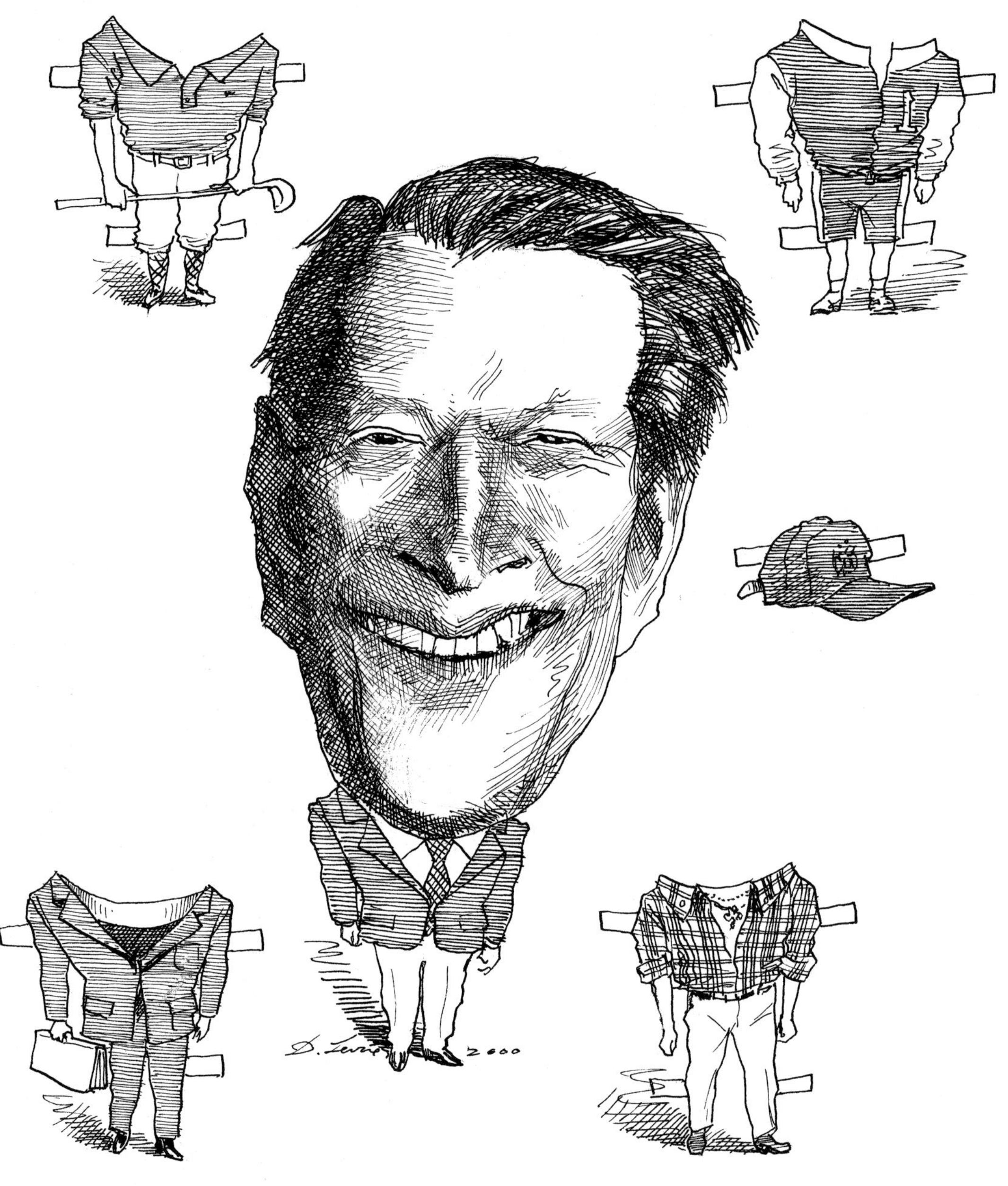

Al Gore

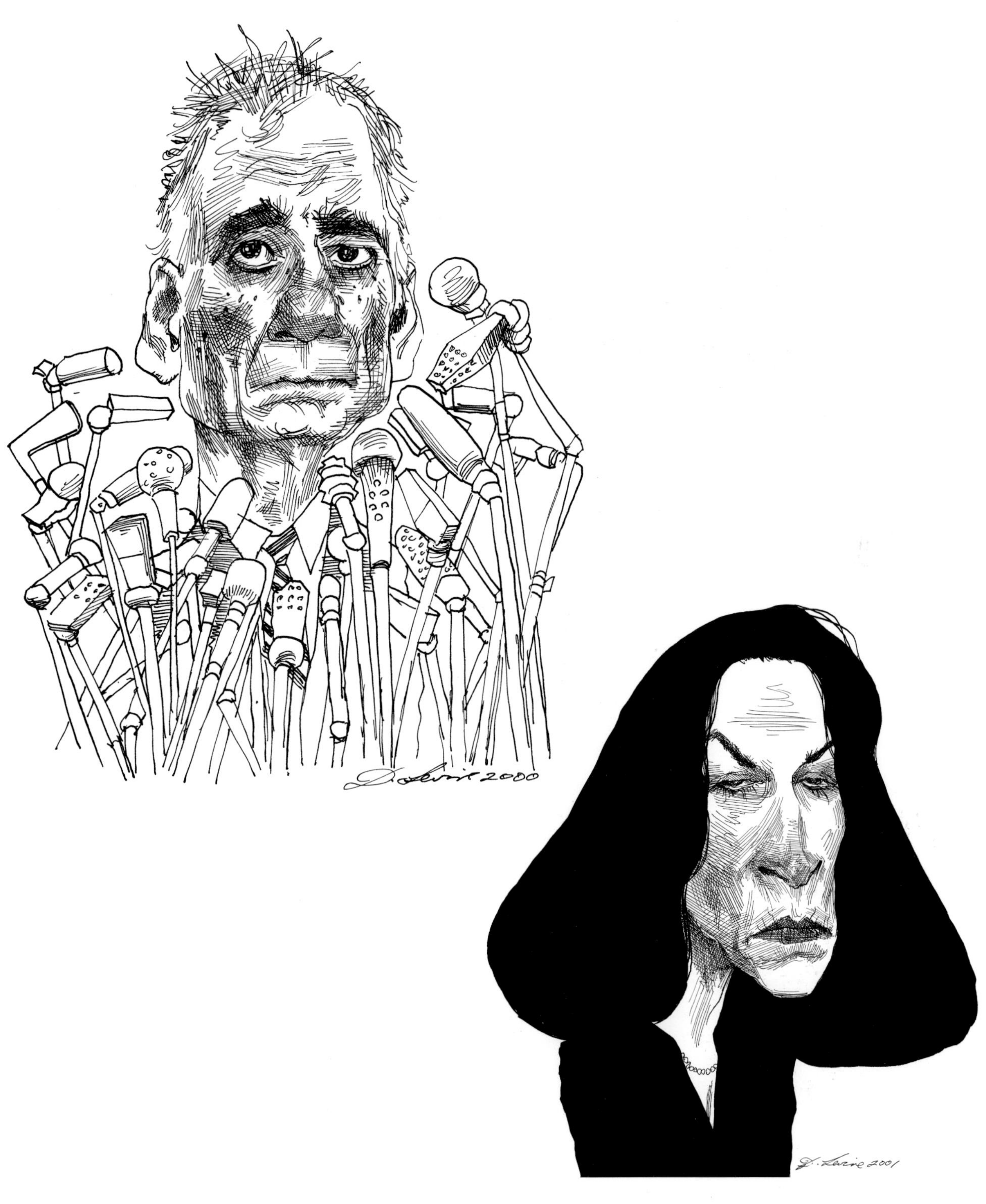

Perennial candidate **RALPH NADER**; Bush Florida campaign co-chair, Florida Secretary of State **KATHERINE HARRIS** certified that in her state, Bush had defeated Gore.

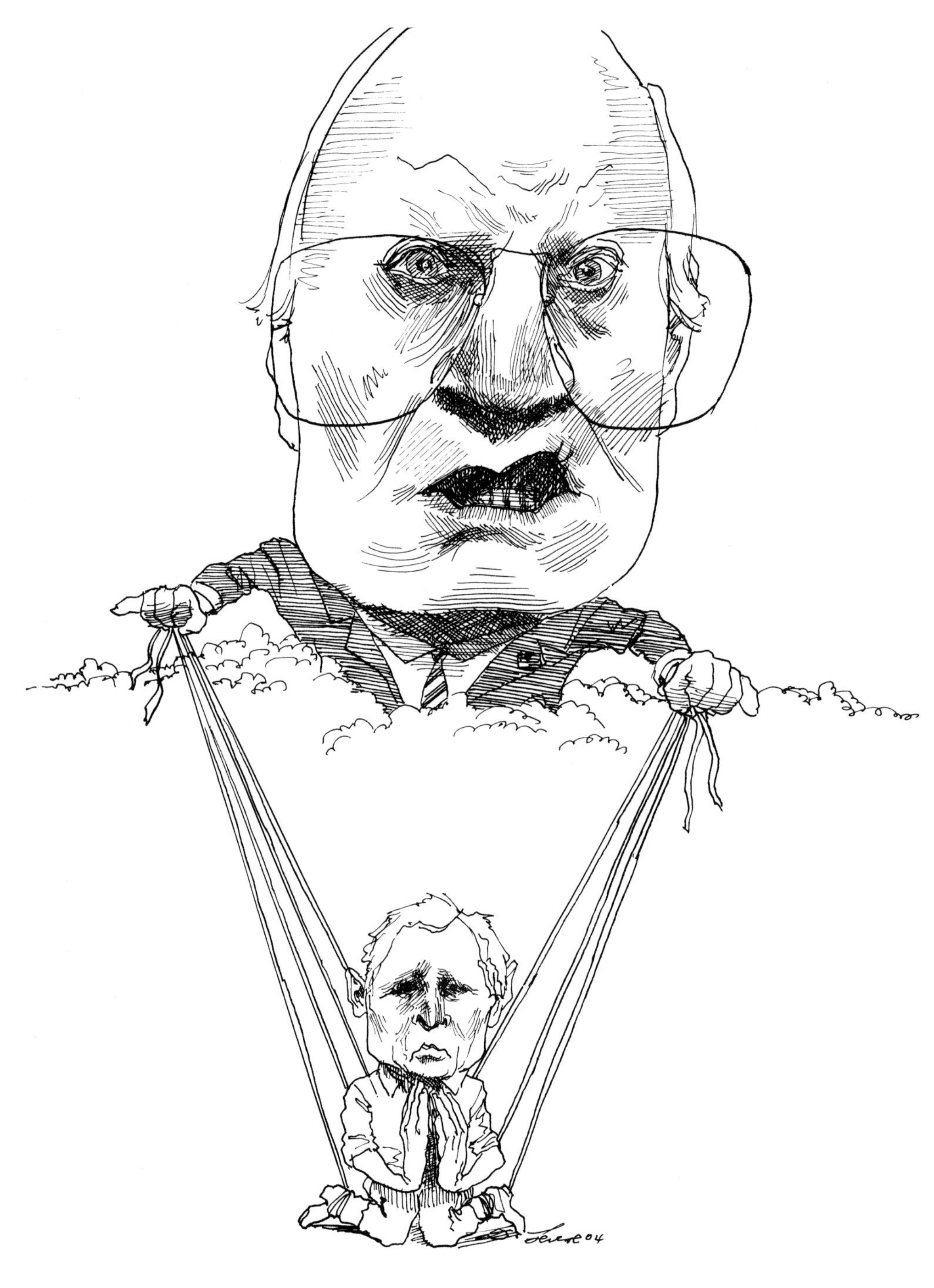

"Praying to a Higher Authority": **Dick Cheney** and **George W. Bush**

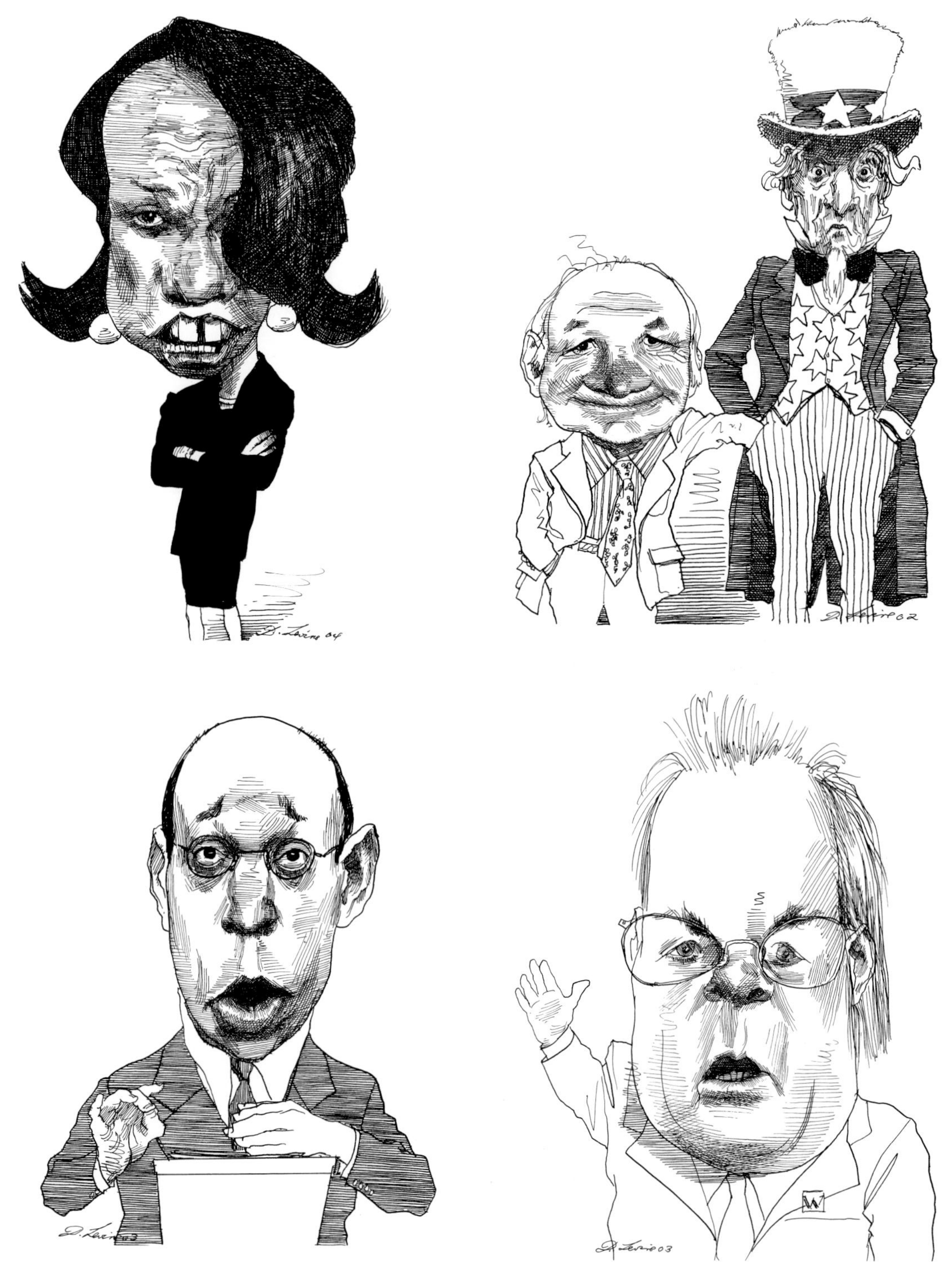

Bushites (clockwise from top left): National Security Advisor and Secretary of State **"Congaleeza" Rice**; Enron Corporation CEO **"Kenny Boy" Lay**; Deputy Chief of Staff **Karl "Turd Blossom" Rove**; Press Secretary **Ari Fleischer**, "Mouthpiece for Bush."

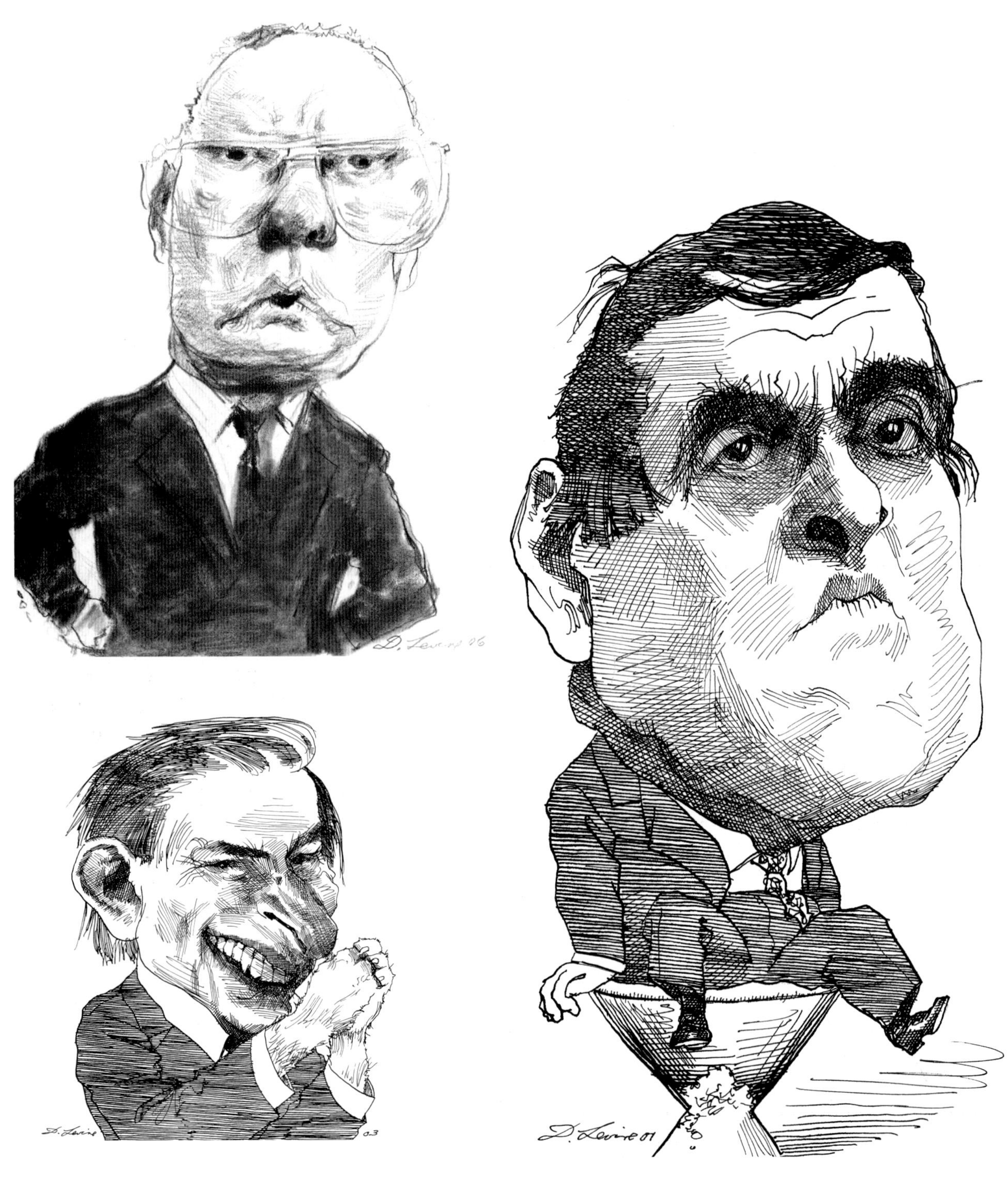

More Bushites (clockwise from top left): Secretary of State **Colin Powell**; CIA Director **"Brother George" Tenet**; Deputy Defense Secretary **Paul Wolfowitz**.

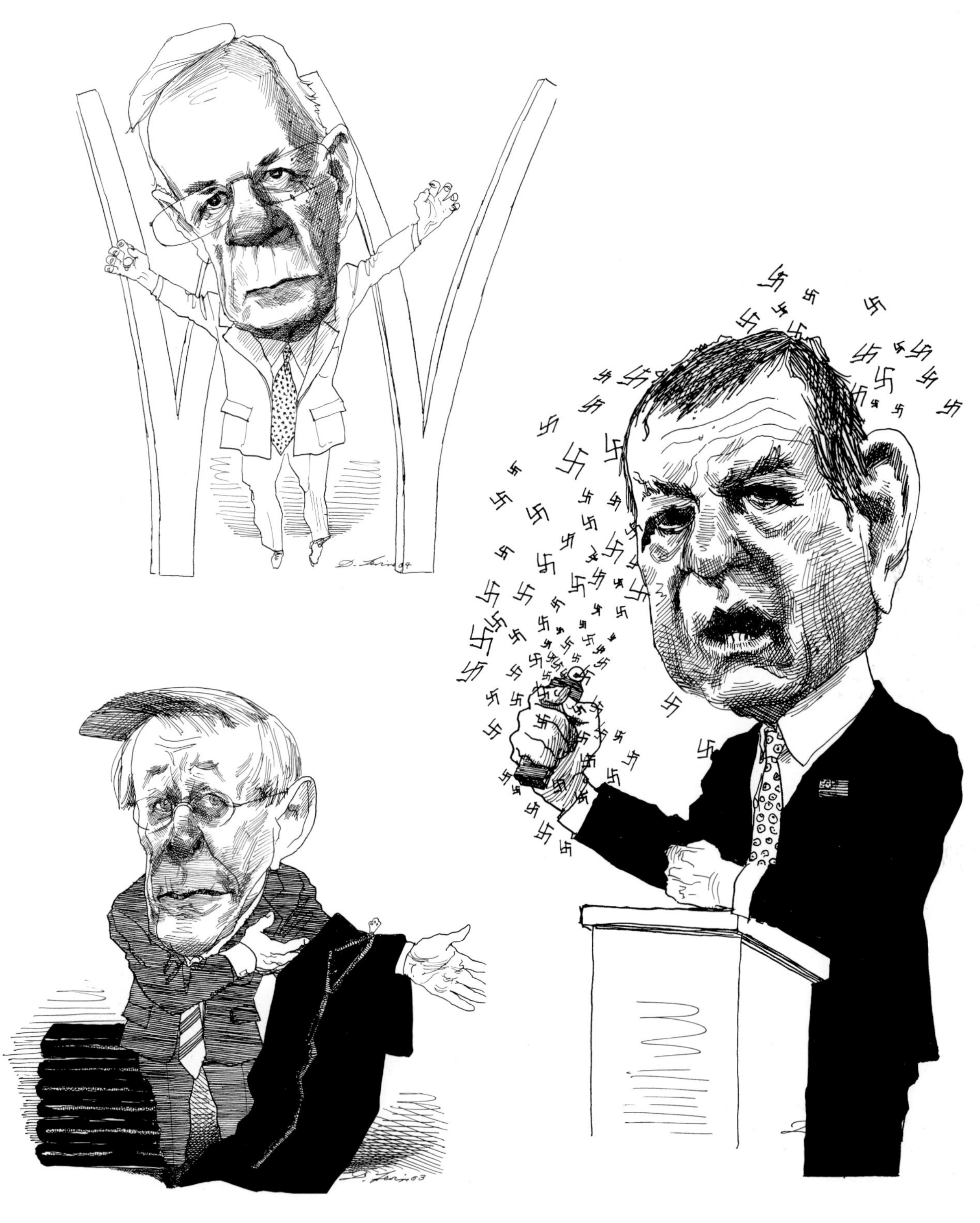

Even More Bushies (CLOCKWISE FROM TOP LEFT): Treasury Secretary **PAUL O'NEILL**; Attorney General **JOHN ASHCROFT**; Defense Secretary **DONALD "OLD BODY BAGS" RUMSFELD**.

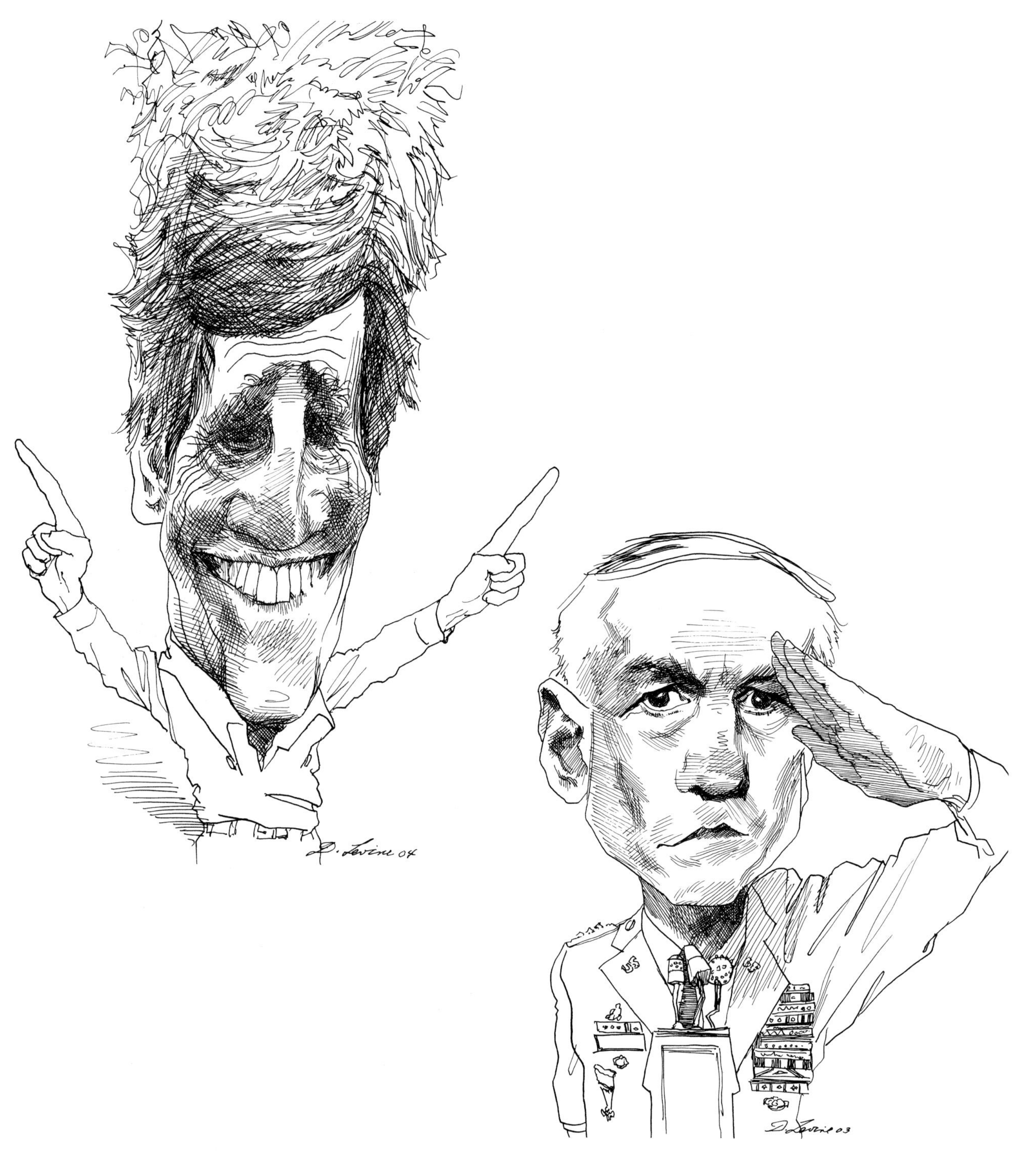

2004 Democratic contenders: Senator **JOHN KERRY** (TOP), General **WESLEY CLARK** (BOTTOM)

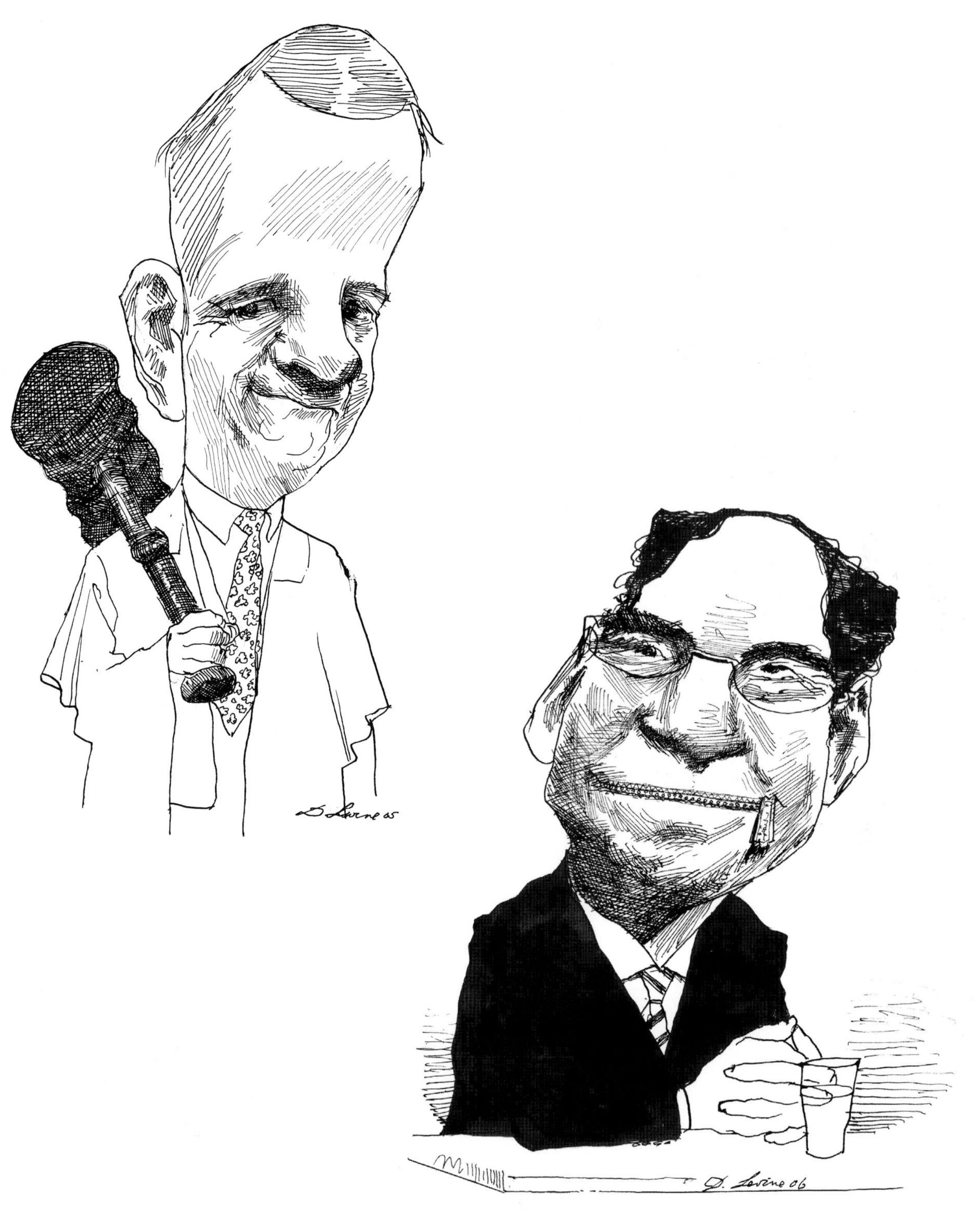

Supreme Court Nominees: **JOHN ROBERTS** (TOP) and **SAMUEL ALITO** (BOTTOM)

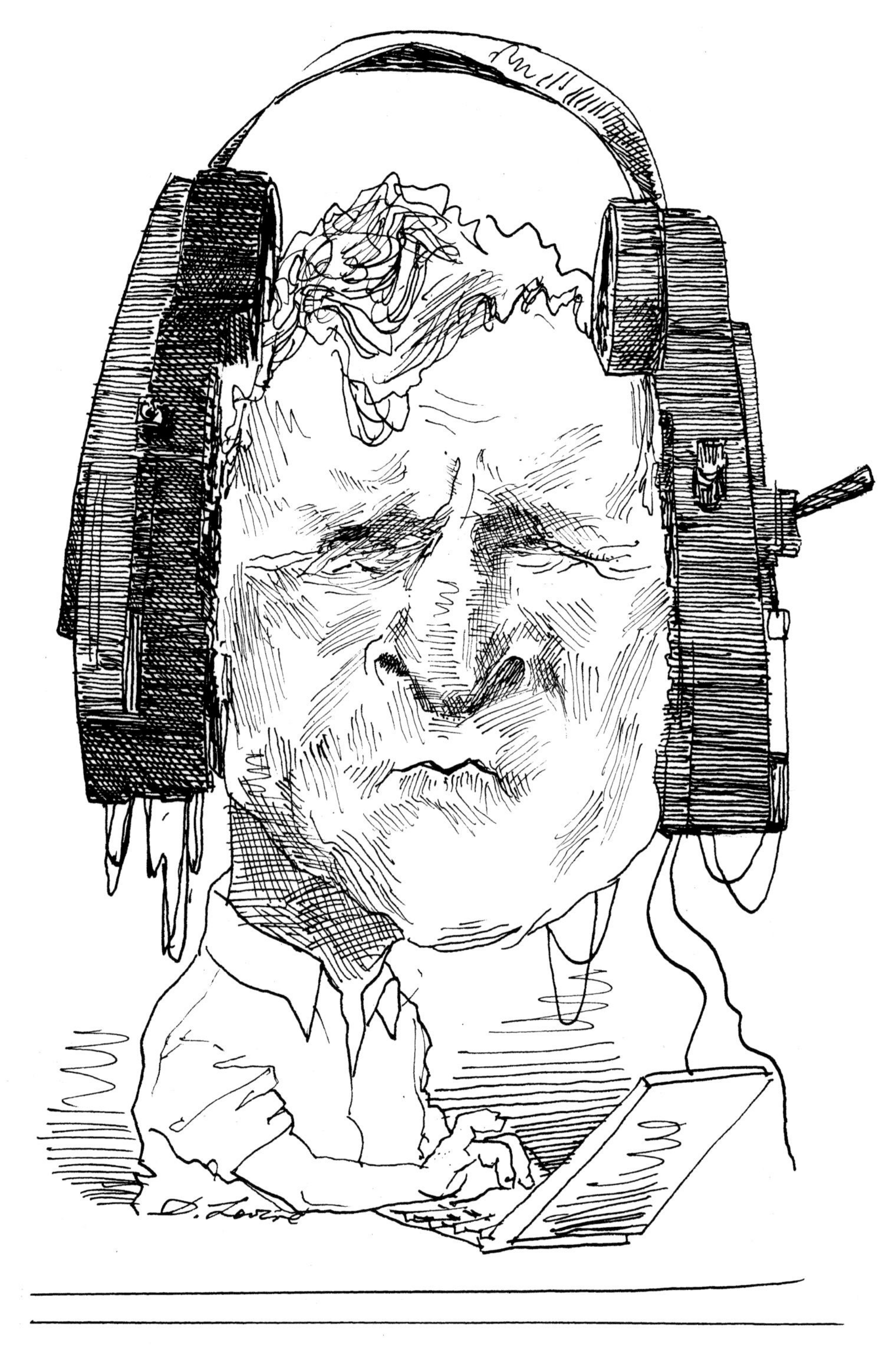

"The Listener," **George W. Bush**

★2★0★0★8★

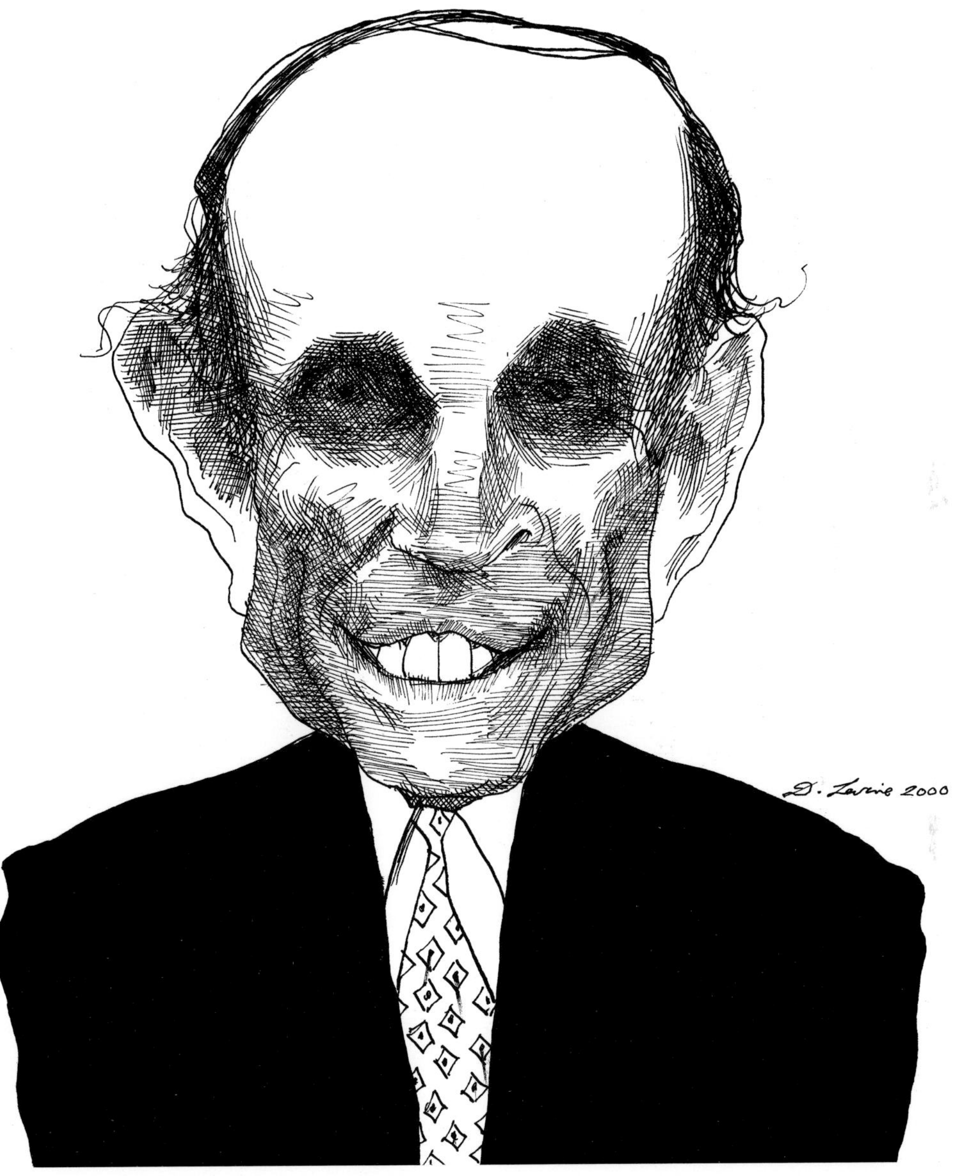

➽ The presidential campaign began with a sense of achieving something through the primaries. A woman president. A black president. A Mormon president. But soon we lost all the talk of the issues and devolved into name calling. At least now, everything is under an enormous magnifier. Finally people are actually looking at the people running. Candidates now have to show consistency. We all come to this with our own bias: "They are wrong and I am right." Presidents have the power to hurt, we only have the power to question. Caricature is very hopeful in the belief that a drawing is going to help make change. It will be a long wait until we see the character of the next administration. No matter who is elected, I will look at the next presidency with a cocked eye. ABOVE: **RUDY GIULIANI**

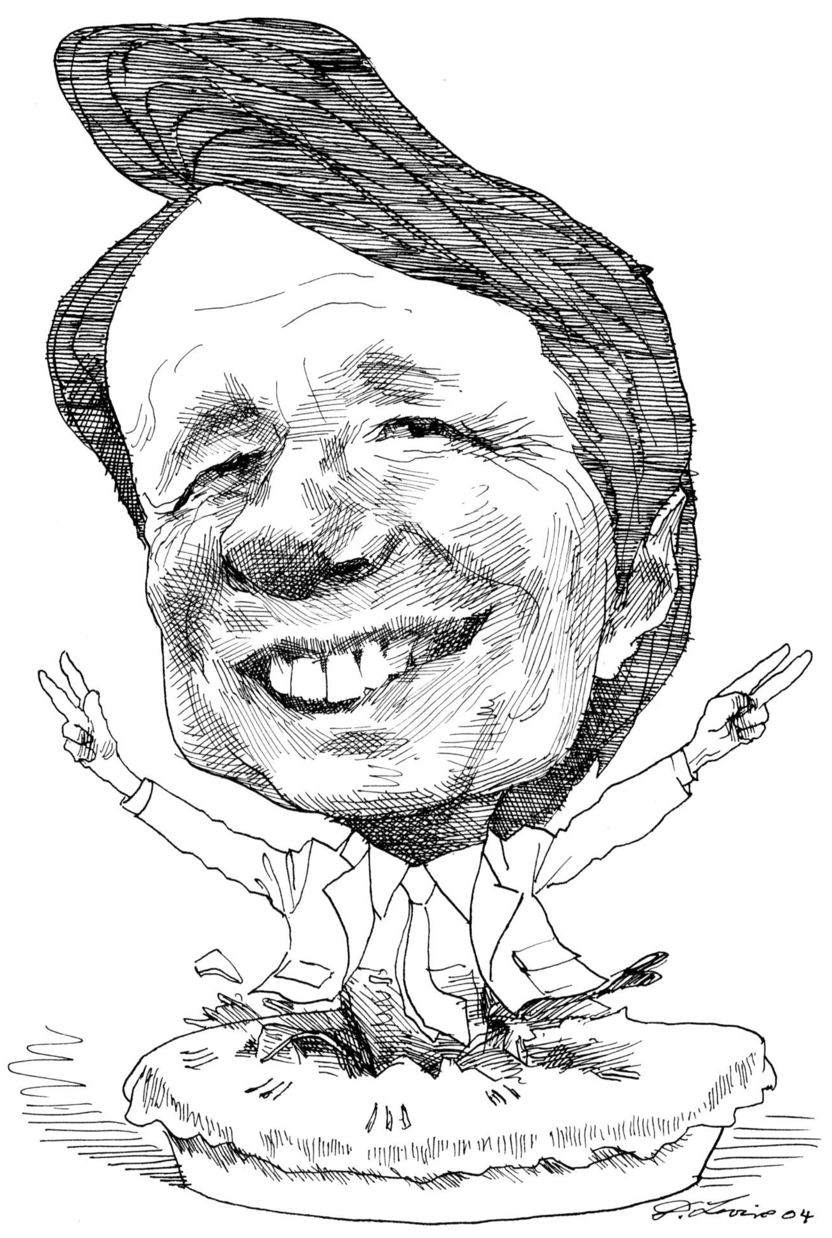

JOHN EDWARDS

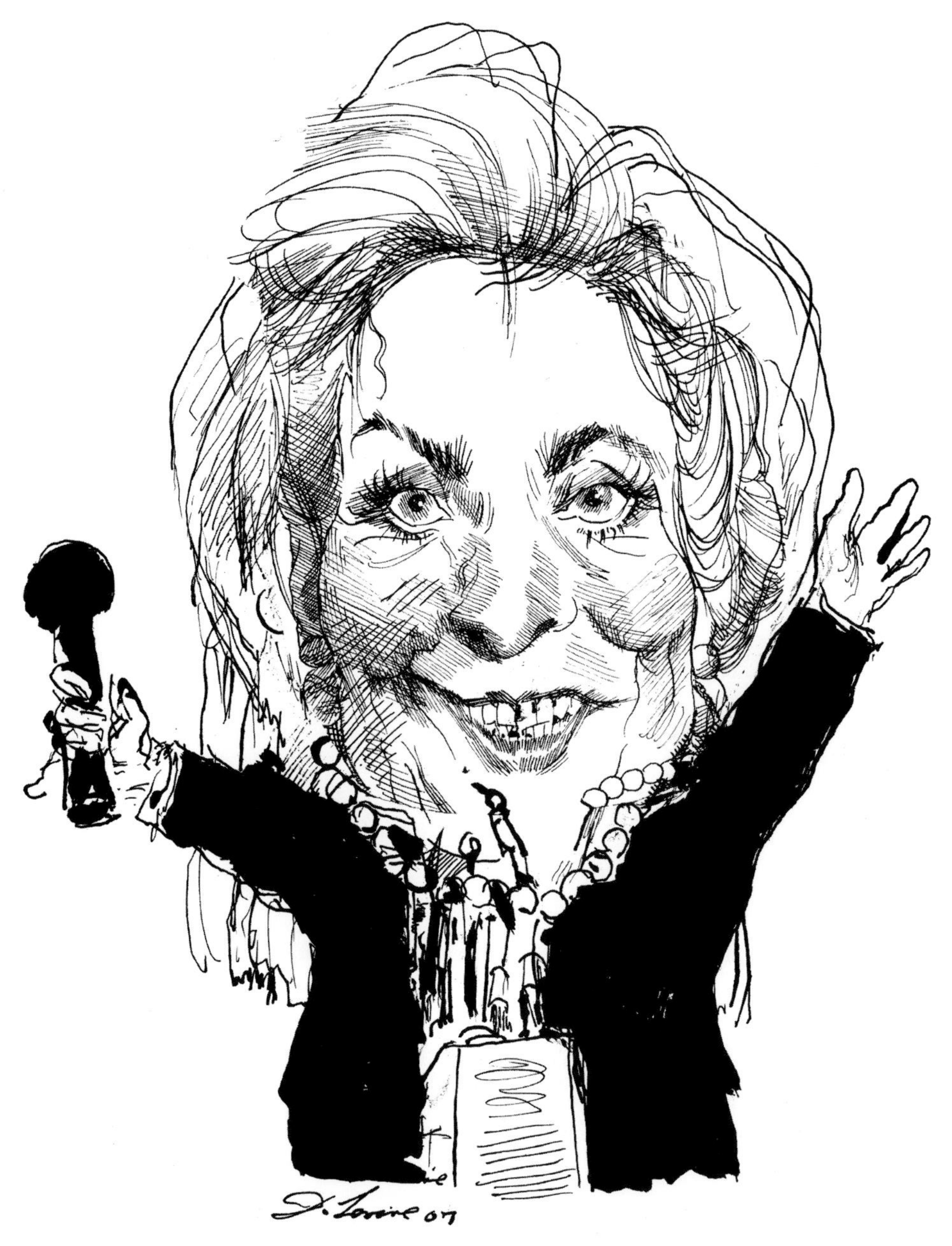

HILLARY CLINTON

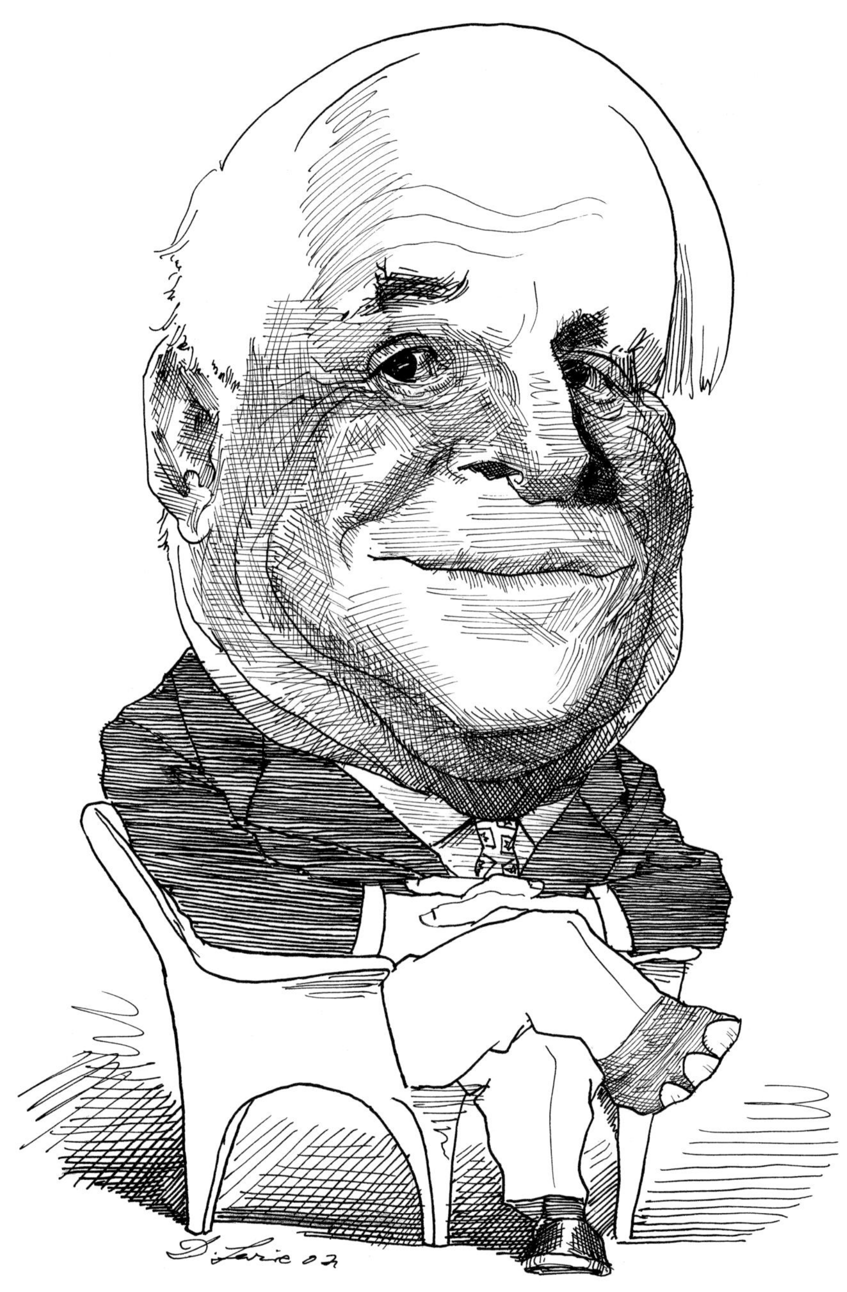

John McCain

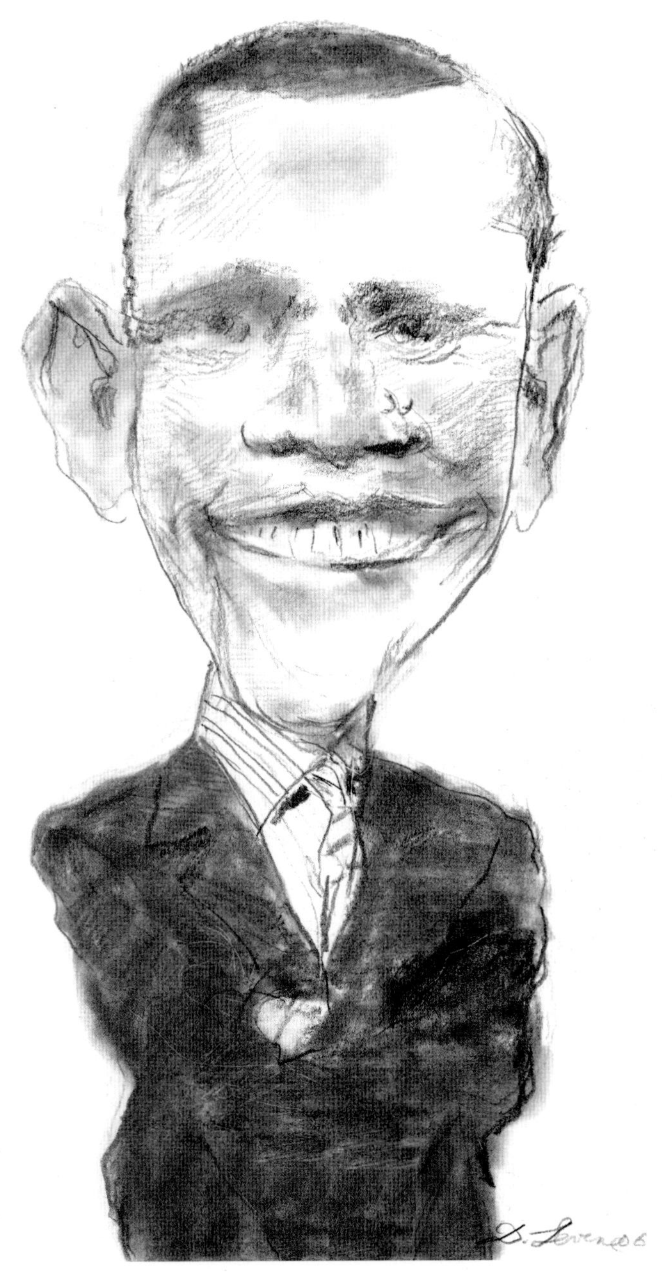

Barack Obama

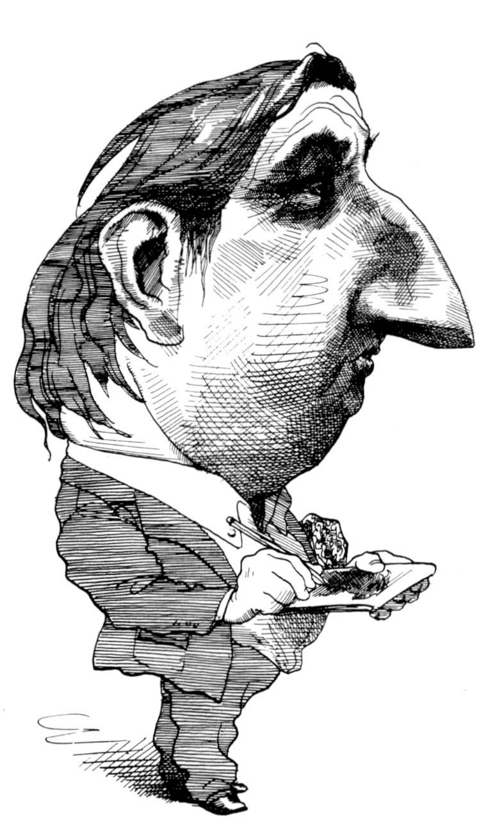

David Levine was born in Brooklyn, New York in 1926 and studied at the Brooklyn Museum of Art School, Pratt Institute, the Tyler School of Art at Temple University in Philadelphia, and the Eighth Street School of New York with Hans Hoffman. His many awards include the Louis Comfort Tiffany Foundation Award in 1955, the Isaac Maynard, Julius Hallgarten, and Thomas B. Clarke awards (all from the National Academy of Design), the George Polk Memorial Award, a Guggenheim Fellowship, the Childe Hassam Purchase Prize (American Academy of Arts and Letters), the John Pike Memorial Prize, and the Gold Medal of the American Academy and Institute of Arts and Letters in 1993. Internationally, David Levine has received the French Legion of Honor award and the Thomas Nast Award in Landau, Germany.

Levine exhibited paintings with the Davis Gallery in New York from 1954 to 1963, then joined the Forum Gallery. In addition to 15 one-person exhibitions at Forum, he has had exhibitions in Paris, Stuttgart, Washington, Munich, Oxford (England), Beverly Hills, and Columbus, Georgia.

Levine's caricatures have been seen in *Time*, *Newsweek*, *Esquire*, *Playboy*, *The New Yorker*, *New York Magazine*, *The Nation*, and, for 45 years, every issue of *The New York Review of Books*, as well as in numerous solo and group shows.

His caricatures and paintings are part of permanent collections at the Metropolitan Museum, the Library of Congress, the Cleveland Museum of Art, the National Portrait Gallery, Brooklyn Museum of Art, the Hirshhorn Museum, England's National Portrait Gallery, the New York Public Library, and the Pierpont Morgan Library in New York.

Six books have been published of David Levine's art, including *The Arts of David Levine* (Knopf, New York, 1978) and *Pens and Needles* (Gambit, Boston, 1969). A long, career-spanning interview with the artist appears in *Drawing the Line* (Fantagraphics Books, 2004). David Levine lives and works in Brooklyn, New York.